MW01234652

The Butterfly Effect in Competitive Markets

The Butterfly Effect in Competitive Markets

Driving Small Changes for Large Differences

Rajagopal
Professor, EGADE Business School, ITESM Mexico City and Visiting Professor, Boston University, Boston, MA

© Rajagopal 2015

Foreword © Tom Breur 2015

All rights reserved. No reproduction, copy or transmission of this publication may be made without written permission.

No portion of this publication may be reproduced, copied or transmitted save with written permission or in accordance with the provisions of the Copyright, Designs and Patents Act 1988, or under the terms of any licence permitting limited copying issued by the Copyright Licensing Agency, Saffron House, 6–10 Kirby Street, London EC1N 8TS.

Any person who does any unauthorized act in relation to this publication may be liable to criminal prosecution and civil claims for damages.

The author has asserted his right to be identified as the author of this work in accordance with the Copyright, Designs and Patents Act 1988.

First published 2015 by
PALGRAVE MACMILLAN

Palgrave Macmillan in the UK is an imprint of Macmillan Publishers Limited, registered in England, company number 785998, of Houndmills, Basingstoke, Hampshire, RG21 6XS.

Palgrave Macmillan in the US is a division of St Martin's Press LLC, 175 Fifth Avenue, New York, NY 10010.

Palgrave is the global academic imprint of the above companies and has companies and representatives throughout the world.

Palgrave® and Macmillan® are registered trademarks in the United States, the United Kingdom, Europe and other countries.

ISBN 978–1–137–43495–1

This book is printed on paper suitable for recycling and made from fully managed and sustained forest sources. Logging, pulping and manufacturing processes are expected to conform to the environmental regulations of the country of origin.

A catalogue record for this book is available from the British Library.

A catalog record for this book is available from the Library of Congress.

Typeset by MPS Limited, Chennai, India.

*To Arati, and my little grandson Akhilesh, who
gave me scope to relax from always sitting
upright and working on this project*

Contents

List of Figures and Tables

Figures

Table

Foreword

Markets are less predictable than ever. All around us we see the unexpected rise and spectacular demise of products and services. Companies like Facebook can quickly grow to a $200 billion market capitalization, while others (like Kodak, for instance) suffer spectacular demise. Some products become almost ubiquitous overnight, but there are also products with years of steady sales that suddenly vanish. Markets display spectacular turbulence. We "experience" chaos at work in many settings. More than ever we need to understand its origins. We also need to identify corporate strategy, preferably a steady course, to cope with the resulting uncertainty in our pursuit of success in this chaotic environment.

Complex, mathematically "chaotic" phenomena are difficult to "see": it seems that our brains are more inclined to attribute observations to causality rather than complexity (Appelo, 2011). Our minds favor linear thinking. Weinberg (1992) has dubbed the human preference for easily explainable events with simple causes and simple effects the "causation fallacy" – "Complexity science teaches us that applying linear thinking to complex problems can lead to painful mistakes."

Many authors (and so does Rajagopal) draw parallels between the chaos in markets and a Darwinian (biological) model of survival of the fittest. A Darwinistic approach to optimizing your marketing mix implies trial and error, with an emphasis on measurement and experimentation. We expect and accept many innovation attempts to fail. Then drop those products from our portfolio. By rational allocation across our offerings, you evolve to sustainable growth. This way we leverage the consequences of chaos, rather than falling victim to it.

The last few decades have seen the emergence of complexity theory. It is hard to pinpoint exactly where this branch of science started, but certainly Edward Lorenz (1917–2008) was an early thought leader. It was Lorenz who coined the term "butterfly effect" in his landmark paper from 1972 called "Predictability: Does the Flap of a Butterfly's Wings in Brazil Set Off a Tornado in Texas?" Lorenz was a meteorologist and mathematician by background. Early in his career (1950s) he appreciated that there were serious flaws in the linear models being applied to weather forecasting in those days. Most atmospheric phenomena behind weather forecasting are non-linear, and therefore Lorenz challenged the appropriateness of linear models to describe these processes (Lorenz, 1972). Lorenz discovered a mechanism of deterministic chaos in computer models. Simple systems, with (very) few variables, can still display complicated and unpredictable behavior. Lorenz showed that even deterministic systems have limits to their predictability.

The well-known Cynefin framework distinguishes between complicated and complex systems. Simple systems, with few variables, can nonetheless show unpredictable and sometimes chaotic behavior. Although this could be demonstrated in simulations, it took a while before these phenomena could be demonstrated in real-world, physical systems. It wasn't until 1977 that Libchaber conducted a series of seminal experiments. He created a small system in his lab to study convection (chaotic system behavior) in a cubic millimeter of helium. By gradually warming this up from the bottom, he could create a state of controlled turbulence. Even this tightly controlled environment displayed chaotic behavior: complex unpredictable disorder that is paradoxically governed by "orderly" rules.

The "butterfly effect" refers to the phenomenon that a seemingly stable system (as in Libchaber's 1 ccm cell of helium) can be exposed to very small influences (like heating it up a mere 0.001 degree), and can transform from orderly convection into wild chaos. Although governed by deterministic phenomena, we are nonetheless unable to predict how such systems will behave over time. The scientific study of chaotic system behavior took off. Initially in hard sciences like Mathematics. Then Biology, and later in social sciences like Economics and Sociology. Some people have called this the third scientific revolution of the twentieth century. After relativity, quantum mechanics, now complexity science (sometimes called chaos theory) is an idea whose time has come.

We live in an interconnected, or rather a hyper-connected society. Organizations and markets "behave" like networks. This triggers chaotic (complex) rather than linear behavior. Although this may all be blatantly obvious to the layman, science has been rather slow to evolve from almost exclusively linear models to system dynamics and complexity science. Another example of linear models is that of the "rational customer" who always maximizes economic utility. When I was in university I vividly remember hearing about the assumptions that needed to be made in order to justify working with economic (regression) models. Interestingly, it was clear to everyone that these were evidently inaccurate assumptions. There was (and is) undisputed scientific evidence that consumers do *not* behave like rational agents. They do *not* constantly try to maximize economic utility.

Dan Ariely's book *Predictably Irrational* was a bestseller, and few people dispute his findings. It strikes me as odd that *still* the overwhelming majority of economic theories rest squarely on the assumption of the rational consumer (Ariely, 2010). It seems we are at the fray of a change in research tradition. As this paradigm shift unfolds, it is only natural to see more and more applications of complexity science. *The Butterfly Effect in Competitive Markets* by Rajagopal pertains to marketing and business strategy, and aims to enable forward-thinking marketers to *benefit* rather than *suffer* from butterfly effects.

We all seem to be looking for the Holy Grail, the nexus point in a complex system. This is where a small change in the marketing mix will yield a large improvement in marketing dynamics. Many memorable innovations in hindsight seem remarkably small adjustments to existing products. Like the change from mp3 players to iPod didn't seem such a big deal at the time. Yet some of these innovations drive enormous revenue growth.

The nexus point in a complex system is where you have (the most) leverage. In any other place, you may well be pushing and pushing, only to spend more money and create more waste, without seeing any sustainable change. Systems have a tendency to "bounce back," to "resist change" as system dynamics (Sterman, 2000) has taught us. Were the early smartphones all that different from the existing mobile devices? Isn't a tablet computer "merely" an intelligent compromise between a smartphone and an ultra-portable laptop? Yet both have defined new product categories, essentially creating a new market. But many other seemingly "brilliant" improvements faded into oblivion.

Unless the customer is getting more value, he is unlikely to be willing to pay a premium. At least not for long, until a competitor comes along that steals your thunder. Rajagopal answers the question how you carry innovation forward to enhanced products and offerings, on the road to a *sustainable improvement* of value for your customers.

Tom Breur
VP Data Analytics, Cengage Learning Inc., Boston, MA

In the past 15 years Tom Breur has specialized in how companies can make better use of their data. Teaching at universities, MBA programs, for the IQCP (Information Quality Certified Professional) and CBIP program (Certified Business Intelligence Professional), his focus is on Agile approaches to data-driven decision-making and business intelligence. In 2013 he published a book on Big Data. *Tom is author of several papers in peer-reviewed journals, an active blogger, and regular keynoter at international conferences. At the moment he is a member of the editorial board of the* Journal of Targeting, *the* Journal of Financial Services Management, *and* Banking Review. *He is Chief Editor for the Palgrave* Journal of Marketing Analytics. *He was cited, among others, in* Harvard Management Update *about state-of-the-art data analytics. Tom works as VP of Data Analytics at Cengage Learning, Inc. in Boston, Massachusetts, USA.*

Preface

I have argued in my previous book, *Architecting Enterprise: Managing Innovation, Technology, and Global Competitiveness*, published by Palgrave Macmillan, that most global firms are penetrating bottom-of-the-pyramid market segments by introducing small changes in technology, value perceptions, marketing-mix strategies, and driving production on an unimagined scale of magnitude to derive a major effect on markets. This book is an outcome of the continuum of the thought process of the previous book, which gave a platform to address the issues concerning how small changes could lead to large differences in driving business at the global scale. This phenomenon has been explained as the butterfly effect in market competition and indeed most multinational companies in consumer goods sector, for example, Colgate-Palmolive, Procter & Gamble, Kellogg's, Unilever, Nestlé, Apple, and Samsung, have experienced this effect in their business growth in the global marketplace. Well-managed companies drive small changes in their business strategies by nipping the pulse of consumers on issues such as customizing globally standardized products that are advanced, led by competitive technology, are functional and reliable, and offered with competitive benefits to sensitize the market. These companies benefit from enormous economies of scale in production, distribution, marketing, and management. Successful new enterprise in the global marketplace needs enormous efforts in innovation, competitiveness, and application of technology for sustainable growth.

A fundamental management challenge, particularly in large diversified global companies, has emerged as stress in engaging toward continuous innovation to stay competitive in the market. Wise companies in the competitive fray are catching up with the concepts of the butterfly effect and driving low-cost and customer-centric moves in their business strategies to embed an emotional appeal among consumers to lead to competitive advantage in the market. The butterfly effect driven by emerging firms is seen as widespread in the taxonomy of markets ranging from macro to niche levels, and prompts short-run growth of firms in the competitive marketplace. Most firms use such effect by making a small change in their strategy in reference to produce, price, place, promotion, packaging, pace (competitive strategies), people (salesforce), performance, psychodynamics (communication through

social networks), posture (developing corporate image), and proliferation (value-driven diversifications in product and services attributes,
and marketing strategies) to gain higher market share and profit in a
short span. The butterfly effect is obvious in the market during peak
sales season as even a small discount leverages higher market share of
competing firms.

As the globalization of firms has increased during the early twenty-
first century, the need for innovation and technology application has
swiftly drawn the attention of emerging firms to make sustainable
moves in the competitive marketplace. Most firms that are new and at
the grassroots of the market have started to redefine key aspects of their
marketing-mix, and by using innovation and customer-driven technology solutions have grown stronger to sustain the market competition.
Most companies, thus, lean toward investing in market-oriented technology and encourage the co-creation of differentiated products and
services. A large number of firms operating in mature markets have the
resources to launch unique and superior products with a compelling
value proposition. However, contemporary studies show that sustainable customer-centric innovations are relatively few, while improvements and modifications to existing products are increasing.

Globalization and frequent shifts in consumer preferences toward
products and services have accelerated chaos in the market due to the
rush of firms, products, and business strategies. Chaos theory in markets
addresses the behavior of strategic and dynamic moves of competing
firms that are highly sensitive to existing market conditions triggering the butterfly effect. Accordingly, small differences in the strategy
of marketing-mix elements, brand, and corporate business conditions
yield widely diverging outcomes in market dynamics, rendering long-
term impacts. Chaos in the market happens as a result of random
changes in the marketing strategies of firms, even though at a small
scale. It has been observed that the larger the number of firms in the
market the higher the degree of chaos. The sensitivity to small changes
in marketing strategy is identified as the butterfly effect.

It is argued in the book that most firms look for gaining competitive
advantage in the marketplace by driving tactical moves, inculcating
small, cost-effective changes in marketing approaches. Sometimes such
small changes are introduced into niche markets, which yield macro
effects in large markets. Often the butterfly effect is initiated by user-
friendly innovations that enable consumers to realize that with such
interventions in the market they could not have gained such value
before at the offered price. Such consumer perceptions may have a large

impact on the market in terms of market share and profitability. This book explains how to "refresh" consumer value with small changes in marketing policy to larger and sustainable effects in threshold markets to gain competitive advantage. As competition among the firms in the marketplace across territories and market segments is perennially growing, the butterfly effect has become much more dispersed, complexity in market predictions has increased, and tactical interventions have turned to business models involving consumers and social media in demonstrating effects on a much larger scale. Companies successfully driving the butterfly effect in the global–local marketplace need to overcome the organizational barriers and transaction costs involved with innovation, technology application, and managing intellectual property besides developing effective production, operations, and marketing strategies. Firms must also evaluate how best to appropriate value to innovations and technology interventions within the organization and marketplace. The arguments in this book harness the power of firms toward sensitive market interventions through marketing-mix strategies, innovation, and technology application to click larger effects with smaller differentiations.

The discussions in this book follow a linear path of cause and effect on various organizational and market-driven factors to analyze the butterfly effect in the marketplace. It is illustrated through logical market behavior analysis how chaos in the market drives tactics among market competitors that cause shifts in consumer preferences and guides their buying behavior. Such shifts in consumer behavior are often radical and face initial resistance; however, consumers' thrust to break out of social conformity drives their adaptability behavior to change over time. Strategies of firms that emerge out of market chaos help these firms in growing their business in local markets and achieve sustainability and global competitiveness. Consequently, every small change emerging out of market chaos contributes to a global and sustainable effect in the market.

This book is divided into ten chapters spread across three sections, which comprise analyzing market chaos, building global–local marketing effects, and unveiling future effects. Chapter 1 discusses the attributes of growing competitiveness in the global marketplace that cause chaos among companies and affects sustainability in the market. The critical issues concerning chaos in markets in reference to complexities of competition, and random and rational choices of consumers are addressed in this chapter. The chapter argues that manifold increase in market competition at the macro, meso, and micro levels creates chaos in the market, while it also seeds many opportunities for companies to grow via differentiation.

Chapter 2 analyzes the reasoned action and planned behavior of consumers toward new and competitively differentiated products, and argues that consumers initially are critical to changes in view of differences in culture, awareness, and socioeconomic positioning, but companies need to maneuver such behavior to develop their marketplace and drive strategic differentiations to spark the butterfly effect. The chapter also maps the mindset of consumers in adopting competitively differentiated products and services. In this context the chapter also addresses how the consumer learning curve and social media deliver a new cognitive push to small competitive differences for large socioeconomic benefits for consumers.

Chapter 3 critically examines the market shifts toward innovation and technology application in products and services for creating competitive differentiation among consumers and various market players. A systematic discussion on interrelated issues on organizational learning, transformation of competitive differentiation and innovation, and managing market uncertainties is presented in this chapter. The market environment for spreading small competitive differentiations for large benefits across the consumer and market segments to optimize the butterfly effect is also discussed. It is argued that emerging firms are aggressive in innovation of products and services, and are competent in managing the dynamics of butterfly effects in global markets.

Most companies invest resources and make efforts to analyze market trends continuously to track consumer preferences and the need for developing competitive differentiations in products, services, and strategies to gain competitive advantage in the marketplace. Chapter 4 focuses discussions from the above perspectives and addresses issues on market trend analysis, behavioral resistance of consumers to change, opportunities and threats in product differentiation, and how small differentiations can drive large benefits, like the butterfly effect in the market. The discussions in this chapter also explain the disruptive tendencies in markets that affect the performance of new or competitively differentiated products at a global scale.

Chapter 5 discusses customer value management in reference to new and differential products by improving organization capabilities and competencies of companies in carrying out competitive innovation and value chain management. While discussing the issues related to managing improvement of products and services, this chapter argues that the most effective way for companies to approach competitive differentiation is through co-creation, involving consumers in the process.

The chaos in the market can also be explained with the Darwinian theory of biological evolution, which states the axioms of the struggle for existence and the survival of the fittest govern the process of evolution. In the global marketplace both axioms appears to fit as multinational companies are moving to bottom-of-the-pyramid segments and regional companies are aspiring to upscale their operations to the global level. Such bidirectional competitive moves cause chaos, and companies in market competitions lean on differentiation to establish their unique posture in the market. Chapter 6 accordingly discusses evolution and growth in business, marketing competition, and managing low-end differentiation. One of the salient features of the discussion is the differentiation and chaos matrix, which analyzes the effect of differentiation in reference to advertising and communication, price, quality and perceived value, and technology.

Chapter 7 addresses business growth and local effects on competitive differentiation, and discusses five key drivers of competitive differentiation. The chapter explains the complexity grid that companies face in reference to strategic, marketplace, tactical, and cognitive complexities. This chapter also analyzes the causes of differentiation failures and risk factors.

Chapter 8 explores sustainable marketing, considering business growth and the factors driving marketing decisions. It is identified that consumer value, environmental issues, decision-making, competition management, business governance, organizational culture, and understanding the market are key factors in determining business sustainability and company growth. This chapter also addresses issues of market competition and corporate sustainability, and argues that companies should refrain from short-run, myopic strategies if they want to grow sustainably in the marketplace.

The social psychology of consumers as an attitudinal environment in consumers developing perceptions of competitive differentiations is discussed in Chapter 9. Consumer culture and associated ethnographic factors are also addressed by laying emphasis on cultural shifts, changing psychographic paradigms, and demographic congregations.

The final chapter of the book, Chapter 10, addresses issues related to the dynamics and challenges associated with the competitive differentiation process and examines how companies can make small changes for large benefits in the global market using technology and innovations. This chapter argues that this phenomenon in global markets drives the butterfly effect as competitive differentiations move boundaries in global markets from a niche to larger markets and vice versa.

This book provides a comprehensive introduction to the concept of market transitions and radical business management. It covers complex elements of market management by analyzing behavioral theories such as chaos theory, the theory of reasoned action and planned behavior, the theory of change, resistance theory, and the theory of acceptance and diffusion from the perspectives of business growth, sustainability, and market competitiveness causing butterfly effects in the market. A broad foundation of this subject beginning with a discussion of the concept of market dynamics followed by analysis of change behavior of markets and its components form the core discussion in this book. The arguments on butterfly effect in markets delineate critical insights on the significance of leadership, building consumer value through innovation, tracking the external environment for organizational change, and relevant general factors as well as important emerging trends toward building an innovative venture.

Various perspectives of market growth and development of emerging firms in the global context are addressed in this book in reference to the impact of market chaos, change behavior, and consumer preferences on growth of firms and competitiveness. The content and coverage of the book range from chaos theory to managing global competitiveness. In reference to the butterfly effect on market competitiveness this book argues that technological innovations, which are triggering changes in niche markets, are driving market competition at local and global levels. Policymakers and business strategists are examining new theoretical frameworks to understand the underlying dynamics of this global reshuffling of production and marketing activities of firms, and how small changes cause large effects in business. This book examines the butterfly effect in reference to innovation, competitiveness, and shifts in business strategies in regional and global perspective, and discusses the impact of globalization on innovation, production, and marketing activities. The book reviews categorically behavioral theories on marketing and previous researches, and analyzes the strategic and tactical stewardship of firms in business for sustainable growth in the global marketplace. The book discusses new concepts related to market efficiency and co-creation approaches to manage recurring changes in the market in reference to innovation, technology, and disruptive behavior. This book significantly contributes to the existing literature and will serve as a learning post and a think-tank for students, researchers, and business managers.

The principal audience of this book lies among corporate managers, including CEOs, and students of undergraduate and graduate management studies, research scholars and academics in different business-related disciplines. The book has also been developed to serve as a principal text for undergraduate and graduate students who are pursuing studies in international management, marketing, and administrative studies. Hence, undergraduate and graduate students of major business and economics schools on the American continent and across Europe and Asia are the potential audience for this book. Besides serving as a textbook in undergraduate and graduate courses, this would also be an inspiring book for managers, market analysts, and business consultants to explore various solutions related to product management.

There were several brainstorming sessions with students and peer researchers on innovation and technology management by emerging and large existing firms in the global marketplace that supported the framing of new ideas for discussion in this book. Such discussions brought new insights on redefining the significance of innovation and technology in a competitive marketplace, highlighting the role of disruptive practices in the market by new entrants. The discussion in the book also surveys several consumer-centric strategies to associate consumers as pivots in driving new products and technologies by companies in the market. Initially, I worked out a teaching agenda on developing innovation and technology process, and diffusion and adoption models for global companies, and discussed them at length in the classroom, encouraging open discussions on the subject. These helped in developing new conceptual frameworks on the subject. Some of my research papers on the services innovation process and customer-centric marketing in the emerging markets were published in international refereed journals that had driven new insights on the subject. Such refined work has been presented in this book, endorsed with applied illustrations and updated research on innovation, technology, and management of market competition in order to architect enterprises.

I hope this book will contribute to the existing literature and deliver new concepts to students and researchers to pursue the subject further. Reading this book, working managers may also realize how to converge innovation and technology with market competition in emerging global business.

Rajagopal
Mexico City
September 2014

Acknowledgments

Writing this book has been supported by the discussions of my colleagues within and outside the EGADE Business School. I am thankful to Dr Kip Becker, Chair of Administrative Sciences Department of Boston University and Dr Jack McCann, Dean, School of Business, Lincoln Memorial University, Harrogate, Tennessee, who have been encouraging me to take up new topics in the area of marketing, develop new insights, and contribute to the existing literature prolifically. I express my gratitude to Dr Vladimir Zlatev, Professor of Practice and Dr Barry Unger, Professor of Marketing at Boston University for sharing valuable insights on the subject that helped me in improving the quality of discussions in the book. As this book is an outgrowth of my previous book, *Architecting Enterprise: Managing Innovation, Technology, and Global Competitiveness*, which I have used as principal text in a course, I thank all my students at Boston University for sharing enriching ideas during the classroom discussions that helped in building this book on the framework of innovative ideas. I sincerely thank Tom Breur, Vice President, Data Analytics, Boston, Massachusetts, USA, and Editor of *Journal of Marketing Analytics*, for agreeing to write the Foreword to this book despite his busy schedule.

I also acknowledge the outstanding support of Palgrave Macmillan team, particularly Virginia Thorp, Liz Barlow, and Kirandeep Bolla. I extend my thanks to Virginia Thorp, Senior Commissioning Editor of Palgrave Macmillan, who critically examined the proposal and took the process forward. Special thanks to Kirandeep Bolla who gave her full support in seeing this work through the press. My sincere thanks are also due to M. Bhuvanaraj of MPS Limited and his team who took all care in copyediting the manuscript and preparing it meticulously for the production of this book.

I am thankful to various anonymous referees of my previous research works on globalization, consumer behavior, and marketing strategy, who helped me in looking deeper into the conceptual gaps and improve the quality of my work through their valuable comments. I sincerely thank my colleagues at EGADE Business School and students for their cooperation in gathering literature on the subject. I express my sincere thanks to Shweta Ramesh Santhebennur, Graduate Assistant, who has helped in drafting preliminary versions of charts, organizing the bibliography, and developing the index for the book. My thanks are also due to Amritanshu and Anaya, who have always been inspiring me with their critical thinking, which often rejuvenated my thought process and added value to this book.

Finally, I express my deep gratitude to my beloved wife Arati Rajagopal, who has been instrumental in completing this book, like all other works of mine. I acknowledge her help in copyediting the first draft of the manuscript and for staying in touch till the final proofs were cross-checked and index was completed.

About the Author

Dr Rajagopal is Professor of Marketing at EGADE Business School of Monterrey Institute of Technology and Higher Education (ITESM), Mexico City Campus, and Fellow of the Royal Society for Encouragement of Arts, Manufacture and Commerce, London. He is also Fellow of the Chartered Management Institute, and Fellow of the Institute of Operations Management, United Kingdom. Dr Rajagopal is also Visiting Professor at Boston University, Boston, Massachusetts.

He has been listed with a biography in various international directories including *Who's Who in the World* since 2008, and *2000 Outstanding Intellectual of the 21*st *Century* published in 2009 by International Biographical Center, Cambridge, UK. He offers courses on Competitor Analysis, Marketing Strategy, Advance Selling Systems, International Marketing, Services Marketing, New Product Development, and other subjects of contemporary interest to the students of undergraduate, graduate, and doctoral programs. He has imparted training to senior executives and to date has conducted 55 management development programs.

Dr Rajagopal holds postgraduate and doctoral degrees in Economics and Marketing, respectively, from Ravishankar University in India. His specialization is in the fields of Marketing Management, Rural Economic Linkages and Development Economics. He has to his credit 42 books on marketing management and rural development themes, and over 400 research contributions, which include published research papers in national and international refereed journals. He is Editor-in-Chief of *International Journal of Leisure and Tourism Marketing*, *International Journal of Business Competition and Growth*, and *International Journal of Built Environment and Asset Management*. Dr Rajagopal is also Regional Editor of Emerald Emerging Markets Case Studies, published by Emerald Publishers, UK. He is on the editorial board of various journals of international repute.

His research contributions have been recognized by the National Council of Science and Technology (CONACyT), Government of Mexico by awarding him the status of National Researcher-SNI Level-II during 2004–2012. Currently Dr Rajagopal has been conferred the highest level of National Researcher-SNI Level-III (2013–2017).

Section I
Analyzing Market Chaos

1
Chaos in Markets

Globalization has created new challenges for firms to survive in the competitive marketplace. Most firms have adapted their policies to stay innovative and have applied new technologies in products and services to gain competitive advantage. Simultaneously consumer buying dynamics have also become unstable due to continuous innovations and improvements in products and services using user-friendly technologies. This chapter discusses how small changes drive large effects in the market amidst the chaos of market competition. The chapter will argue that expectations of companies on market behavior, and the degree of freedom consumers have to drive demand for products and services, prompt problems and challenges for companies in the competitive marketplace. By allowing changes in the products and services offered through innovation and technology, firms encourage small market changes to drive macro and sustainable shifts in consumer behavior. Companies that encourage such strategies are prone to spread chaos in the market by driving high vulnerability into competing companies and their business growth. The chapter addresses the explanation for this apparent paradox, which lies in the butterfly effect of a firm through the convergence of market dynamism, globalization, and the evolving role of the consumer from passive recipient to active co-creator of market behavior. This chapter also discusses the attributes of random versus rational consumer decision-making in chaotic markets.

Freedom in doing international business since the mid-twentieth century has been one of the rewards of globalization. The World Trade Organization has played a pivotal role in driving trade policy liberalization among its member countries, and emerging markets such as Brazil, Russia, India, China, and South Africa have immensely benefitted from open market policies. Emerging markets have grown manifold internally and could develop external trade relations to enhance the outreach of their products and services in global markets. However, the race to global markets has time and again created market chaos through price wars and subsidized transactions by some countries. Over the last three decades market liberalization has reduced the protectionist barriers in developing countries. Consequently, multinational companies were able to secure easy access into emerging markets, driving a Darwinian thrust in the marketplace. As the multinationals began penetrating local markets, a business retaliation triggered among the local and regional companies a vigorous hit-or-miss competition that caused competition for survival and sustenance. In the Darwinian struggle for existence and survival of the fittest against the penetration by large companies, many local companies lost market share or sold off businesses, while some fought back. India's Mahindra and Mahindra, a principal automobile and tractor manufacturing company, and China's Haier Group can be given special mention in this context. The governments of most developing countries have developed and implemented the policy of special economic zones to nurture export-oriented units in export-processing zones to encourage exports and overseas business orientation of their companies as a survival strategy. These policies have certainly strengthened the domestic economy of many countries and also forced intensive market competition in the local and international markets, again causing chaos.

Multinational companies in developing countries have overpowered the market by restructuring their businesses to customer-centric strategies and exploiting new opportunities. Most companies employ emotional marketing strategies to maintain brand awareness in the minds of consumers and achieved higher market share than their domestic macro- and meso-level counterparts. The bidirectional market chaos from international to domestic and domestic to global markets has become diverse in the twenty-first century. In order to develop new markets some multinationals have capitalized on their knowledge of local product markets. As an example of the struggle of companies to survive in this chaotic arena, the Philippines' Jollibee Foods has profitably battled McDonald's because it understood that Filipinos like their burgers to have a particular soy and garlic taste, while Hamburgesas Memorable, a traditional fast food company in Mexico, has lost business to McDonald's. Most companies have incorporated local talent and accessed capital markets to span their operations in serving customers both in domestic and destination markets by staying cost-effective (Khanna and Palepu, 2006). India's software companies had recognized the possibility of penetrating into the offshore services business as a survival strategy as they felt the threat of penetrating low-cost technology electronics from China in the domestic market, which was eating into their market share, besides the growth of disruptive technology.

Evolution of global markets

The process of globalization, networking companies and markets as a global platform began with fierce strategies in the mid-twentieth century. The shift in corporate governance and business philosophies among multinational companies across the world has driven the process of globalization and created the concept of global markets. The transformation of business philosophy from "marketing to customer" to "marketing with customer" has triggered business decisions among companies to develop customer-centric marketing strategies in order to conquer both high- and low-end markets. As multinational companies of the western hemisphere tend to penetrate developing regions and bottom-of-the-pyramid market segments in their search for growth, they have no choice but to compete in the big emerging markets of Brazil, Russia, India, China, Indonesia, and South Africa. The dynamism for globalization has come from political thinkers and business managers, with dual perspectives of building diplomatic relationships by narrowing trade and economy barriers across the world and equalizing the power play among nations, resulting in more space for multinational companies to do business in far-reachable markets. Although globalization has driven bidirectional efforts of multinational and local companies to share their marketplace in home and destination countries, the question remains as to how these companies can play SMART to gain competitive advantage and grow sustainably in the given marketplace.

Playing SMART indicates that companies should develop Strategic, Measurable, Accessible, Responsive, and Trustworthy postures in the destination markets to gain the confidence of consumers and drive the pull effect that generates sustainable demand and allows companies to operate with economies of scale. During the 1980s multinationals gained first-mover advantage in emerging markets and developed meticulously every element of their business. Some companies presumed that they could gain competitive advantage as the emerging markets would merely be new markets for their old product models, and proceeded with an imperialist mind-set. But the strategies developed with such thinking narrowed down the success of multinational companies in most emerging markets like India and China, which appeared to be innovative in bringing out new products at low cost in the market against the multinationals. Thus going global has become a big challenge for multinational companies, and to evolve in the new marketplace several critical questions remain to be resolved. Some of these include:

- What is in the growth target in the emerging markets: affluent, middle-, or bottom-of-the-pyramid market segment?
- How do the distribution and logistics networks operate?
- What mix of local and global leadership is necessary to foster business opportunities?
- Should there be a consistent strategy for doing business in a new marketplace, or are diverse marketing strategies needed to serve the niches?
- Should there be global–local partnerships promoted to seek a win–win market share in the local markets?

In order to compete in the big emerging markets companies need to reconfigure their strategies by ascertaining appropriate responses on their competitive fitness and redesign costs and operational dynamics (Prahalad and Lieberthal, 2003). It is observed that though premium consumer segment may attract the companies with global vision bottom-of-the-pyramid markets appear to be more promising from the perspectives of building the brand equity and customer-centric posture of the company. Companies entering into the premium segment may push themselves toward a high-profile niche, but this segment might not support the objective of increasing market share and staying in touch with mass customers. The new commercial reality is the emergence of omnipresent global companies across consumer segments and leaning toward marketing more standardized products and services than offering customized products on a previously unimagined scale of magnitude. The marketing technology for global, multi-domestic, and transnational companies today is to move to digital platforms and give consumers convenience and cost advantages over the conventional wisdom of laying down non-flexible marketing standards. Those companies with globally standardized products enjoy the benefits of economies of scale in production, distribution, marketing, and advanced management with reference to functional, reliable, and price competitiveness (Levitt, 1983).

Breaking social, cultural, economic, and political barriers for moving the business in various destination markets is a tough challenge for multinational companies. Though globalization of business has become the lifeline of most companies, creating a sustainable corporate strategy in tune with local market conditions is difficult. Thus, most companies do not stay competitive in the local markets and lose their market share to low-cost customer-centric companies. Multinational companies largely employ natives in the destination countries to inculcate the cross-cultural organizational behavior that can enable the company to compete on a worldwide basis without straying far from headquarters control. One of the effective inspirations for foreign companies is the implication of the comparative advantages on product factors comprising land, labor, capital, workplace talent, and technology that drive companies to perform effectively. Overseas companies tend to meet the demands for local convergence and build distinctive competitiveness (Kogut, 1999).

There have been many notions on globalization of business comprising various social, economic, political, and ethnic points of views. However, from the perspective of empowering people to access global markets demand for products and services has been identified as crystallization of the world into a single place and as the emergence of global human needs (Robertson, 1987). The integration of various digital socio-economic communication platforms is argued to explain that globalization is a reflexive process and brings global markets into one boundary-less playing field. The development of new technology allows mass media to become universally available to consumers, and this combines with cross-border marketing opportunities for the multinational companies (Ritzer, 2007). These market trends lead to a homogenization of consumer needs and develop pro-innovation and overseas cultures in emerging markets through new consumption trends, standardization, intercultural collaboration and coordination, and cross-border competition (Zou and Cavusgil, 2002). Consistent with the globalization trend, many international companies begin to utilize a global approach in which companies market their products on a global basis to replace the traditional multi-domestic approach in which local subsidiaries market local products to local markets (Kotabe and Helsen, 2010).

Many factors are driving the world toward greater globalization. These factors include the rise of worldwide networks for investment, production, and marketing; advances in telecommunication technologies and the Internet; increases in world travel; and the growth of global media (Yu et al., 2014). Globalization involves the homogenization of international markets and an increasing similarity in the needs and habits of international customers. Using globalized strategies can help international companies create consistent brand images worldwide and utilize their resources more efficiently (Alden et al., 1999). However, any attempt to globally standardize service delivery may encounter difficulties, and it may be argued that every market is unique, such that a globalized approach cannot adequately take account of cultural differences in ethnic markets. Some leading multinational consumer products companies, like Unilever, have leaned toward a localized approach, based on the continued desire for maintaining local culture. Indeed, it is clear that many people prefer local consumption imagery, because they can more easily identify with local lifestyles, values, and attitudes. Some studies suggest that neither consumption nor marketing can be made globally uniform. These studies emphasize the powerful influence of local cultures, and demonstrate how customers are developing hybrid cultures or growing with both global and local cultural influences (Steenkamp and De Jong, 2010).

Global and bottom-of-the-pyramid market segments

Most companies also experience a countervailing trend as many consumers seek unique services that reflect their local cultures, lifestyles, and customs. In response, some companies have begun to design their business strategies to fit the special needs and distinct tastes of consumers in particular regions. This localized management approach requires international companies to invest large amounts of time and resources into research and development in an effort to better understand and respond to specific local markets. Companies moving into mass markets and bottom-of-the-pyramid markets in developing countries grow through localized strategies in different regions (Liu et al., 2014). In view of the experiences of companies engaged in market expansion amidst thriving market competition in both the high-end and low-end markets, it may be argued that the globalization of consumer preferences does not necessarily imply convergence in management practices. Globalization (or convergence) and localization (or divergence) are two extremes in the formation of company strategies. Companies often find themselves somewhere in the middle, on the continuum between these two extremes (Yu et al., 2014).

Evolution of the market at the lower end of global markets is identified as a set of localization processes through which the forces of globalization move into the destination markets (Hansen, 2002). The success of McDonald's, Pepsi-Cola, Coca-Cola, etc. is based on variation, which means not offering the same products everywhere around the world, which evidences that globalization does penetrate local markets and acquires them or threatens competition to local firms but also in a curious way contributes to its revitalization. For example, consider Cadbury's expansion into the Chinese market as an experiment to investigate whether a company needs to modify its products, production process, product names and other factors to compete in a new local market (Wood and Grosvenor, 2003). Similarly, chains of small convenience stores, such as the Seven-Eleven Group, have achieved global success through localized strategies. These cases stress the continued desire of customers to maintain their local culture, because people in different markets have different goals, needs, uses for products, and ways of living (Steenkamp and De Jong, 2010). The concept of *glocalization* is a hybrid strategy that embraces elements of global culture and integrates them into the local culture. Robertson developed the term *glocalization* to explain that global forces do not override locality and that heterogeneity in consumption is an important feature of modern society (Robertson, 1995).

The process of localization of global companies has emerged as the penetration of global marketing strategies into ethnic business across a wide range of products and preferences, resulting in rapid business growth for the global firms in different geo-demographic consumer segments. For example, McDonald's uses hybrid, *glocalized* approaches to incorporate local food preferences and lifestyles by serving spicy cottage cheese burgers in India, beer in The Netherlands, and wine in France (Alden et al., 2006). Management experts in favor of *glocalization* argue that consumers often show their preferences by blending available global and local, and continental and traditional information. Consumers use products to position themselves in local age, gender, social class, religion, and ethnic hierarchies (Ger and Belk, 1996).

As market competition increases and the threat of consumer defection to international companies is sensed by local companies, they develop defensive marketing strategies and engage in alluring their consumers with similar or identical product and services offers. Often such defensive strategies subtly grow into disruptive products and cause a serious threat to large companies. Local firms compete with transnational firms if their actions are firmly based in the local culture, and if they move from local strengths with an in-depth understanding of global production and consumption dynamics. Creative firms also offer alternatives to global products that are positioned in local markets. Such firms develop innovative perspectives of global products with a focus on local cultural use values but adopt the acquired marketing skills and practices to stay competitive in the market. Such firms can successfully travel on their alternative road within the global arena and may also pose a potential threat of disruptive marketing (Ger, 1999). However, there is a growing number of small native companies that are affected by various unforeseen technologies, product designs, and marketing strategies of multinational companies that penetrate into local markets. However, the strategy for globalization, which appears to be effective for local companies, is to develop cooperation with multinational companies and their subsidiaries instead of trying to compete with them (Prashantham and Birkinshaw, 2008).

On academic platforms since the global marketplace concept was proposed by Levitt (1983), debate has continued over whether international companies should take a globalized, *glocalized*, or localized management approach during their worldwide expansion process. Among several arguments to emerge on the sustainability of global–local market management, Coca-Stefaniak et al. (2010) point out that the interaction between global and local factors can often be complex and difficult to predict, while Ritzer (2007) suggests a framework for understanding the causes and effects of hybridization. Steenkamp and De Jong (2010) conducted a global investigation into the constellation of consumer attitudes toward global and local products, and suggest that international companies should be careful in relying too much on the globalized approach because this strategy may not work well with large segmentations of consumers. Coca-Stefaniak et al. (2010) examine the localization impacts on the business practices and marketing strategies of small retailers in Spain and Scotland, with the purpose of helping lessen the gap between the concepts of globalization and localization. They find that the localization process often drives the diversity and richness of cultural mosaics between customers and businesses into globally blended consumer products and services.

Going global seemed to be a glamorous vision for every company in the world till the end of the twentieth century. However, the political ideology in the twenty-first century moved to meticulously develop a global market platform in all destinations by driving cooperation between domestic and international companies for ensuring mutual business growth of the companies and national economic development. But there are many incidences of multinational companies cannibalizing the market share of local companies and positing economic threats to the country in terms of money laundering, disrupting primary consumer markets, and causing national security concerns. Accordingly, governments of most developing countries have raised the concept of guarded globalization to protect economic, consumer, and national security. Such concerns have prompted developing countries to improve their stakes in public sector industries. Indeed, the rise of state capitalism in some of the world's most important emerging markets has altered the playing field. Multinational companies must understand globalization's new risks but project their strategic importance to the host government and their home government, and play safe in entering the destination markets by developing alliances with local players, exploring new ways to add value abroad, and expand business in multiple sectors both at home and the overseas destination (Bremmer, 2014).

Most developing countries are pro-globalization but act prudently in promoting globalization to domestic markets. These countries guard against globalization to protect their country's political and social systems, extent of functional openness, product markets, labor markets, and its capital markets. However, when companies match their strategies to each country's contexts, they can take advantage of a location's unique strengths. But first firms should weigh benefits against costs. If they find the risks of adaptation are too great, they should try to change the contexts in which they operate or simply stay away (Khanna et al., 2005).

Global consumer flows

The new information technology is becoming an important factor in the future development of the consumer services industry, and especially banking. The growth in e-banking has significantly influenced customers interacting with retailers to a greater extent through remote technological channels. Though there is much variation in online banking registration and adoption levels, little is understood about actual customer motivators and perceived barriers to registration for online banking services. The impact of the Internet on bank–customer relationships has emerged as a key determinant amidst global competition that has driven customers, motivators and inhibitors toward adapting online banking services (Durkin, 2007). Developments in information and communication technology have significantly contributed to the exponential growth and profits of companies worldwide. This evolution had transformed the way retailers deliver their services, using technologies such as automated teller machines, phones, the Internet, credit cards, and electronic cash. However, retailers face a number of important questions on choosing strategies for taking full advantage of new technology opportunities and tracking electronic development changes affecting interactions with customers.

In general terms, increasing convenience is a way of raising consumers' surplus provided new technology is adopted by retailers in order to

offer convenience to the customers, such as through an electronic transaction as a substitute for a trip to the branch. Technology-based services
imply different combinations of accessibility attributes (time, distance,
and search costs), ease of use, and price. Another factor in determining
the magnitude of the surplus that the bank can command is the relative
importance of cross-selling. The bundle of services provided electroni-
cally is usually not the same as that available at a branch. For this reason
new technology-based banking services with high customer value may
offer better service conditions to harmonize the flow of information
and services across the spatial and temporal dimensions.

The spread of the Internet and of digital technologies is transforming
all types of flows and creating new ones. Global online traffic across
borders grew eighteenfold between 2005 and 2012, and could increase
eightfold more by 2025. Digital technologies, which reduce the cost
of production and distribution, are transforming flows in three ways:
through the creation of purely digital goods and services; "digital wrap-
pers" that enhance the value of physical flows; and digital platforms
that facilitate cross-border production and exchange. The enormous
potential impact of digitization is only beginning to emerge. Consider
that international Skype-call minutes grew to 40 percent of the present
level of traditional international calls in just a decade. Or that cross-
border e-commerce has grown to represent more than 10 percent of
trade in goods in less than a decade. The network of global flows is
expanding rapidly as emerging economies join in. Rising incomes in
the developing world are creating enormous new centers of consumer
demand, global production, and commodities trade, as well as sending
more people across borders for business and leisure. Existing routes of
flows are broadening and deepening, and new ones are emerging as
more countries participate. Developing economies now account for 38
percent of global flows, nearly triple their share in 1990. South–South
goods flows between developing countries have grown from roughly
$200 billion (6 percent of goods flows) in 1990 to $4.2 trillion (24 percent) in 2012.

In global markets, various initiatives of using the mobile phone to
provide consumer services to customers to gain value-added services
benefits over the traditional outlets by mobile marketing and mobile
payments systems have been introduced. This innovation in the retailing system has revealed three cross-cutting customer-centric benefits,
namely amplification of services, simultaneous payments, and multidimensional trust (Donner and Tellez, 2008). Trust has been identified as
the key to e-commerce because it is crucial wherever uncertainty and

interdependence exist. The strong association between a high level of trust and the banking sector has not yet been fully translated in the electronic world as Internet banking is still not used by customers to its fullest potential. It is observed that trust and perceived risk are direct antecedents of intention, and trust is a multidimensional construct with three antecedents, namely perceived trustworthiness, perceived security, and perceived privacy (Yousafzai et al., 2009). When a major technology innovation arrives, a wave of new firms enters the market, implementing the innovation for profits. However, if the innovation complements existing technology, some new entrants will later be forced out as more and more incumbent firms succeed in adopting the innovation. Such a situation has revealed that the diffusion of Internet technology among traditional brick-and-mortar firms was indeed the driving force behind the rise and fall of dotcoms as well as the sustained growth of e-commerce (Wang, 2005). However, in reference to banking reforms in India, technology has been found to be the major input in driving competition, which has been evidenced in a study revealing a positive relationship between the level of competition and banking efficiency. However, a negative relationship between the presence of foreign retailers and banking efficiency is found, which contributes to a short-run increase in costs due to the introduction of new banking technology by foreign retailers (Ali and Hang, 2006).

Global markets are not like consumer product markets to be built across product categories and product lines within a given time in a destination. The global evolution of markets is proximity-bound and moves product by product and market by market, generating sustainable consumer experience. The process of the globalization of consumer products is relatively slower than traditional consumer products as they are embedded with risks and uncertainties. The global evolution of markets that intend to drive risk-embedded products is full of complex adaptive systems. The complexity can be explained with an analogy of the behavior of an ant colony. Business leadership drives from top to bottom of the pyramid and vice versa as each ant has a decision role, but it works only with local information, having no sense of the global system. Ants proceed ahead by continuously exploring their path and cooperate with incoming partners to seek information of the destination. Ant colonies solve very complicated, very challenging problems with no leadership or strategic plan. However, companies aiming to expand their business territorially need to generate awareness about the prospective business environments and develop adaptive systems to meet local socio-cultural, political, and legal requirements.

Multinational companies penetrating in the emerging market destination to do business should surround themselves with cognitive diversity and extract unshared information for building value-added business propositions (Sullivan, 2011).

Complexity of competition in markets

Globalization has created complex conditions in markets by triggering manifold competition. Companies striving to gain higher market share have impelled competition across rivals, customer segments, and also across products and services within their product lines. As market competition grows across consumer market segments, companies are moving to unexplored areas to gain competitive advantage. Most companies aim to gain first-mover advantage either in upstream or downstream markets. In developing markets most companies gain competitive advantage in upstream activities related to making new products by way of building manufacturing infrastructure, sourcing cheaper raw materials, and improving manufacturing and marketing efficiency. However, such opportunities are diminishing in urban markets due to market saturation, and now appear promising in downstream market segments.

A pertinent question that drives business is how to add value to existing markets by manufacturing and marketing something different. The new center of gravity in the internationalization of business demands rethinking of small changes to drive larger effects in low-cost and high-gains propositions. This notion in international business prompts potential companies to drive butterfly effects to earn global benefits and sustain market competition with long-standing strategy principles. In order to attain a butterfly effect in competitive markets through small changes for larger differentiation, companies should attempt to co-create new products that add to the perceived use value of consumers and deliver sustainable competitive advantage against profit-oriented business houses. Such strategy grows with experience and knowledge of consumers and company respectively. As the butterfly effect is triggered, the pace of change in markets is driven by shifts in customers' purchase criteria and improvements in products and applied technology (Dawar, 2013).

Most markets exhibit some form of imperfect or monopolistic competition. There are fewer firms than in a perfectly competitive market, and each can create barriers to entry to some degree. A firm may own a crucial resource, such as an oil well or power generation, or it may have an exclusive operating license, which restricts other competitors from entering the business. Operating on economies of scale for a large firm may also have a significant competitive advantage as it may enjoy a large volume of production at lower costs, which may further lead to price leadership with low retail prices. Such a strategy would also prevent potential competitors from entering in the business. An incumbent firm may make it hard for a would-be entrant by incurring huge sunk costs with high-budget advertising. New entrants facing such a strategy may be able to compete effectively but may lose market share if their competitive attempts fail. Sunk costs are costs that have been incurred and cannot be reversed, unlike spending on advertising or researching a product idea, and can be a barrier to entry. If potential entrants would have to incur similar costs, which would not be recoverable if the entry failed, they may be scared off. Another radical strategy may be used by powerful firms to discourage entry by raising exit costs, for example, by making it an industry norm to hire workers on long-term contracts, which would increase escalated cost barriers for rival companies. Thus firms can earn excess profits without a new entrant being able to compete on prices (Rajagopal, 2012).

In the contemporary analysis of competition and related strategies, it is observed that competitive firms intend to ascertain a continuous organizational learning process with respect to the value creation chain and measure performance of new products introduced into the market. In growing competitive markets large and reputed firms are developing strategies to move into the provision of innovative combinations of products and services as "high-value integrated solutions" tailored to each customer's needs than simply "moving downstream" into services. Such firms are developing innovative combinations of service capabilities such as operations, business consultancy, and finance required to provide complete solutions to each customer's needs in order to augment customer value toward the innovative or new products. It has been argued that the provision of integrated solutions is attracting firms traditionally based in manufacturing and services to occupy a new base in the value stream centered on *systems integration* using internal or external sources of product designing, supply, and customer focused promotion (Davies, 2004). Besides the organizational perspectives of enhancing customer value, functional variables like pricing play a significant role in developing customer perceptions towards the new products.

Since the 1960s, sophisticated economic theories of how firms work have been developed. These have examined why firms grow at different rates and have tried to model the normal lifecycle of a company, from fast-growing start-up to lumbering mature business. The more competition there is, the more likely are firms to be efficient and prices to be low. Economists have identified several different sorts of competition. In perfect competition every firm is competitive and plays in the market as a price taker. Where there is a monopoly, or firms have some market power, the seller has some control over the price, which is probably higher than in a perfectly competitive market. By how much more will depend on how much market power there is, and on whether the firm(s) with the market power are committed to profit maximization. Firms earn only normal profits, the bare minimum profit necessary to keep them in business. If firms earn more than this (excess profits) other firms will enter the market and drive the price level down until there are only normal profits to be made.

Market power may be stated as when one buyer or seller in a market has the ability to exert significant influence over the quantity of goods and services traded or the price at which they are sold. Market power does not exist when there is perfect competition, but it does when there is a monopoly, monopsony, or oligopoly. Monopsony may be described as the market dominated by a single buyer, unlike a monopoly wherein there exists a single seller.

In oligopolistic market competition there are only a few firms that make up an industry. This select group of firms has control over the price and, like a monopoly, an oligopoly has high barriers to entry. The products that the oligopolistic firms produce are often nearly identical and, therefore, the companies, which are competing for market share, are interdependent as a result of market forces.

The fostering of successful private companies becomes particularly attractive in global markets. The clearest example is the Internet, in which China's state-controlled news providers and broadcasters have the resources and content to succeed but have failed to create much noise. There is no single theory of how firms determine price and output under conditions of oligopoly. If a price war breaks out, oligopolistic firms will produce and price much as a perfectly competitive industry would; at other times they act like a pure monopoly. Oligopoly is considered to be a healthy ambience for market competition. In this pattern of competition, market leaders need challengers to keep them dynamic in the marketplace. For example, consider Microsoft Corporation's curious love–hate tango with Netscape Communications Corporation. In the ongoing government antitrust trial, Microsoft faces allegations that it first proposed dividing the Internet-browser market with Netscape, creating an oligopoly for the two of them, and then attempted to crush the fledgling company when it refused. Microsoft denies that this occurred. Still, it is clear that Netscape's existence prodded Microsoft to pour huge resources into improving its own browser (Zachary, 1999).

The contemporary ideology on competition lays emphasis on the competitive environment, which contributes to various dimensions of rivalries. It has been observed that a low-end competitor offering much lower prices for a seemingly similar product has been the common fear of industry leaders managing their business among competitors. The vast majority of such low-end companies fall into one of four broad categories, namely strippers, predators, reformers, or transformers (Potter, 2004). Each of these is defined by the functionality of product and the convenience of purchase. Industry leaders have significant advantages for combating low-end competition, but they often hesitate because they are afraid their actions will adversely affect their current profit margins. The solution then may be to find the response that is most likely to restore market calm in the least disruptive way. An industry leader could choose to ride out the challenge by ignoring, blocking, or acquiring the low-end competitor, or it could decide to strengthen its own value proposition by adding new price points, increasing its level of benefits, or dropping its prices. Such tactics can be effective in the short term, but the industry leader also needs to consider the option of strategic retreat, particularly when certain conditions make future low-end challenges inevitable. In rapidly changing global economic and competitive market conditions in respect of customer location, flash market recessions across countries, currency valuation, labor and transportation costs, and rapidly changing technology, many multinational companies are looking at exploring small changes to introduce as effective competitive drivers that can offer large benefits. In this process companies may need to move to different geographical locations (Tate et al., 2014).

Competition may be analyzed in reference to the characteristics of products as either breakthrough, competitive, or improved. A *breakthrough product* is a unique innovation that is mainly technical in nature, such as the digital watch, VCR, and personal computer. A *competitive product* is one of many brands currently available in the market and has no special advantage over competing products. An *improved product* is not unique but is generally superior to many existing brands.

For example, let us assume Aubrey Organics is interested in manufacturing shampoo for tender hair in Turkey and seeks entry into the emerging market in the Middle East. The company finds that in addition to a number of local brands, Johnson & Johnson's baby shampoo and Helene Curtis Industries' Suave Shampoo are the competitive products in the market. Procter & Gamble has recently entered the market with its Pantene Pro-V brand, which is considered to be an improved product. Most of the competition appears to be addressing existing demand. However, no attempts have been made to satisfy latent demand or incipient demand. After reviewing various considerations, Aubrey Organics may decide to fulfill perceived latent demand with an improved offering through its Camomile Luxurious brand. Based on market information, the company reasons that a hair problem most consumers face in that market is dandruff. No brand has addressed itself to that problem. Even Procter & Gamble's new entry mainly emphasizes the health of hair. Thus, analysis of the competition with reference to product offerings and demand enables Aubrey Organics to determine its entry point into the Middle Eastern market.

Companies engaged in competitive business should aim at conducting competitor analysis to build competitive advantage. This cannot be done in isolation from the market and the rest of the industry, because being better than a competitor will not guarantee success if what is offered gives little value to the customer. Hence, it should be understood by firms that any inferences that might be drawn from competitor analysis must be considered in conjunction with other environmental factors. Every company has strategic options, although this does not mean that all options are sensible for every company. A company may choose to operate within the rules of the industry, without major change to what it offers. The options may include stronger focus on a niche strategy, seeking to identify and exploit segments where the company's products would have an advantage, or what might be termed improvement strategies. A competing firm may be attacked in various ways by a new and prospecting business firm in a given territory in order to optimize market advantage. The most effective way for a firm to attack may be through implementing a creative and entrepreneurial strategy on a sound knowledge analysis in view of changes in the competitive arena. Alternatively, a firm may attempt to pre-empt a competitor by getting into the market first with a new product, in an area of strategic importance. However, attacking the strategy of a competitor can leave a firm in a weaker position.

In a competitive business arena the competitors may be categorized as hard or soft players. Hard competitive players in business single-mindedly pursue competitive advantage and its benefits including leading market share, improved margins, and rapid growth. They pick their shots, seek out competitive encounters, set the pace of innovation, and test the edges of the possible success of their products and services in the market (Sutthijakra, 2011). Soft players, by contrast, may look good, but they are not intensely serious about winning. They do not accept that they must sometimes hurt their rivals, and risk being hurt, to get what they want. The commonly employed methods in taking up hard competitor strategies in bursts of ruthless intensity may include devastating rivals' profit sanctuaries, deceiving the competition, unleashing massive and overwhelming force, and raising competitors' costs (Stalk and Lachenauer, 2004). Soft players, by contrast, do not play to win; they just participate in the business and try to survive. This approach envelops issues such as leadership, corporate culture, knowledge management, talent management, and employee empowerment.

Every firm is risk averse in facing its business competition as it is a fact of business life, but many companies fail to manage it well. Good risk management not only protects companies from adverse risk but also confers a competitive advantage, enabling them to be more entrepreneurial and, in the end, to make bigger profits. Companies should clearly articulate their risk strategies, understand the risks they are taking, and build an effective risk-management organization that helps foster a responsible risk culture.

Companies in developing countries are often focused on chasing growth by investing in improving innovation, operations, and brand management. However, often despite potential for market share and efforts to increase demand for differentiated products, their business growth is slow while the market competition from regional and multinational companies keeps intensifying. Such a situation can be explained with reference to once high-flying Chinese automakers BYD and Chery, which have landed hard. By contrast, another automaker, Great Wall, and the appliance maker Haier have won early competitive advantage. The lessons from the experience of such companies is that companies should invest in basic innovations that meet latent demand at low organizational, manufacturing, and marketing cost. Change-driving companies also need to build their strength through licensing or contract manufacturing from established companies to reduce their organizational and manufacturing costs, operate on economies of scale, and focus on fast-moving products (Jullens, 2013).

Chaos theory in business

Dynamic behavior with referred uncertainty in business drives the chaos in markets. Chaos is a natural phenomenon in any dynamic state unless it is regulated or controlled through the set principles of action. The theory of chaos behavior has emerged as a field of study in mathematics, with applications in several disciplines including meteorology, sociology, physics, engineering, economics, biology, and philosophy. Of late this theory has also been interpreted meticulously in business as it leads to various uncertainties in market competition. Chaos theory studies the behavior of dynamic systems that are highly sensitive to initial conditions, a paradigm popularly referred to as the butterfly effect.

In reference to business the butterfly effect drives through small changes in marketing-mix, corporate policies, organizational culture, and competitive strategies that lead to larger effects in stimulating market share, business growth, and acquiring and retaining customers. Chaos in the market is commonly caused by congestion of competitors, frequent introduction and withdrawal of products and services, and extensive price promotions. Small differences yield widely diverging outcomes in dynamic market systems, often rendering long-term prediction impossible in general for a market or a business. This happens even though market systems are deterministic, meaning that their future behavior is fully determined, overruling the uncertainties. In consumer markets the chaos is frequent as these markets are very susceptible to butterfly effects, notably in fashion products and consumer electronics. Market chaos largely affects low-end markets, as exhibited in Figure 1.1.

The figure illustrates that the success of any innovation that has been a target for the mass market may trigger market chaos as fierce competition begins in the low-end markets. Such competition would divert consumers from the principal brands and toward low price-utilitarian or social status products. The growth of virtual channels would also drive the competition and chaos in the market. Market chaos in low-end markets is generally prompted by local companies, which give way to the international and virtual companies to push through the market space. On the other hand, chaos in high-end markets occurs through the rush of identical products by high-priced brand icons. Such competition in the high-end markets fragments the market share of companies and drives most consumers to adapt to fashion consumption behavior without developing loyalty for any brand. Many firms that enter with one touch technology fall into high-end market chaos.

Chaotic market behavior is predictable for a while and then appears to become random, posing consumers with a dilemma over responding to the uncertain marketing strategies of the concerned companies. The amount of time for which the behavior of market chaos can be

21

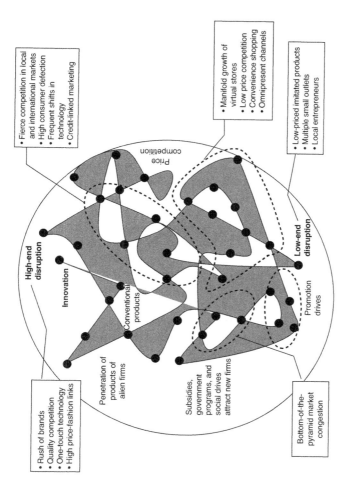

Figure 1.1 Market chaos and attributes of disruption

effectively predicted depends on three things, namely the tolerance limit of uncertainties in the market; how accurately market dynamism and chain causes and effects can be measured; and how effectively a temporal and spatial scale can be created to monitor and control market uncertainties in a given time. Chaos in the market is often initiated by companies that would like to leap frog the competition by earning higher market share through applying price-driven tactics. Companies in such market conditions experience high uncertainties and are unable to develop strategic plans. Thus, embracing chaos seems to be the opposite of discipline and planning. However, uncertainty is embedded in negotiations, and negotiators who ignore this fact and follow rigid strategies blind themselves to unexpected threats and miss potential opportunities (Wheeler, 2004).

Chaos in global as well as local markets has been caused by the introduction of new products as an outgrowth of continuous innovation and growth in technology, the free entry and exit of firms, frequently changing consumer preferences, and high substitution effects that makes the trust and loyalty of consumers fragile. Chaos in the market prompts abrupt changes and also triggers distractions in the business growth of companies. Chaos in market through innovation and technology breakthroughs is akin to the lifecycle of many industrial and consumer products in comprising the stages of introduction, acceleration (growth), acceptance (maturity), and renewal/diversification (decline). Each big idea catches hold slowly and moves through these stages in the market, but chaos occurs in the market as many ideas grow simultaneously. Yet, within a relatively short time, the new approach becomes so widely accepted that it is difficult even for old-timers to reconstruct how the world looked before. As market competition grows and consumers rapidly shift their preferences, most companies face creative destruction as survival options in the market narrow down to a change or perish philosophy. Accordingly most companies are leaning toward continuous innovations to differentiate their products and services but at the same time they are also susceptible to failures due to random and non-tested efforts. Thus, business in modern times poses uncertainty and moves on the common rationale of no pain, no gain. Understanding changing market and consumer behaviors, creative destruction may be necessary, and even preferable, in certain situations (Abrahamson, 2004).

The community-creation model in managing new businesses across diverse market segments is a governance mechanism for managing innovation that lies between hierarchy-based (closed) mechanisms and market-based (open) systems for new product management and driving the butterfly effect. The community-centric model shifts the focus of innovation and drives the change process beyond the boundaries of the firm, to a community of individuals and firms that collaborate to create joint intellectual property. Such strategies involve the community in spanning the change instituted by the company, setting ground rules for participation, and developing sustainable consumer behavior with differentiation. The community-of-creation model allows innovation-led changes to initially pass through a complex environment by striking a balance between order and chaos in the market (Sawhney and Prandelli, 2000).

With the high advancement of information technology and business forecasting tools, most companies are able to sustain short-run market chaos by predicting future market dynamics. Most companies are also able to determine and interpret the signals of competitors in chaotic markets. The foreseen uncertainty arising from chaos in the market is characterized by radical marketing elements comprising market communications that lay loose ends for free interpretations, marginal differences with existing and substitute products, and varied use values. In order to manage market uncertainty and chaos, companies need to play pro-customer roles, drive loyalty toward corporate brands, and build confidence in changing technology-led lifestyles to gain strategic competitive advantage. Companies must learn to ascertain the best mix of tools and techniques to select while driving changes though the differentiation in products and services and managing a market in chaos (Meyer et al., 2002).

Companies often make substantial efforts to innovate their products, and the processes to improve profit margins are often expensive and time-consuming, requiring a considerable upfront investment. Most companies step back from entering into the risk of engaging in driving change to gain butterfly effects and refrain from making large consumer products involving research and innovation investments (Economic Intelligence Unit, 2005). A similar global study conducted by IBM, in which over 750 corporate and public sector leaders were interviewed on the subject of innovation, found that competitive pressures pushed the business model innovation much more strongly than expected by multinational companies seeking global expansion and exploring markets in developing countries (Raphael and Christoph, 2012).

Managing chaos in the market needs to be learnt through constructive strategies and analyzing multiple perspectives by companies engaged in driving change in consumer behavior. In a growing market chaos among several competitive products that have marginal differentiation, global organizations need to develop customer values quickly to streamline the desired change in market and consumer attitudes. Large organizations, if led well, can do more for more people and flip the chaos, complexity, and pressure to manage the new market endeavors. Nissan Automobiles has been able to cope with crises in the Asian automobile industry and the chaos of low-cost cars penetrating potential emerging markets like India and China. The chaos was triggered by the Nano brand of Tata Motors Corporation in India, which promised low-end pricing in the mass market. Similarly in China, Faw Automobiles has driven its low-priced cars to global markets. Nissan tried to cut through the chaos by generating diverse values concerning the quality and services among consumers in global markets (Barton et al., 2012).

Random vs rational choices

Rational choice theory describes rationality of consumer choice as a conventional, learned, acquired, or shared wisdom in making buying decisions toward products and services considering the comparative advantages in value for money. The rationality associated with consumer choice in business is different from the colloquial and philosophical use of the word, which typically denotes rationality as sane or thoughtful. Rational choice theory uses a specific and narrower definition of rationality, explaining that individuals act in the buying process by balancing costs against benefits to arrive at action that maximizes personal advantage. Rational choice theory also suggests that consumers with a strong self-reference criterion would exhibit independent and measurable decisions in the market. Thus rationality is seen as patterns of choices, rather than individual perceptions.

Rational choices of consumers can be explained as reversible decisions in terms of the risk of delivering low value in comparison to alternative decisions. In the rational choice process individuals are seen as motivated by their needs, which offer options for strategic or tactical decision-making. The consumer in the present digital era acts within the community and develops preferences by analyzing the given information on products and services. Rational choice theory holds that individuals must anticipate the outcomes of alternative courses of action and calculate what will be best for them. Rational consumers choose the alternative that is likely to give them the greatest satisfaction. The rational decision of consumers generally applies not only to an individual consumer but also works as a conscious preferential move by a social actor engaging in community strategies. The behavior of consumers is shaped by the gains and losses that emerge as a consequence of their involvement in decision-making. Reinforcement of right consumer choices through gainful promotions of products and services needs to be technically driven by companies as conditioning in driving positive attitudes among consumers (Homans, 1961). Most consumers learn from their past experiences and streamline their future decision-making process. Not all rational choice of consumers leads to the best benefits in the competitive market, but many consumer decisions remain subtle without revealing the desired benefits to them (Scott, 2000).

The problem of collective action poses great difficulties for many consumers seeking a rational choice, which explains why some individuals refrain from joining groups and associations in driving their decisions. Consumer choices can be better nurtured if companies develop appropriate information platforms for consumers to analyze the pros and cons of the probable decisions that would benefit them. A good consumer–company relationship would benefit both company and consumer by driving simplified decision-making, enhanced customer satisfaction, reduced risk, and profitable bargains at both ends. On the other hand, if companies diffuse unclear information about their products and services, and do not offer the necessary support to consumers in making the right decision at the right time, this will fuel adverse consumer reactions, and put customers at risk of making inappropriate choices, causing bilateral damage to both consumers and company.

Despite consumers' high stakes in the business, sometimes companies pay little attention to default choices. Driving consumers toward a right choice requires companies to balance a complex array of interests, including customers' wishes and the company's desire to maximize profits while minimizing risk. Most companies strive to align their customer relationship strategies to help consumers in developing right and rational choices. The Audi automobile manufacturing company disseminates all required information to consumers from individual and community perspectives, and has found that consumers often align their choice with the company. Audi preselects silver metallic as its default color because it is the most popular. Of course, the random choice of consumers can be awkward and may not match with that of the company. Hence, a right buying perspective of consumers can be well developed by the company in addition to the community influences (Goldstein et al., 2008).

There are a number of assumptions made by rational choice theorists. Abell (2000) noted several such assumptions, as follows:

Individualism: Individuals, as actors in society, behave and act always as rational entities, self-calculating, self-interested, and self-maximizing for developing choices in a given business environment.

Optimality: Individuals choose their actions optimally, given their individual preferences as well as the opportunities or constraints that face them.

Structures: The structures and norms that dictate a single course of action are merely special cases of rational choice theory. In other words, the range of choices in other circumstances differs from choices in a strong structural circumstance, where there may be only one choice.

Self-Regarding Interest: This assumption states that the actions of the individual are concerned entirely with his or her own welfare.

Rationality: This appears the most predominant assumption of rational choice theory. All individuals, according to this assumption, act in ways that would benefit them more as compared to the alternate choices available in the market.

The rational choice exercises begin from the viewpoint of the consumer and seek endorsement through social institutions. The emphasis on the individual interest is always the starting point of the preference arguments. Despite several social interventions it is only individuals who ultimately derive buying preferences between several competitive options of products and services. Upon the foundation of individualism, the rational choice process may go further to portray how sharing, cooperation, or norms emerge, and the role they play in the buying decision.

Innovation and market competition

Innovation should always be customer-centric. For example, innovation in consumer health evolves through novel options around dietary products, consumer convenience, higher perceived value, and improved delivery mechanisms. Consumers intend to seek quick and effective solutions to prevent and treat minor ailments, and access low-fat, high-fiber diet products. Improved formulations provide relief via novel delivery mechanisms that make drugs easy to swallow or apply. New product development concepts have shifted toward herbal and quasi-traditional products, and dietary supplements, as regulatory procedures are being revised in various markets across the world. In the case of consumer products in developed markets, health is one common theme for many new soft drinks products. Other areas of innovation are in creating products that combine the characteristics of two categories, and using packaging to create a product with unique benefits.

There is a different set of opportunities for new products in developing markets than in developed markets. Global new product development in soft drinks was driven in 2012 by manufacturers' desire to add value to their products across developed and emerging markets alike. Key drivers for these products included the continued demand for beverage functionality, the consumer search for healthier soft drinks, and the expansion of both exotic and traditional flavors. Successful organizations that are engaged in the continuous innovation of products, services, and strategies are often dominated by the idea of staying ahead of the competition and their positioning as market leader. As against a long presence in the market and achieving high growth, innovation firms pay little attention to matching or outmaneuvering their rivals, seeking instead value innovation (Kim and Mouborgne, 2004).

As competition among firms manufacturing identical and similar products manufacturers increases, customers are expecting better service. Such consumer behavior has also resulted in brand-switching tendencies from dissatisfaction with services and low customer value. Those firms with predetermined business process tend to offer better customer services than those that do not follow a systems approach toward customer relations management. The process dynamics in developing and implementing strategies is a continuous process that should not be taken as an ad hoc requirement. The completeness of the process and proper strategy alignment would result in firms succeeding in a given marketplace. Hence, firms need guidelines and frameworks for addressing these expanding requirements.

The concept of process dynamics and completeness helps to consider service from the customer's viewpoint, arguably the major perspective to consider for market leadership in a competitive business environment. Process completeness is achieved when a firm's service delivery system matches the typical customer's breadth of expectations (Piccoli et al., 2009). There are four basic stages of process dynamics and strategy development systems in a competitive marketplace, namely:

- Transaction: to execute a basic request of customers through various routes to market.

- Process: handling all firm-related marketing and services requests through a hierarchical or a one-stop delivery point.
- Alliance: handling the process requests through a single touch point via stitching together a predetermined firm-selected alliance of service partners.
- Agility: handling process requests through a single touch point via stitching together a dynamic customer-selected alliance of business partners.

Developing an appropriate marketing strategy and its implementation involves making choices meticulously about whom to target as customers, what products to offer, and how to undertake related activities efficiently. The most common cause of strategic failure is the inability to make clear, explicit choices in these areas. It is very common for aggressive competitors to imitate attractive strategies but, perhaps more importantly, new strategic positions emerge continually. Successful incursions into established markets by strategic innovators such as Canon and the brokerage firm Edward Jones are based on strategic innovation proactively establishing distinctive strategic positions that are critical to shifting market share or creating new markets (Markides, 1999).

Most companies play a proactive role in launching innovative products and prepare marketing strategies in reference to existing market competition and competitors' business goals. New products often do not achieve the desired success because of the lack of organizational policies and teamwork. Thus it is required to inculcate team behavior in developing new products and popularizing them in test market segments. The results of the test markets may be further carried out in larger segments. It is essential to drive adequate brainstorming to map the basic (consumers' perceptions) and secondary market (operational market players such as distributors, retailers, inventory managers and the like) requirements for the product, listing the product attributes, and identifying the forced relationship of other goods and services with the new product (Rajagopal, 2014). Innovation-led products are susceptible to imitations by infringement of intellectual property rights and disruptive technologies with the increase of market competition against the innovative product. Most firms invest in building product brands at this stage and enhance services support to inculcate confidence among consumers and augment their loyalty toward the product and company. Innovation-led products become sustainable in the mature stage as they gain the desired market share and are positioned strategically against the market competition with long-term goals. At this stage both consumer value and brand equity for innovation-led products and services are enhanced.

Intensive competition from reputed brands of global firms have not only decreased the brand share in the premium and regular consumers' market segment but have also created price wars that reduce profit margins and limit the market growth of firms. This situation has motivated companies to consider positioning brands in the suburban and rural segments, which are largely unexplored. By targeting these segments with products in small packs at lower price points, companies have experienced great success (Dubey and Patel, 2004). The bottom-of-the-pyramid market segment, which constitutes a mass of small consumers, has become the principal target of most of the consumer brands emerging from multinational firms. The brands penetrating at the bottom-of-the-pyramid market should provide constancy and agility at the same time. Constancy is required if the brand is to build awareness and credibility, while agility in the brand builds perceived values among consumers. Agility is required if the brand is to remain relevant in a free marketplace (Blumenthal, 2002).

In changing global markets the concept of choice, and the ability to exercise it, is seen as a healthy practice to allow consumers to build confidence in the company and develop long-term relations with it. Most multinational companies believe that a sense of autonomy and consumer well-being can be developed among consumers by providing them the right to choice on a more transparent information base. Accordingly, the global business philosophy delineates that the "choice is good" thinking, and the number of offerings in a wide variety of product and service categories, can significantly drive consumer confidence in the company as well as help the company to stay competitive in the marketplace over time. Companies in the competitive marketplace are engaged in encouraging attribute-based decision-making models for helping consumers make the right decision.

2
Reasoned Action and Planned Behavior

Chaos in markets drives random buying behavior among consumers. Consumer behavior in general exhibits mixed cognitive attributes of risk-averse and creative enthusiasm during periods of market chaos. The ideal circumstances for consumer behavior are driven by a competitive business environment in the market. Intention is the cognitive representation of a consumer's readiness to accept or reject changes in the market and perform induced or self-referred behavior. The butterfly effect in the market triggers such cognitive conditions among consumers. This intention is determined by three things: consumers' attitude toward the specific behavior, their subjective norms, and their perceived behavioral control. This chapter argues that at the initial stage consumers face a decision crunch, a narrow scope of idea transformation, returns on investment, and self-references versus peer review pressures in making buying decisions. The chapter addresses the issues of reasoned action and differentiation strategies that drive the thought process among companies for reaping better advantages of the butterfly effect. The chapter also maps the mindset of consumers in managing the challenges and opportunities within and outside the market ambience. The chapter also considers the attributes of cognitive push for overcoming complex decisions in marketing, as a way to deliver value for money to consumers. Besides cognitive attributes of consumers, this chapter also discusses issues of knowledge development, business thought process, and managing the consumer learning curve.

Reasoned action and planned behavior cannot be interpreted while chaos exists in the market. Consumers are unable to develop logical analysis for making the right choices in a chaotic environment. Hence, most companies streamline their marketing strategy in a selected market segment to avoid competition conflicts and offer consumers enough space toward making right choices. The streamlining efforts of companies' marketing strategies should be duly coordinated through a bottom-up process and should take into account the competition realities surrounding markets. Emerging companies put forth enormous resources and managerial efforts to develop a market environment conducive to competition for consumers to help them in building planned behavior to support appropriate decision-making.

The developing marketplace

Marketplace strategy includes elements of product and customer segments, competitive posture, and the goals, moves and directions of the firm. Products and customers are categorized in different ways. Customers are segmented on the basis of the products and services they use at any point in time, along with customer demographics. The needs of customers relate more directly than any of the demographic profiles. A competitor's position and direction are better known to the distributing channels than any other external agency. Tapping the right information by taking the distribution channels into confidence would be more appropriate than any other means for the company. Rival business firms often choose distinctly different channels to reach end users. Competitive posture reveals how a competitor competes in the marketplace to attract, win, and retain customers.

The customer is the kingpin in determining competitive posture. The competitive posture of a company consists of product line, product attributes, functionality, service, availability, image, sales relationship, and pricing pattern. The *product line* broadly refers to the range of products available to the competitor. Distributors and retailers are more concerned with the width (that is, item in the product range). Some companies focus on a narrow range of products and build a high image among customers. The *product attributes* vary in terms of shape, design, style, color, and added advantages. Further, customers may view the functionality of the product as the satisfaction derived from the products. The dimensions of *functionality* are highly product-specific. In competitive markets, the efficiency of the *services* discharged and extended to buyers also contributes in building or breaking the marketplace strategy. Products, in the same market or competitive domain, largely vary in their *availability* often because of weak or faulty supply chain management. Competing firms must study this situation and develop strategies accordingly. Beside all, *pricing patterns* of mercantile and service sector companies are sensitive and may carry enough strength to destroy rivals' business.

Such market tactics among companies dealing with fast-moving consumer goods (FMCGs) and services have been observed time and again. An example of price war is seen in the low-cost airlines of India. Jet Airways, Kingfisher Airlines, and Indian Airlines drive campaigns to attract potential customers as well as prevent the switching of existing customers by slashing prices on domestic trunk routes. The position of products and services, and the level of competition in the marketplace may be assessed by measuring the dynamic moves (strategic and tactical) in the given product-customer segments in a competitive marketplace.

A niche domain involves a narrow product line and customer segment. A competing company must take note that the rival is always expert in terms of product and customers. The spread domain entails narrow product ranges targeted at a large segment of customers. Such firms invest more time and resources in building brands and securing customer segments (e.g. Bata India Ltd has a narrow product-mix but a wide customer segment). The proliferated domain involves a wide range of products aimed at narrow customer segments. Many companies offer a wide range of products in a restricted range. A blanket domain is attained when the competitor has positioned its products and services in all the available segments (e.g. Bajaj Scooters Ltd in the Indian automobile sector). Marketing organizations in a competitive marketplace follow different organizational designs to optimize their advantage over rival firms. In an *international business division structure*, a firm's activities are separated into two units comprising domestic and international operations. The main function of such an international division is to draw a distinction between the domestic and international business.

A worldwide *geographic structure* of organization can overcome the problems associated with an international division structure. In this structure, foreign and domestic operations are not isolated, but are integrated as if foreign boundaries did not exist. Worldwide markets are segregated into geographic areas. Operational responsibility goes to area line managers, whereas corporate headquarters maintains responsibility for overall planning and control. Major attributes of the geographic organizational design of multinational companies are as below:

- Product lines are less diverse.
- Products are sold to end users.
- Marketing is a critical variable.
- A similar channel is used for marketing of all products.
- Products are based on local consumer needs.

This organizational design has various advantages, markedly in delegation of line authority and explicit responsibility. Specifically, the merits of this system include:

- Responsibility and delegation of line authority.
- Manufacturing and product sales coordination.
- Large number of executives.
- Conflicts of roles and responsibilities.
- Lack of specialists in the product sales line.

An important disadvantage in geographic organizational design may be the involvement of a large number of top-level executives in operational tasks, which leads to conflict in terms of power play and command execution in the organization. Beside the agglomeration of top management personnel, the individual products may suffer, as responsibilities cannot be fixed easily on specific operational executives.

A product led organizational design is different from a geographic design wherein a worldwide responsibility to product group executives at the line management level is assigned, and emphasis is placed on the product line rather than on geographic differences. The coordination of activities in a geographic area is handled through specialists at the corporate staff level, but in the product organization focus is laid on the performance of the product-mix in a given area. Multinational companies, which operate within this kind of structure, have a variety of end users, handle diversified product lines with high technological capability, and divert logistics costs to local manufacturers. This type of organizational design has several benefits, including:

- Decentralization of authority.
- High motivation of divisional heads.
- Adding or dropping new products have marginal impact on operations.
- Control of product through the product lifecycle.

In organizational structure, a firm is segregated along product lines considering each division as a separate profit center with the division head directly accountable for profitability. Decentralization of operations is critical in this structure, and more decisions are likely to be left to the local manager, who is then usually more highly motivated. Decentralization of authority is a prime advantage of this structure wherein division heads are highly motivated. This structure allows product managers to add new products and product lines and with-draw old ones with only marginal effect on overall operations. Another advantage of this structure is that the control of a product through the product lifecycle can be managed more readily and securely. However, firms following this organizational structure often face problem of coor-dination among product and territory managers. In addition, it is felt that executives quickly become biased toward the regional and corpo-rate staff in managing any product process.

In recent years, a synergy of all the above organizational structures has emerged among multinational companies, defined as a *matrix structure*. Matrix structures offer greater flexibility than the single line-of-command structures already discussed and reconcile this flexibility with coordination and economies of scale to maintain the strength of large organizations. The attributes and advantages of matrix organiza-tions include:

- Multiple command lines.
- Product and geographic coordination.
- Product lines in a national setting.
- Organization design reacts quickly to local environment demands.

For multinational firms, matrix organization is a solution to the prob-lem of responding to both economic and political environments. General Electric Company in Asia operates with a matrix structure and has been successful. A matrix organization can encompass geographic and product-management components. However, some of the disad-vantages in this organizational design are power struggles among the supervisory personnel and parallel decision-making.

Many technology-driven firms consider establishing strategic alliances to be an effective strategy to sustain market competition. They recog-nize that alliances and relationships with other companies of repute are fundamental to outwit, outmaneuver, and outperform competitors by way of better branding, better service, and tagging global brands for assuring the quality of goods and services. Alliances and relationships thus transform the concept of the competitor. Strategic alliances may be in various forms, such as branding, logistics, research and development, production and operations management, packaging, services, sales, and customers. Business alliances have to be identified by doing a rigorous exercise: the company has to list all alliances that it is planning to have to outperform competitors, categorize all available alliances by activity, value chain, and resources, and identify key alliances, which will give it an edge on the marketplace strategy of the competitor. It is essential to identify alliance partners and know about their marketplace strategies. The purpose of the alliance has to be made transparent at the very beginning of the deal. The type of alliance and context of the alliance are the relevant competitive conditions, leadership, and motivations for the partners. The company has to draft the terms of the alliance clearly for striking a final deal. The terms of the alliance must delineate the resources contribution of each partner, the roles and responsibilities of both partners, duration of the alliance and the quality benchmarks. The company proposing the alliances must assess the evolution date of the alliance, its attributes, marketplace signals, and consequences for the competitor in terms of changes in marketplace strategy. The company should also identify the indicators to monitor the terms of the alliance with a view to reorient business needs, mutual interests, and commitment. The marketing environment for a competitive environment is a combination of factors that the customers use as tools for pursuing marketing objectives in the identified markets for achieving targets. These factors have to be strategically mixed in marketing planning for offering quality services and optimizing customer value. It is an integrated approach for promoting services with a view to expand the area in the services market. The traditional components of marketing-mix, including product, pricing, place, and promotion, are further supplemented by another set of "11Ps" consisting of product, price, place, promotion, packaging, pace, people, performance, psychodynamics, posture, and proliferation.

A company trying to outwit, outmaneuver, and outperform competitors must also keep a constant watch on their future movements and should draw up projections for building counter-strategies to check or defuse competitor moves. The company must assess the marketplace strategy alternatives being considered by the competitor firm. The analysis of competitor strategy plots need to be conducted carefully. There are a number of options for examining the competitor firm, including:

- Aggressive penetration of high-price markets.
- Low-price market entry.
- Maintaining present strategy.

Multiple signals typically emerge out of the projected strategy of the competitor and have to be interpreted appropriately. The signals must be assessed in reference to the supporting logics, competitive consequences, and the implications thereof.

Companies intending to expand their business to various destinations look into the ethnocentrism, polycentrism, and geo-centrism in driving a sustainable market development process. An executive with an *ethnocentric orientation* views international business as secondary, a place to dispose of "surplus" products left over after fulfilling domestic demand. The differences in these approaches have been illustrated by choices of branding policy. A firm following a *polycentric orientation* establishes subsidiaries located overseas to operate independently from each other and encourages the company to follow its unique marketing strategy. In such a situation each company will have independent planning for brands, products, and services, consistent with local criteria. A company with a *geocentric approach* takes a perspective of one world market and considers the global market as a whole, with no demarcation between domestic and international business. Such a firm will have a global marketing planning and strategic focus.

Reasoned action and differentiation strategy

The theory of reasoned action may be explained in the context of consumer choices in market competition that consumer behavior is determined by the intention to lean toward a choice of product and service and develop norms of association with it (Fishbein and Aizen, 1975). The intention to choose a product or service is the cognitive representation of a consumer's readiness to explore satisfaction and derive comparative use values and value for money. The consumer's intention to buy products and services is determined by their attitude toward the specific behavior, value gains through comparative advantages, and perceived behavioral control. Supplementing the variables of consumer purchase intention behavior, the theory of planned behavior argues that attitudes of consumers derived from social media and peer influences help in fostering their preferences for products and services in competitive markets. Most companies engage market research agencies to monitor and measure the dynamics of consumer attitudes that are governed by continuously updating their knowledge, changing beliefs, and social interactions. The perceived behavioral control of consumers also influences intentions (Aizen, 1991).

Some studies counter-argue against cognitive intricacies between behavioral intention and actual behavior in determining consumer preferences and giving a lead to the brand in a given marketplace. Perceived behavioral control analysis also helps companies in predicting behavioral intention and probable shifts in consumer behavior. In addition, consumers are also driven by the socio-cognitive elements such as motivation and performance, and feelings of frustration associated with repeated failures determine effect and behavioral reactions. In a competitive marketplace, where determining comparative advantage is complex, consumer behavior is largely determined by self-efficacy and value-expectancy parameters. *Self-efficacy* may be defined as the conviction emerging from the ACCA model, comprising accessibility to products, comprehension, conviction, and action. An attitude of self-efficacy successfully executes the behavior required to produce the desired values. *Value expectancy* refers to a consumers' estimation of the degree of satisfaction that will lead to certain outcomes. Self-efficacy is the most important precondition for behavioral change, since it has the potential to induce community behavior (Rajagopal, 2011).

The theory of planned behavior (TPB) emerged in the late twentieth century as an outgrowth of the theory of reasoned action, and has been used successfully to predict and explain a wide range of organizational behavior of business companies in the global marketplace. Most companies growing amidst market competition drive their efforts to change the purchase intentions of consumers in their favor to gain sustainable advantage over the competition and inject the butterfly effect into the market. The TPB states that consumer behavior is largely driven by motivation, which develops an intention, while behavioral control demonstrates the ability of consumers to turn their buying intentions into action. Such planned behavior and reasoned action distinguishes between beliefs, normative behavior, and behavioral control. The TPB exhibits the following constructs that collectively represent the analytical insights and carry dynamic expulsion of small changes for a large difference that explains the butterfly effects:

- Attitudes – This refers to the critical evaluation of purchase intentions and expected benefits of the buying behavior of consumers. It entails a consideration of the outcomes of right buying decisions.
- Behavioral intention – This exhibits the motivational factors that influence a given behavior, which demonstrates that the stronger the purchase intention, the stronger the consumer behavior.
- Subjective norms – This refers to the belief about whether most consumers approve or disapprove of the behavior and seek a second opinion from their peers or consider public opinion. Subjective norms relate to consumers' beliefs about whether peers and people of importance guide their personal insights to engage in the right analysis and decision-making.

- Social norms – This refers to the social codes of behavior in a group of people or larger cultural context. Social norms are considered normative, or standard, in a group of people that most consumers set as their decision-making benchmark.
- Perceived power – This refers to consumers' bargaining power and perceived value analysis on the decisions that may facilitate or impede the judgmental behavior of consumers. Perceived power contributes to a consumer's perceived behavior also in reference to competitive products.

The butterfly effect thought process

As market competition is increasing diversely, companies are actively engaged in differentiating products, services, and marketing strategies to gain competitive advantage. In this process companies are investing resources enormously in product and process innovation to stimulate consumers toward product differentiation. However, small changes combined with the right psychographic segmentation can lead to large benefits in the business and drive competitive advantage. For instance, Bonafont S.A. de C.V., a purified water bottling company in Mexico, positioned its purified bottled water gender-sensitively to a female segment though a TV commercial aired in 2003. The commercial focused on promoting the concept of drinking water to reduce weight and stay petite. This small change resulted in high customer loyalty in the consumer segment, and the company is currently ranked third in the bottled water segment.

Parallel to global markets, local markets are growing manifold in the twenty-first century and large firms are stimulating regional and local enterprises to become dynamic in order to face increasing market competition. Consequently a large number of enterprises have agglomerated in emerging markets and are driving continuous innovation in products, services, and marketing strategies to acquire a profitable posture in the marketplace. Managers are putting various strategic efforts to sustain the company in a time of highly competitive and unpredictable markets. During the latter half of the twentieth century there was a dramatic shift in the pace of market competition. Consequently most managerial firms, irrespective of their size of operations, have given up the traditional manufacturing and marketing model, with its user-friendly innovation and technology, and have adopted competitive and less bureaucratic ways of managing their firms. In the process most managers attempt to learn from trial and error experiments on organizational and strategic change. This resulted in many small changes introduced by companies in reference to product design, technology, use value, price, and competitive advantage that brought larger benefits to the company on the global marketplace. The transformation in consumer attitude following a small change, such as adding Aloe Vera to cosmetics to identify them as on par with organic cosmetics, has resulted in high market share for the cosmetic division of consumer goods manufacturing companies such as Unilever, Procter & Gamble, and Revlon.

In the recovery and learning process of the consequences of small changes driving large effects, companies often realize that emotional recovery from failure happens when loss in the business is sustainable and not a threat to future growth. In the process of shift in the business strategy, a major threat appears as the loss of competencies, market share, and profit. Hence, managers are often concerned to develop strategies of restoration. The thinking of managers toward shifts in the managerial strategy is illustrated in Table 2.1.

However, most companies remain locked into the mechanical mindset of the industrial age, assuming that for any management challenge an optimal solution can be found. In the increasingly unstable and unpredictable market environment that exists in the global marketplace today, managers find it difficult to develop a precise marketing strategy for achieving competitive advantage. Companies should engage in open-ended conversations with business counterparts, market players, and customers as a way to interpret and respond creatively to

Table 2.1 Causes and effects of transforming markets with the butterfly effect

Risk-oriented	Recovery-oriented
• Involves working through and processing small change experiences in products marketing with less emotional bonds and competitive advantage. • Product differentiation might create loss in reference to the eventually changed viewpoint. • Changes introduced by companies to gain competitive advantage confront consumer use value. • The changes introduced by companies might also drive negative emotions.	• Most changes are pro-active and lead to build sustainable consumer behavior toward the products, brands, and competitive gains. • Involves high consumer psychodynamics and builds the change effect for larger impact within the consumer segment. • Enhances the value-added benefits to consumers and increases value for money. • Builds "me too" feeling among consumers for the products and services following a butterfly effect.

differentiate manufacturing and marketing strategies to gain competitive advantage (Lester et al., 1998).

The differentiation process demands a continuous flow of new ideas. Ideas for innovations are the precious currency of the new market economy, but generating them is a mysterious process. Businesses that constantly innovate have systematized the production and testing of new ideas, and the system can be replicated by practically any organization. The best innovators use old ideas as the raw materials for new ideas. Managers need to develop their thinking process in the following way:

- Nurture good ideas from a wide variety of sources.
- Keep those ideas alive by developing them, discussing them among peers, and applying them in niche environments.
- Visualize new uses of conventional wisdom and encourage cross-pollination of ideas within the organization to allow peer interaction.
- Turn promising concepts into real services, products, processes, or business models to gain competitive advantage in the marketplace.

Leading companies may use the above thought process to generate innovative strategies. Most dynamic enterprises tend to move new ideas from one market to another and intend to build full-fledged consulting groups to refine the thought processes and internal knowledge on managerial leadership by innovations. The most important issue in cultivating such thought processes is to strike a balance between organizational responsiveness to innovative thinking and organizational work culture (Keidle, 2013). Competitive mind-set of companies involves the ability to rapidly sense, act, and mobilize even under uncertain conditions. Most managers learn in a dual-process way. This process suggests two-level interactive learning platforms based on the idea of interaction by means of explicit and implicit learning through reinforcement. It accounts for many unexplained cognitive perceptions and phenomena based on casual and peer interactions. The dual process of oscillating between loss-orientation and restoration-orientation enables an manager to:

- obtain the benefits of each,
- minimize the costs of maintaining one for too long, and
- accelerate the recovery of market process.

There are many applied implications of a dual learning process, leading to the following attributes of the managerial thinking process:

- Companies acquire knowledge through feelings and reactions as experienced in real situations.
- Realizing that psychological and physiological outcomes caused by the feelings of loss of appropriate thought processes are symptoms in an innovation process may reduce secondary sources of stress among managers.
- There is a process of recovery to learn from failure, which offers some comfort that the current feelings of loss will eventually diminish.
- Recovery and learning process can be enhanced by some degree of co-creation or peer interactions.
- Recovery from loss offers an opportunity to increase one's knowledge of managership and regenerate the thinking process.

There is often an imbalance between the flow of ideas and implementing them to arrive at solutions in a growing managerial firm. Companies face a problem in fitting the ideas to resolve complexities in innovation and growth, and most managers immediately focus on crash solutions, devoting little time to analyzing why the problem exists in the first place. This is one of the flaws in traditional thinking, which may lead to conclusions without any rationale. In the marketplace today, consistent thinking for continuous innovation becomes increasingly important for the simple reason that the challenges enterprises face are becoming more complex (May, 2012).

Seasoned enterprises in the marketplace know that the opportunities for competitive advantage lie in market muddle, but they recognize the need for developing critical strategic processes. In traditional strategy, most managers derive advantage by exploiting resources and stable market positions for the products and services of their firms. A simple rule of strategy implementation suggests that advantage on outcome appears upon successfully seizing opportunities. Most firms found good innovation opportunities toward key strategic processes, such as product innovation, partnering, or spinout creation. They need to create simple rules for the innovation process to help managers in pursuing such opportunities in reference to practical approaches to innovations, market limitations, priority rules, scheduling, and exit rules. Managerial firms must follow the set rules meticulously to avoid the distraction to the innovation process caused by frequent rule changes. A consistent strategy helps managers and managers in sorting out promising opportunities and gaining short-term advantage by exploiting them (Eisenhardt and Sull, 2001).

Sometimes a dynamic idea – the change agent – which emerges and spans the business in a given market, creates the butterfly effect to yield large benefits. These ideas may thrust a product or process innovation by making small changes that could drive large effects in the market in terms of shifts in consumer behavior, retailing, distribution, competitive performance, and profiteering of the company. However, to make the butterfly effect happen in the market, companies need to evaluate innovative ideas that have the potential to drive large changes and reset organizational behavior in tune with understanding the market scenarios and developing a rationale for building market development strategies. In the process of resetting organizational behavior and work culture, companies review their existing beliefs, normative behavior and organizational control process to foster the potential butterfly effect change agents. The butterfly effect process in the market is exhibited in Figure 2.1.

In order to drive small changes to gain large competitive benefits companies should adapt their organizational behavior to understand the existing market scenario by analyzing chaos among competitors and changing consumer behavior as shown in Figure 2.1. Various elements of organizational beliefs, normative behavior, and organizational behavioral control contribute in developing marketing strategies to incubate the butterfly effect. While nurturing the butterfly effect companies are required to change their organizational beliefs toward introducing long product lifecycles, making strategic moves, and enhancing competitive responsiveness to introduce small and dynamic changes for gaining competitive advantage in the marketplace. Companies also need to reorient their normative behavior toward strengthening risk absorption and tolerance on gaining market share in the competitive marketplace. Strengthening strategies on acquiring and retention of consumers, cost and profit management, and developing marketplace ambience for seeding competitive differentiation would help companies to drive butterfly effects.

Butterfly effects emerge in the market through differentiation management, penetrating into the competitive market by using marketing-mix injective strategies as illustrated in Figure 2.1. The marketing-mix, as mentioned, consists of the "11 Ps" of product, place, price, promotion, packaging, pace, performance, people, psychodynamics, posture, and proliferation. However, companies should also develop reactive strategies to sustain competition shocks and reviving values. As companies experience the global spread of the butterfly effect they may decide to develop macro marketing strategies or favor niche development. Such strategies may lead to significant corporate effects in reference to increase in market share, corporate posture development, enhanced

43

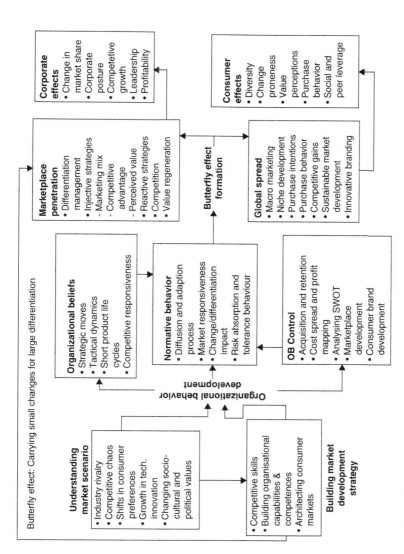

Figure 2.1 The butterfly effect: backward and forward linkages

business growth, and profitability. Accordingly, consumers develop a positive attitude toward change proneness, and augment their value perceptions.

The consumer market has now exceeded one billion, which gives the right opportunities for multi-scale retailing companies in consumer products to move their innovative products, marketing strategies, and processes to drive the butterfly effect. China is often viewed as a land of limitless opportunities. The country has experienced multiple sea changes that, collectively, have created one of the most appealing business destinations in the world. China is a pioneer in manufacturing and marketing mobile communication devices but its retailing is still largely observed in a conventional way. Most companies are engaged in digitizing the retail trade to offer more convenience to local Chinese consumers. The fact is that China's consumer market today is a collection of many different consumer archetypes that incorporate many groups of consumers with different preferences and behaviors. Digital channels are prevalent today and digital consumption continues to become popular. Hence, developing smarter, seamless, and secure retailing experiences using new retailing technologies may evoke the butterfly effect not only in China but also in the large demography markets of India, Russia, and Brazil. China's urban consumers remain very pragmatic shoppers, leveraging multiple channels before they purchase.

Omni channel experience

Differentiation and change management in a market is a continuous process, which should be linked to *kaizen* – a Japanese term for continuous improvement. Improvement or *change for the better* refers to a philosophy or practices that focus upon continuous improvement of processes in manufacturing, engineering, and business management. *Kaizen* refers to activities that continually improve all functions, and involves all employees from the CEO to assembly line workers. It also applies to processes, such as purchase and logistics, which cross organizational boundaries into the supply chain. By improving standardized activities and processes, *kaizen* aims to eliminate waste (as in lean manufacturing). *Kaizen* was first implemented in several Japanese businesses after World War II, influenced in part by American business and quality management teachers who visited the country.

Every small idea in a company may be a powerful means to initiate a business revolution by putting the organization first in acquiring market and customer value. Putting the customer first has sparked a revolution at Hindustan Computers Limited, the services giant of India in information technology. This company banked in conventional wisdom of valuing the customer first, then turned the hierarchical pyramid upside down by making management accountable to the employees. By catalyzing both employees and customers, the emerging enterprise may be able to pave a path of transformation through innovation to enable the firm to grow fast and stay profitable among competing firms. Managers may create a sense of urgency for innovative thinking in the organization by enabling employees to realize the need for change and inculcate a culture of trust by pushing transparency in communication and information sharing. Enterprises can grow as think-tanks like Toyota and General Electric by developing a bottom-up organizational hierarchy and enabling the ideation process and functions accountable to the employee as performance indicators (Nayar, 2010). Innovative thinking can become a work culture as firms encourage liberty of expressions among employees to unveil their potential with the following goals:

- foster a managerial mind-set,
- decentralize decision-making, and
- transfer the ownership of "change" to the employee in the market and consumer value zones.

Competitive thinking is the ability to view the market and its ambience business platform and develop both market-oriented and customer-centric strategies necessary to exploit the available opportunities. The drive to differentiate products and services in a company involves looking into future and visualizing collective initiatives within the industry. Most firms are increasingly turning toward business model innovation as an alternative or a complement to product or process innovation. A business model may be defined as a system of interconnected and interdependent activities that determines the way the company does business with its customers, partners, and vendors. Business model innovation may occur by adding innovative activities like forward or backward integration and by linking activities in novel ways. Managers may develop their innovative business model by considering the following issues (Amit and Zott, 2012):

- Identifying perceived needs that can satisfy the innovative business model, which has a potential to trigger the butterfly effect.
- Listing novel activities that are needed to satisfy the perceived values of consumers.

- Finding how the required activities could be linked to each other in novel ways.
- Identifying the key players to perform each of the activities that are part of the business model.
- Identifying ways to create value through the novel business model.
- Developing a revenue model that fits with the company's innovative business model.

In a traditional enterprise, innovative thinking is often centralized. However, modern firms focus on developing new aesthetically attractive products and enhancing brand perception through smart, evocative advertising. Growing firms are inducing employees, consumers, and market players to create new ideas instead of simply improving existing products, services and processes. Creative thinking in a company drives creative designing to cater to the consumer needs in a technologically feasible and strategically viable way. A good thinking process in a firm may be generated through collaboration between frontline employees and market players, including distributors, retailers, and consumers, to reengineer existing products and services or create new ones through innovation and technology. Competitive thinking should be based on close observation on demand shifts, competitor product portfolios, and changes in consumer preferences combined with brainstorming and rapid prototyping of innovative products (Brown, 2008).

Developing the product-market differentiation is one of the strongest self-growth challenges. However, it is necessary for companies to know the market attributes that arise to carry on the thought process and set up a pro-innovation and pro-growth mind-set. Some of these issues are discussed below:

- Negative attitudes, habits, and beliefs override the growth challenges and hinder managers from achieving their own potential.,
- Fear of loss of money on introducing new products, new designs or shifting technologies can hold back the innovation or change process.
- Procrastination and lack of focus may cause managers to get poor results from the efforts on time and resources invested.
- A random approach without proper planning may cause disruption in the thinking process and may jeopardize the growth of the enterprise.
- Low self-confidence of managers reduces their effectiveness and affects the growth of the enterprise.

- The "bright shiny object syndrome" means to grab the newest, hottest idea or strategy and can lead to managers endlessly changing the ideas.
- Lack of action on plans can push new ideas away from proper implementation and leave innovations stranded.

Companies should address these issues with the help of a mentor and break the cognitive barriers to see the light on the other side of attitudinal issues. Applying innovation and technology to small business is usually challenging as operational and marketing plans are largely based on short-run profits. Change management involves facing major challenges. Managers should value the particular twists and abilities of employees if they contribute to the growth of the business. Emerging firms should plan to capitalize on each employee's uniqueness and encourage employees to share ideas on innovation and technology to strengthen their capabilities and competencies. The focus on employees would also make them accountable in their task and help in capitalizing on their on-the-job experience and thereby build a stronger sense of team-playing (Buckingham, 2005).

Most companies believe they make decisions by pursuing market analysis. To refine their decision-making skills they must understand that real-world decisions are not always made through logical steps. Using the convergence of conventional wisdom with innovation and technological growth, managers should learn to define the problem, diagnose its causes, design possible solutions, choose strategic options, and finally implement the best choice. Companies should focus on thinking first before choosing to interfere with a concurrent market situation and taking a decision on the complex issues. The decision-making process for managers consist of the three stages of thinking, visualizing, and applying. Thinking in depth is required when the innovation issue or market situation is clear, data are reliable, the context is structured, thoughts can be pinned down, and discipline can be applied – for example, in an established production process. Companies may visualize their ideas when many elements are combined into creative solutions. Applying ideas may work effectively when the situation is innovative and a few simple relationship rules are designed to carry out creativity in innovation and technology projects. Such an approach could help the firm move forward in the marketplace (Mintzberg and Westley, 2001).

Despite differences in their personal attributes, successful companies stand by their commitments and excel in business operations. Their commitments may vary from capital investments to personnel decisions to stakeholder management that would have enduring influence on the company. Meticulously accomplishing the set commitments by all in an organization helps in shaping the posture of the firm in the marketplace, defines the strengths and weaknesses of firm, establishes its opportunities and limitations, and sets its future direction. Competing companies often take actions in view of the current business situation that might result in short-run benefits but may not necessary help in complying with long-term business goals (Sull, 2003). The effective small changes that have potential to create larger market advantages for a company make the lifecycle of the butterfly effect sustainable in the market.

Strategic differentiation and market development

Market differentiation is a useful first step for retailers or developers who are trying to identify the best locations in a large market territory. In the context of increasing market competition firms undergo a comprehensive market differentiation process prior to developing market attractiveness for sustaining market competition. In order to survive market competition, most firms also explore the possibility of strategic marketing alliances with strong firms. In the strategic partner selection process competing firms look for finance, business know-how, and knowledge of local markets, a shared understanding of the business and brand, and ultimately homogeneity between the partners (Doherty, 2009).

The following differentiation process will help managers to zero in on visible prospects for growth. Once identified and prioritized the process can be converted into long-term and short-term marketing objectives, and strategies and tactics.

1. **Present markets:** To identify the best opportunities for expanding present markets, it is necessary to investigate emerging businesses or acquire new users for a product. Determining how to displace competition is a particularly significant factor in no-growth markets. Firms need to increase product usage by current customers and redefine market segments where there are changes in customer buying patterns. Firm may opt to work in association with customers on innovative ideas to reformulate or repackage the product according to their specific need. It is important to identify new uses (applications) of products and services, and reposition the product to create

a more favorable perception over rival products. The investigation should be carried out where to expand into new or non-served market niches.

2. **Customers:** Distribution channels need to be assessed to identify the best opportunities for expanding, improvement or expansion in the customer base. Managers should refine the product pricing policies to match market share objectives, enrich communications, including advertising, sales promotion, and publicity, and deploy the sales force to target new customers with high potential. There is a need to consider enhancing customer service, including technical services and complaint handling. Identifying the changes in trade buying practices, where the buying process may have shifted from manufacturer to distributor or to end-user, makes the marketing strategy good for effective implementation.

3. **Growth markets:** Firms operating in a competitive marketplace should target key geographic locations, developing appropriate market segments and building substantial long-term potential to identify growth markets.

4. **New product development:** In order to give priority to creative ideas for new product and services development that will impact on immediate and long-range opportunities, the company should focus on new products that can be differentiated and that have the potential for an extended lifecycle. Firms need to search for ways to diversify into new or related products, product lines, and/or new items or features. Firms should examine the techniques to modify products by customer groups, distribution outlets, or individual customer applications, and initiate the work on improving packaging to conform to customer specifications and to distinguish their product from rivals'. Simultaneously there is a need to establish new value-added services.

5. **Targets of opportunity:** Innovative attitudes and managerial thinking would develop the focus on areas outside the current market segment or production line not included in other categories. However, strategic directions or mission statements need to be maintained as a guideline to assess how far a company can realistically diversify from its core business and still retain its vitality.

During the early stage of economic transition, it was presumed that the newly liberalized economies in Central and Eastern Europe would experience high rates of sustained economic growth, with rapid convergence toward the trade and economy of the major industrialized economies in the West. A key factor of the transition process was structural change from the reallocation of resources on the basis of market incentives. Variability in production and consumption behavior was therefore a potentially useful concept in analyzing the structural changes that actually occurred in Eastern European transition economies. Among these economies, the Polish transition can be viewed as most successful in terms of growth levels. The overall impact of political and economic disintegration on trade among the former constituent republics of three former federations in Central and Eastern Europe – the Soviet Union, Yugoslavia, and Czechoslovakia – has been followed by a sharp fall in trade intensity, although the legacy of a common past remains strong. However, the process of integration into the world economy has not been uniform across the transition countries. After long inward-looking trade policies and import-substituting industrialization, several Latin American countries undertook comprehensive trade liberalization and macroeconomic adjustment in the 1980s, and the experience of these countries has been relevant for the economies in Eastern Europe and the former Soviet Union in the transition from socialism to market economies (Rajagopal, 2009).

Business partnership strategies should be developed keeping in view the heterogeneity in economic development, culture, and institutional modalities that exist in both regions, while seeking globally balanced relations. The relationship should be based on fundamentally shared principles and values, which in turn can be translated into clear political messages and a general sustained process of dialogue and cooperation. Relationships can be deepened at the bi-regional, regional or bilateral levels, taking advantage of the special circumstances of country groupings. Building relationships should proceed at different levels and speeds among the countries of the region. Considering the multiplicity of forums, it is necessary to focus the trade partnering negotiations at bilateral and multilateral levels and avoid overlap between distinct dialogues and similar initiatives taken at other forums. Bilateral negotiations should be strategically pursued in removing/reducing non-tariff and investment barriers. The trade-related negotiations among the Latin American and East Asian countries should also focus on technical norms and standards, rules of origin, anti-dumping, subsidies, countervailing measures, other liberalization and deregulation measures (privatization), sub-regional, regional and hemispheric integration processes, and convergence and divergence between regional integration and multilateral trade regimes. The negotiations should also deal with simplifying the customs rules and procedures, including non-transparent and inefficient infrastructures, differing customs, improper application of rules of origin, customs valuation, pre-shipment inspection, and import licensing. Customs problems can be especially difficult for small and medium enterprises that have less experience and fewer resources for handling these problems.

There is a rapid change observed in world markets resulting in new emerging markets around the world. In this century China, India, and Latin America and the emerging market-based economies in Eastern Europe promise new opportunities for global trade. The European Union provided an outlet, initially for unskilled labor-intensive products of Central and Eastern European countries and more recently for skilled-labor intensive and technology-based products. Knowledge-intensive imports from the European Union have also contributed to industrial realignment in the Central European countries. Trade liberalization between Eastern and Western European countries has led to gradual normalization of trade relations, and liberalization within CEFTA (Central European Free Trade Agreement) has reversed the fall in trade intensity among Central European countries. Emerging markets in developing countries showed a strong potential for change in preference during the late twentieth century. The birth rate is declining in most of the advanced countries while it is increasing in the developing countries. The growing trade agreements in the countries indicate some likelihood of success because when the level of tariff and non-tariff barriers is already low, a preferential agreement is more likely to have an adverse impact than a beneficial one. However, the reduction in tariff barriers and duties, and the liberalization process worldwide has further given a stimulus to international marketing across regional boundaries.

Consumer learning curve

Consumer learning is a continuous process involving cognitive, internal and external sources. Cognitive learning sources comprise static and dynamic thinking, emotions, observations, and ambitions, while internal sources that induce consumer learning emerge within the organization through peer interactions, innovation and design research, and voluntary employee contributions to organizational growth. Companies also learn from market behavior driven by competitors' moves, new entrants' market approaches, rivalry within industry and conflicts, and government interventions. Most companies learn business models through trial and error by experimenting with innovative ideas on products, services, and strategies on a small scale in a niche market.

Leading learning theories suggest two dimensions of the learning process: conceptual learning and operational learning. Conceptual dimensions of learning yield *know-why* knowledge while operational learning offers *know-how* learning. Ideally managers should acquire the rationale of business development by learning know-why perspectives and later reinforce knowledge on innovation, technology, and strategies by acquiring know-how information. A production line in a factory may specifically be set to create technological knowledge, which would consistently deliver both *know-why* and *know-how* learning dimensions. However, reorientation of the learning process within the same firm may be required in the long run to transfer knowledge to new-generation employees and deliver the balance between conceptualization and operationalization of knowledge. It is observed that consistent learning in the corporate environment with continuity in resources helps in enhancing knowledge creation and stimulating knowledge diversity (Lapre and Van Wassenhove, 2003).

The cognitive factors in learning are largely influenced by interest in learning among individuals driven by peer influence in a business organization. Employees engaged in learning new concepts in developing products and services evaluate meticulously their time invested in learning with reference to the application of acquiring new skills in the organization. Where there is weak potential in applying their skills in future, resistance would develop toward learning. However, organizations should demonstrate effecting leadership to promote learning on new technologies, product designs, operations, and business strategies among employees. Besides leadership a pro-learning workplace culture with effective diffusion of knowledge also affects the learning process among employees of an organization. Business organizations should create continuous learning opportunities for employees as exemplified in large multinational companies like GEC, IBM, and 3M. It is necessary for organizations also to provide adequate learning opportunities on attributes of market competition, consumer needs, substitution effects, and trends in product lifecycles. It has been observed that in most organizations employees initially resist investing time in on-job learning.

Continuous improvement programs through creativity workshops, discussion syndicates, and innovation seminars are proliferating in the global industrial environment as firms are intending to stimulate more innovative thinking for their employees to gain competitive edge in the marketplace. However, most companies have failed to grasp a basic truth as they provide less time on knowledge creation and thrust their employees into achieving higher market share and economic gains against competitors. In order to improve the learning process of organizations the meaning, management, and measurement issues associated with learning must be addressed (Garvin, 1993). Many managers feel that the learning curve may get out of date over time, but developing strategies on the basis of the experience curve can improve competitive performance in some clearly defined situations (Ghemawat, 1985). There are several benefits that managers may find in conceiving the right learning process for innovation and business growth. Experiential learning would help decision-makers in the firm to develop an appropriate marketing perspective. In many companies, not everyone who has marketing responsibilities has a well-defined set of marketing skills. Often, an organization is founded and developed around a specific technical skill or innovation and, as the organization grows, attempting to meet market uncertainties firms must plan for an analytical skills learning process. The consumer learning curve will furnish an organization with a pattern for analysis that will guide them more successfully through the product evolution. The consumer learning curve has several cause and effect indicators, as discussed below:

- Ideas: Generic, shared, induced, and goal-driven.
- Learn from business failure.
- Deal with loss.
- Achieve emotional recovery.
- Casual, opportunity cost-based:
  - Peer pressure.
  - General social norms in the community.
  - Pressures from competitors.

Most managers develop generic ideas from their own observations and goals toward developing the firm. Sharing ideas among peers within the organization helps in brainstorming innovative ideas, and choosing to work with prolific ideas on innovation can drive the business growth of the company. Transfer of ideas and knowledge is associated with the exchange of knowledge within networks, which consist of innovators and imitators of knowledge. On the contrary, knowledge diffusion describes the diffusion of knowledge within the group of innovators and imitators. Firms should encourage the generation of new ideas and diffusion and transfer of knowledge to integrate the organizational thinking process. Knowledge transfer and diffusion would accelerate the consumer thinking process and generate involvement of all employees in the innovation process of the firm. From this point of view, innovative ideas are mainly expected from knowledge diffusion, which can be directly or indirectly enforced by knowledge transfer. Therefore, the intensity of knowledge networks in enterprises affects the diffusion pattern of knowledge (Klarl, 2009). Some managers go further, and believe that failures offer them better opportunities to think afresh on innovations and drive the process of business growth. The benefits of the new knowledge management initiative are considered by managers as drivers to growth specific to the market or new products and services. This includes the potential contribution of employees to be made to the organization's design to "teamwork-through-innovation" and sharing the tacit knowledge in the firm. If knowledge is to be more widely created, shared, and used, the innovation process could be streamlined within the organization. The interrelationship between knowledge sharing, knowledge creation and organizational change needs to be understood and realized. Managers should refrain from reverting to traditional ways of thinking and operating based on low trust and direct command as these do not encourage integrated knowledge management in a firm to meet business challenges collectively (Storey and Barnett, 2000).

As global competition is increasing, the demand for management skills is also growing. It is observed that the current trend in managerial learning is toward developing strong management skills across broader levels and layers of the workplace. While technical hard skills such as financial management remain vital, the most important skills are those focused on bringing out the best in people and teams. The skills most in demand are those that have been called "soft skills" but are increasingly seen as the hardest to deliver, such as managing people, leadership, teamworking, and customer focus (Report, 2000). Corporate experience shows that in learning management practice there are very different progressive and step-function methodologies being applied in the preparation and resolution of a valued and effective approach to managing the learning strand.

Business education is becoming challenging today as business schools are interested in developing applied learning paradigms for developing sustainable advantage. Often it has been questioned whether strategic thinking should be the core learning platform in business education (Goldman, 2007). The quality of the next generation of business leaders will be determined by the ways in which business schools respond to the dynamic changes emerging in the environment of higher education.

While specific initiatives will vary widely, one thing seems certain that business schools will need to be more dexterous, more innovative, and more efficient than ever before (Acito et al., 2008). Strategic thinking varies among the firms according to their business attributes and categories. Causal evolutionary drivers of variation, selective retention, and struggle for survival provide a framework for understanding the past and current status of the knowledge and determine the level of strategic thinking among the managers of small business firms. Business education and professional associations in learning play a critical role in inculcating strategic thinking among business managers. Increasing competition and collaboration is expected to lead to higher standards of business education (Sharma et al., 2007).

As the dynamic global business environment continues to force organizations to be agile and adaptive, pedagogy in business education is transforming. While reviewing previous contributions that describe the gaps in pedagogy, there emerges the need for strategic and systems thinking. The greater emphasis on learning outcomes reflects a broader and ideological shift about the role of business schools. Such change is increasingly perceived as an appropriate strategy for serving the "knowledge-based economy," which can be implemented through the educational focus on strategic thinking pedagogy in business education (Boden and Nevada, 2010). Although there is widespread recognition of the need to develop both generic and subject-specific skills, a growing number of researchers emphasize the importance of generic skills, because strategic thinking as a pedagogy of business education is increasingly equated with "being flexible and adaptable in the workplace," suggesting that individuals should possess key transferable skills (Wilton, 2008).

Enterprises, irrespective of their size and market share, are becoming virtual to provide convenience to all market players including consumers. Use of information technology in enterprises has made marketing operations cost-effective and easy. However, countering claims that cyberspace will drive more competition in general and of the firm in particular, it is necessary for consumer firms to foster innovative production and diffusion of market knowledge within the firm. Dynamic organizations help turn the partial insights of individuals and communities into robust, organizational knowledge. Infrastructure for organizing knowledge must overcome a firm's boundaries as knowledge is an asset perceived and possessed by individuals through communication technologies and social organization networks (Brown and Duguid, 1998).

The butterfly and grapevine effect

As competition is increasing in the global marketplace most firms are reorienting their marketing communication strategies through customer-to-customer networking as customer-driven communication is found more trustworthy and decisive. Consequently, consumers are adopting increasingly active roles in co-creating marketing communication with companies and their respective brands. Most emerging firms work hard in developing online social marketing programs and brand campaigns to reach consumers where they "live" virtually. However, the challenge faced by many companies is apparently the way to be active in social media as most firms do not have clear understanding as how to manage social networks effectively, in terms of what performance indicators they should be measuring, and how they should measure them. Further, as companies develop social media strategies, platforms such as YouTube, Facebook, and Twitter are too often treated as stand-alone elements rather than parts of an integrated system. Firms should invest in building strategies in a systematic way to understand and conceptualize online social media, as an ecosystem of related elements involving both digital and traditional media (Hanna et al., 2011). As re-communication in social networks like Facebook and Twitter is becoming common, many companies take advantage of such grapevine communication trends. Recent research identifies factors that increase the likelihood of re-tweeting communication, so that a firm's tweets will be shared with social networks among peers. Re-tweeting is desirable both because the original tweet reaches more people and a re-tweet is essentially an endorsement from recipients to their followers. Opening a communication with an attention-grabbing headline is important to post the communications on social networks. Socializing the brand may drive enormous scope for re-tweeting as peers can use and act on the message, and save time and money on their own information search. The best practice of all communication strategies is when organizations combine several of these practices to get the most out of their marketing messages (Malhotra et al., 2012).

Technology platforms for social media commonly include Facebook, Twitter, YouTube, instant messaging, video conferencing, and web meetings. These and many other techno-communication collaboration and social media platforms have now become the lifestyle of people around the world. Firms are continuously exploring their way to enterprise communications and management strategies using the above social media technology platforms. However the efficiency of firms in using these social media applications and technologies poses a greater challenge and raises one of several questions as how successful the companies are in navigating business changes through social media platforms. Though the efficiency of firms in using social media applications varies, many firms drive through multiple talent and organizational elements in business communication across consumer and peer segments. In this process firms work on creating a shared vision, gaining buy-in across locations and levels, and dealing with consumer expectations and streamlining consumer preferences in the day-to-day competition. Social networking and collaboration applications are extremely effective ways of converging forces of a business communication pyramid comprising the bidirectional flow of information between the firm, consumers, and market players (suppliers, service providers, retailers, etc.). The convergence of communication would help firms in performing new processes together and to share experiences on the innovations, improvements, and temporary setbacks. People with common interests or related role players can form communities to learn from and support one another on social media platforms. Social media can also help firms in cases where there is a need for creating more collaborative culture and drive the change initiatives.

In disseminating business communications, timing is arguably the most important variable of all. Indeed, there are critical moments in a customer's relationship with a business when firms want to communicate with all market players to promote various strategies. If the firms contact consumers with the right message in the right format at the right time, there exists a good chance of a warm reception of the communication. There is a new computer-based experimental platform called *dialogue marketing*, which is, to date, the highest step on an evolutionary ladder that ascends from database marketing to relationship marketing to one-to-one marketing. The major advantages of dialogue marketing over conventional communication approaches are that it is completely interactive and it runs on multi-communication channels. This platform continuously tracks every nuance of the customer's interaction with the business. Thus, dialogue marketing responds to each transition in that relationship at the moment the customer requires attention (Kalyanam and Zweben, 2005). Collaboration and networking platforms are empowering employees, customers, and partners to be active participants in global conversation. Social media tools and platforms provide an effective communications channel for customer-centric business communication and across the organization as a transparent knowledge-sharing initiative. Firms must establish a process for delivering their message through the right communication in social media platforms by disseminating authentic, trusted, and believable information. This reinforces the idea that social media can be promoted by the firms as a tool not only to voice ideas and concerns but also to arrive at accurate and credible solutions on various issues raised by consumers.

Firms may find effective ways in working with social media applications to deliver personalized learning experiences to consumers related to brand equity, promotions, and comparative advantage. Firms should not use social media for general broadcasts of information, but rather as linked innovative collaboration platforms to encourage effective company/consumers/suppliers coordination in information sharing and knowledge building opportunities, including:

- Webcasts with short learning segments delivered before a change in enterprise system, innovations, and marketing strategies of the firm goes live.
- Live web meetings and tele-presence solutions that bring together dispersed teams for a common learning experience.
- User-generated content platforms such as YouTube, which allow staff members to provide short video or audio training segments relevant to the change program.

Social media and collaboration solutions allow information to flow in multiple directions rather than just from top-down. For example, using wikis and micro-blog applications for sharing short bursts of information, marketing firms can *crowd-source* ideas and involve employees more directly in innovative strategies. Firms can build greater internal loyalty by actively soliciting continuous feedback on issues related to the change. Social media is an important addition to a traditional change management program, one that can dramatically increase the acceptance of change and advance an organization more predictably toward its business goals. Collaboration and social media tools can reduce the time an organization needs to navigate large-scale change programs and deliver a better solution for consumer-related marketing issues in the future.

The advancement of information technology in global business has led to the prevalence of online communities that drive the virtual business of many firms. Online communities are connected through social network platforms that allow consumers to exchange information about products or services virtually, and to compare prices among competitors. These platforms have also opened freeways to exhibit products online and for consumers to share their opinion or experience on the products and services. Consequently, marketers have lost control over how and where their products are presented to potential customers. Some of the more sophisticated online retailers have used this trend to their advantage, employing recommendation algorithms, user reviews, and unique customer-generated content to build trust and increase a consumer's propensity to purchase. A variety of online players, including Amazon.com, Netflix and Internet radio site Pandora, are recognized for having state-of-the-art recommendation systems that effectively match customers with the products, movies, and music they love.

Social media has widened opportunities for consumer-oriented firms to expand their market beyond brick-and-mortar stores. Consumer networks are used by most firms to supplement traditional sources of buyer insights with a wealth of information gathered by listening in to community sites such as Facebook, LinkedIn and Twitter, as well as customer forums and product review services. Monitoring the information flow on social media gives firms unique access to unfiltered feedback from customers, which may not be possible to obtain through other means such as focus groups and surveys. Firms intending to experiment with monitoring the Web can outsource the entire process to third parties, or build their capabilities internally. However, as information technologies are evolving rapidly, firms need to choose carefully which of them to use to reach their consumers and avoid locking themselves into a solution that constrains their future capabilities.

New insights of firms on marketing and sales to gain competitive advantage continue to use consumer online support besides advertising their products and services. Social networks also drive traffic to firms' retail websites. Firms can engage employees, customers, suppliers, and other third parties as active participants in the innovation process, expanding the range of ideas and gathering real-time feedback on their potential take-up. For example, Nokia operates an online lab that allows users around the world to download beta applications and provide feedback to its product development teams. This strategy provides an early opportunity to identify potential problems and customer differences across geographic markets.

Social media has become embedded in business culture and has drawn the attention of large as well as small firms. More and more people are getting connected with their computers and mobile devices to build relationships with family and friends, to post their opinions, and engage in conversations. Social media is vital for managers to under-stand this phenomenon, and to learn how to prepare their organiza-tions to thrive when customers exercise more power and influence over businesses than ever before. Some companies have made major strides in leveraging social media to develop more effective growth strategies (Wollan et al., 2011).

The marketing philosophy of firms has taken a turn from a market-oriented strategy to a customer-centric strategy as marketing compe-tition intensified in the wake of globalization. Marketers have been spending millions of dollars on elaborately conceived advertising cam-paigns, but often such campaigns do not drive brands to the favored position of consumers' top-of-the-mind. A word-of-mouth recommen-dation from a trusted source is perceived to be more influential than corporate communication. Consumers attracted by product campaigns may feel the taste of traditional marketing, but word of mouth cuts through traditional advertising methods quickly and effectively makes a place in the consumer's mind.

The grapevine effect triggered by word of mouth is the primary factor among a large segment of consumers in making their purchasing deci-sions. Its influence plays a pivotal role when consumers tend to buy a product or service for the first time or when products are relatively expensive. Social media-driven information factors tend to make peo-ple conduct more research, seek more opinions, and deliberate longer among peers than they otherwise do. The influence of word of mouth will probably grow along with the digital revolution and help consum-ers in making buying decisions. Thus, one-on-one communication architects the consumer opinion analyzing personality of products or services, interventions in decision-making, responsiveness of brand or a company, and trust (PIRT). In the ambience of growing globalization, social media operates on a one-to-many respondents basis as product reviews are posted online and opinions disseminated through social networks. Some customers even create websites or blogs to praise or punish brands. Word of mouth is a potential way to acquire new cus-tomers as well as to retain existing customers through building loyalty and trust in the brand and company. On the other hand this media may also lay negative effects among peers by spreading dissatisfaction within the segment. Such developments in word-of-mouth platforms may even cause firms to lose consumers (Yu, 2007).

There are many companies that have developed their posture in the market on the backbone of social media. IBM has emerged as a social business, in consequence of the way it has layered the barriers of reaching out to people within the organization. Most companies are also leveraging tools of social media in order to develop their image for interacting with stakeholders and customers. IBM operates in 170 countries and functions through development teams to build a product and position it in different markets against competing products. The functional teams feel that in positioning the products there is a need to bring together the right consumers through sustainable social networks. IBM brings the right skills and the right intellectual property together to support the operations of the company with existing and potential consumers. Inside IBM there are almost 70,000 communities that represent science and technology, associated with the products in every industry that the company serves, and with every standard that the products bear. Some communities are made up of a narrow access-controlled list of people, possibly focused on an acquisition, and some are communities with tens of thousands or even a hundred thousand people, sharing information about a particular focus area. The major challenge of social media is to develop collaboration capabilities and the co-creation of brand personality. IBM has developed practitioner portals to leverage content more quickly, to locate relevant people faster, to discover people they do not know who can help them on the project, and to grow their own capabilities by leveraging the tacit knowledge and wealth of information available (Kiron, 2012).

In general word-of-mouth is something about how people react to variability in product and service performance within a niche. However, as the communication circles expand, the reach of informal communication is enhanced at various territorial levels. Customer acquisition, retention and referrals are co-created by consumers and market players associated with the company on social media platforms. Communication delivered through such platforms explains that with better consumer perceptions on products and services, the buying decision would turn positive and more consumers would be likely to remain with the brand or market, which confirms the link between communication quality and customer satisfaction. The power of word-of-mouth communication and its influence on consumer decision-making is well established in various research studies. The recent adoption of online communication by many consumers has facilitated a fundamental change to the structure of many interpersonal interactions by exposing consumers to electronic word of mouth from virtual strangers. The emergence of the Internet and social networking has spawned an interest among consumer communities that help consumers in decision-making (Steffes et al., 2009).

The impact of word of mouth could be strongest when it originates from social contacts as such communication often has greater perceived reliability. By the very nature of such social communication the word of mouth is outside the formal control of an organization. Social media exhibits the ability to influence or encourage word of mouth to make it a powerful marketing tool. Financial service providers have shown long-standing faith in positive word-of-mouth communication as a means of attracting new customers, and a variety of studies on customer choice of bank highlights the significance of personal recommendation. Financial services tend to be characterized by a predominance of experience and credence qualities where word-of-mouth communication is particularly valuable to provide the potential consumer with vicarious experience of the service under consideration (Ennew et al., 2000). The service-dominant logic describes customer-actualized value as being idiosyncratic, experiential, contextual, and meaning-laden. Since positive word of mouth is an expression of customer-actualized value, the social communication philosophy postulates that word of mouth is not only related to a holistic set of assessments of the service experience but also to the idiosyncratic nature of the individual customer. Thus, a question often stands to be analyzed of whether socially oriented individuals have a greater propensity to engage in positive word of mouth leading to construct an effective communication grapevine (Ferguson et al., 2010).

Some studies on the impact of communication on cognitive behavior reveal that word of mouth plays critical role in mobilizing consumer communities. A study observes that the "pester power" phenomenon among young consumers is often driven by the word of mouth that poses the repeated delivery of unwanted requests as influencing purchasing behavior. It has been analyzed in the study that a large number of highly successful products, notably Harry Potter, became popular not through marketing but via word of mouth, and the staying power (or stickiness) of the product illustrates the importance of social learning (Procter and Richard, 2002).

Word-of-mouth communication has three distinct dimensions, comprising cognitive content, richness of content, and strength of delivery. The first two constituents reflect the composition of the message, while the third factor reflects the manner of delivery of communication. Such social communication has strong psychometric properties and can be generalized in the four contexts of sending positive/negative messages and receiving positive/negative messages among peers and referrals segments (Sweeney et al., 2012). Word of mouth in the marketplace and social neighborhood influences both short-term and long-term judgments of consumers on various buying situations. This influence is greater when a consumer faces a disconfirmation experience and when the word-of-mouth communication is presented by an expert. Most companies disseminate the word-of-mouth analytics among various consumer segments to develop buying intentions and loyalty. Interestingly, personal characteristics such as susceptibility to interpersonal influence and product knowledge do not appear to moderate the word-of-mouth observations (Bone, 1995).

The global butterfly effect mind-set

In the early twentieth century most enterprises began as cottage industries focusing on home markets. Later agglomerations of such small enterprises have grown global. However, in the early twenty-first century more and more firms have been born global, chasing opportunities created by distance, learning to manage faraway operations, and pursuing the most advantageous manufacturing locations, the brightest talent, the most willing investors, and most profitable customers from the beginning of the enterprise. The global start-ups of the new age face many challenges, some of which are discussed below:

• The basic challenges for born-global enterprises are apparently the logistics problems and socio-cognitive barriers caused by remote business operations and socio-cognitive concerns pertaining to cross-cultural limitations, language, education systems, religion, and economic development levels. Global companies often also face problems in workplace culture adjustments such as accommodating heterogeneous workweek schedules in a local context, which may put a strain on staff at local level.
• Managing the challenges and exploring opportunities in various PESTLE contexts (political, economic, social, technological and legal).
• Global enterprises must find a way to compete with large firms using low-cost remote resources like virtual retailing, distribution, and competitive price offerings.

Most start-up companies today consider overseas expansion from their inception. Global managers must cultivate four competencies: clearly articulating their causes and effects for going global; learning to build alliances with powerful partners; excelling in international supply chain management; and creating a cross-cultural work ambience within their organization. Of many emerging firms, the most successful ones are those that overcome tensions between resources and opportunities and offer a local business framework with global thinking by anticipating a variety of strategic, financial, organizational, and regulatory factors (Isenberg, 2008). Managers shouldn't fear the fact that the world isn't flat. Being global may not be a pursuit for the fainthearted, but even start-ups can thrive by using distance to gain competitive advantage. The example of the global growth of an air-freight delivery service may be illustrated as a firm that progressed by pursuing local opportunities within local resources with an objective of going global to enjoy cross-border opportunities. Similarly, a consumer-loan provider firm may begin by pursuing a local opportunity with local resources, and then added cross-border resources (Kuemmerle, 2005).

In a recent development in the global market segment, citizen sector organizations (CSOs) have been formed in developed countries that are attracting talented and creative leaders, and managers in changing critical industries such as energy and health care. Profit-oriented companies now have an opportunity to collaborate with CSOs to create new markets for reaching a world market. The power of such collaborations lies in the complementary strengths of the partners in the scale of business, expertise in manufacturing and operations, and financing. Social managers offer lower costs, strong social networks, and deep insights into potential customers and communities (Drayton and Budinich, 2010). The main goal of any international strategy should be to manage the large differences that arise at the borders of markets. Most managers learn from adaptation, aggregation, and arbitrage during the process of expansion of their business activities to the global marketplace. Young managers learn to boost revenues and market share by maximizing their local relevance through adaptation, while they attempt to deliver economies of scale by creating regional, or sometimes global, operations during the process of aggregation of their business. Firms exploit disparities between national or regional markets, often by locating different parts of the supply chain in different places, working through arbitrage. However, to make strategic choice firms require some degree of prioritization, and they must focus on one or two when trying to build competitive advantage (Ghemawat, 2007). Emerging managers should also attempt to address the following issues while developing a global framework for enterprise expansion:

- Comprehension questions help understanding of the nature of the environment before addressing a consumer challenge.

- Connection tasks stimulate thinking about the current situation in terms of similarities and differences with situations previously faced and solved.
- Strategic tasks stimulate thoughts about which strategies are appropriate for solving the problem (and why) or pursuing the opportunity (and how).
- Reflection tasks stimulate thinking about their understanding and feelings as they progress through the consumer process.
- Adaptability drives managers who are able to increase cognitive adaptability develop an improved ability to:
  o adapt to new situations,
  o be creative,
  o communicate one's reasoning behind a particular response.

Organizational integration is increasingly essential. Cutting-edge companies are putting their efforts to meet challenges by integrating organizational issues horizontally into subunits or area autonomies and centralized monitoring and control. Fundamental management challenges of emerging and small enterprises are diversified activities, decision-making, and companywide cohesion. In the mid-twentieth century performance criteria were often ignored by small firms, while empowerment of managers in enhancing the production improved unit competitiveness but deteriorated organizational efforts in diffusing knowledge-sharing within the firm. The consumer philosophy in the twenty-first century has changed to decentralization of power to drive business decisions faster. Managers today are responsible to help other employees to improve both individual and collective performance (Ghoshal and Gratton, 2002). In fact, a company can innovate along any of the performance-driven dimensions, such as product offerings, marketing platform, business solutions, enhancing customer value, customer experience, corporate value, innovating business processes, organizational growth, supply chain management, posture of the business, business networking, and enhancing brand equity (Izosimov, 2008).

3
Managing Market Shifts

Companies that organize their innovation efforts in systematic, well-managed ways are those whose efforts get rewarded. As the level of competition in the market increases consumers face rapid shifts in innovation and technology. This chapter addresses key questions on the complexity of market dynamism caused by small shifts that make greater impacts on consumer behavior as well as the market performance of companies. Change in the market sometimes occurs through forces that are beyond the control of any individual entrepreneur, such as government policies; availability of capital; and wild cards, including oil price volatility, geopolitical conflicts, the rate of economic growth, and public attitudes toward warnings of global market changes. This chapter critically examines market behavior toward strategy shifts, innovations, and technology application in products and services. A systematic model of market shifts, which links strategy, problem solving, and cultural change tailored to the needs of each firm, is discussed. It is argued that market shifts are often aggressive in innovation of products and services and are subject to managing change in the organization. The issues of organizational learning and innovation theory, organizational complexities, taxonomy of innovations, organizational disciplines, innovation models, and transformation of innovations among emerging enterprises are also categorically discussed in the chapter.

Globalization has driven extensive competition in all genres of markets from niche to international markets. Innovations, technology, and consumer preference in global markets shift rapidly as most companies attempt to differentiate their products, services, and image in the marketplace to gain competitive advantage. Thus, companies tend to learn perennially in the market about competitive moves and business dynamics within their industry. In this process companies focus on building their unique business posture to enhance their product attractiveness by matching and beating the competitive strategies of rivals. As a result, their strategies are developed and implemented in parallel with those of competitors. Companies meticulously foster head-on competition based largely on incremental improvements in cost, quality, or both. In order to develop the competencies to gain competitive leadership, many companies invest substantial resources toward executing organizational learning and systems thinking models.

Organizational learning is a continuous process that involves employees at all levels of management in sharing knowledge and innovative insights that support the business growth of the firm. The learning process is generally embedded in an organizational culture that drives employees to invest resources in creative thinking. Organizational culture, comprising the task, thrust, time, target and territory of work, stimulates the learning process. While diffusing knowledge with employees, organizations can source innovative ideas by trial and error experimentation within the organization. Another behavioral dimension that appears to be critical in determining the employer and employee relationship is the opportunity of unlearning knowledge and skills by employees. Firms can convince highly talented candidates to accept lower positions, assuring them that they will be promoted to a position that has a close match with their qualifications and experience, but employees under such circumstances will succumb to frustration as they do not find an appropriate platform to share their knowledge and implement skills.

Learning market dynamics and improving organizational capabilities adds value to innovative thinking and develops a competitive mind-set and a systematic way of looking for opportunities. Companies should look beyond conventional boundaries and managers examine methodically the strategies employed by competitors in the marketplace. By doing so, companies can find new market space to establish their brand and business, and position real-value innovation. Some companies also engage in introspecting their capabilities and competencies rather than looking at competitors by encouraging managers to ask themselves why customers make the trade-off between substitute products or services. Home Depot, a US house construction and utilities chain store, for example, analyzed the existing market competition serving home improvement and developed products and service differentiations to enhance their customer value. Upon critically appraising its own strategies, the company derived powerful insights by reviewing familiar data from a new perspective. Similar insights can be analyzed by looking across strategic groups within an industry; across buyer groups; across complementary product and service offerings; across the functional-emotional orientation of an industry; and even across time (Kim and Mauborgne, 1999).

Forced organizational learning through managerial control also helps employees learn contemporary skills, design thinking, and innovative strategies. It may be appropriate for emerging firms to consider a review of integrated learning designs for improving unit effectiveness. The learning environment in an enterprise is largely governed by the organizational culture, which is affected directly and indirectly by the employee relationship and their behavioral performance (Rajagopal and Rajagopal, 2008). The level of diffusion of knowledge in the organization largely depends on the learning design, comprising individual, peer, and subject-oriented or interdisciplinary patterns. Learning and application of knowledge in an organization is often motivated by reward systems orchestrated to generate a desired synergy in reference to its content and use value. In a global marketplace, which is perpetually changing, learning organizations must support the idea that diffusion and adaptation of innovative ideas, managerial know-how, and business strategy are continuous processes. However, a number of traditional organizations tend to discourage such knowledge process by limiting financial and human resources. Thus, emerging companies should rethink how they choose the most appropriate learning design for the organization in reference to managing information acquisition and diffusion processes, and break conventional knowledge barriers in organizational learning. There are various knowledge-based perspectives that affect the learning process toward innovations and diffusion, as discussed below:

- Inadequate information on innovation, research and development, and design.
- Lack of qualified personnel within the enterprise or in the labor market.
- Lack of information on technology and markets.
- Deficiencies in the availability of external services.
- Difficulty in finding cooperation partners for innovative products, process development, and strategic business alliances.
- Organizational rigidities within the enterprise, including the attitude of personnel or managers toward change and the managerial structure of the enterprise.
- Inability to devote staff to innovation activity due to production requirements.

Organizational learning should be positively related to innovation. If a company is good at acquiring new knowledge and articulating existing knowledge with new knowledge or existing knowledge in a different way, this company should be good at producing innovations of products or processes. Organizational learning is not necessarily related to an innovation's success. Innovation and an innovation's success are two different dimensions (Hurley and Hult, 1998). A successful learning organization leads to the capacity to innovate, which is the ability of the organization to adopt or implement new ideas, processes, or products. Specifically, if the innovation is not in line with the strategy and the environment of the firm, the innovation may fail and thus the learning–innovation link will not be related to performance (Therin, 2002). The attributes of organizational learning and innovation management are illustrated in Figure 3.1.

Figure 3.1 explains the process of organization learning and innovation that drives small differentiation in markets through the positioning of product and services for large advantage over a long period. The organizational learning requirement comprises knowledge management, analysis of market requirement, market-led innovation, and organization performance as drivers. There are many internal and external variables that influence the innovation process and organizational learning. Effective leadership, organizational design, and organizational platforms for transferring skills among the workforce form the core internal drivers stimulating the organizational learning and innovation process. The internal environment of an organization also develops cognitive determinants such as creativity, socialization of ideas, motivation, and demonstrating interpersonal intelligence among employees. Most innovation-driven companies, like Microsoft, Apple etc., spend substantial resources to build the internal environment of the organization in order to support the innovation continuum. The internal environment of a company is administratively controlled and monitored to keep abreast of the interest and knowledge of employees on the innovation process. Besides the internal variable there are many non-controllable factors that constitute the external environment that affects the organizational learning and innovation process; these include the nature of market competition, social and cultural effects, political ideology supporting scientific or commercial innovations, and shifts in consumer preferences.

Knowledge management involves many procedures and techniques to get the most from an organization's explicit and tacit know-how. Information acquisition, sharing of knowledge among the employees

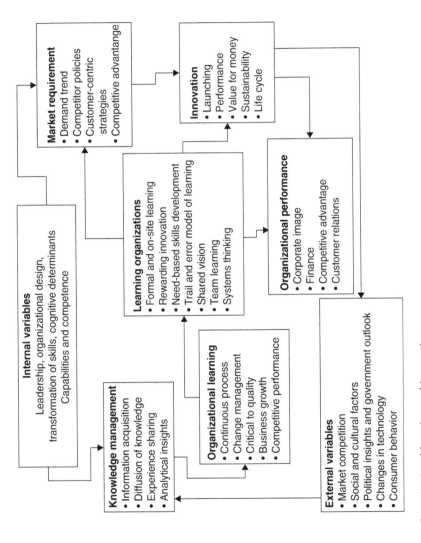

Figure 3.1 Organizational learning and innovation

in the organization, and diffusing experience and analytical skills within the organization form the core activities of knowledge management. Sharing knowledge without personal bias among peers or employees within the organization is the most important critical success factor of all knowledge management strategies. Effective knowledge-sharing practices allows individuals to reuse and regenerate knowledge at the individual and organizational level (Chaudhry, 2005). However, most enterprises observe individual and organizational barriers in knowledge sharing, which include internal resistance, lack of trust and motivation, and inadequate awareness. Learning organizations require a change in focus from a technology-driven approach to a people-driven approach in order to improve their knowledge management. With the evolution of technology, the paradigm of knowledge management is shifting from a conventional approach to an analytical one as a conversational medium by combining formal and informal knowledge within a social context (Hong, 2011). Leaning organizations can effectively acquire knowledge and skills through formal and on-market learning opportunities and develop need-based product innovation and improvement skills. However, most organizations fail to build logical frameworks for learning and push their employees to engage in a trial and error process for gaining the right market-oriented innovation vision. However, the most effective ways of continuous learning occur in organizations through shared vision, systems thinking, and team learning.

Organizational learning

An organization with a strong learning culture always stays abreast of the market competition. A sustainable learning pedagogy for an institution is to be nurtured in a supportive learning environment that comprises openness to new ideas, emotional protection, a positive attitude toward constructive criticism, and allowing time for individual reflection. Sustainable learning processes and practices in the organizational learning environment encompass experimentation, information collection and analysis, and education and training. These attributes are further reinforced by leadership in organizational learning (Garvin et al., 2008). The so-called 3-T determinants lay the groundwork for success inside an organization. The typical work culture of a 3-T power-grid may be described as synergy of task (commitment), thrust (driving force), and time (punctuality). This Japanese synthesis is followed by countries across the world. A 3-T work culture has reflected into the material culture (technology and economy) of Japan, leading to the philosophy of continuous improvement (*kaizen*). In fact, *kaizen* is a social culture, which was later adopted by Japanese organizations. However, *ad hoc* learning focused on tacit knowledge may serve as a tool for organizational survival against market risks and uncertainties. It is perceived by the employees of some organizations that limiting diffusion of corporate strategies and market information often leads to them being unaware of the developments affecting their performance (Carswell, 2005).

Multinational companies largely implement direct management control and influence the learning activities of employees toward improving their efficiency. The extensive monitoring of employees, directing, evaluating, and rewarding activities in an organization intend to guide the behavior of employees through management control processes to achieve results favorable to the organization and its employees. Management control is thus recognized as an important performance indicator of the tasks performed by the employees in an organization. Different organizational structures mean that information is analyzed in different ways by individual decision-makers, potentially creating an informational cascade within the organization (Darr, 2003). The organizational learning environment in the workplace can be made more attractive by considering the following enhancements:

- Improving communication and interaction among different business activities.
- Increasing sharing or transferring of knowledge with other organizations.
- Augmenting the ability to adapt to different client demands.
- Developing stronger relationships with customers.
- Improving working conditions.

Learning performance in an organization is affected by internal and external factors. Internal factors of the organization include work culture, guidance by managers, and administrative support. Coaching is defined as extending guidance toward using skills, experience, and direction to help someone improve their performance. Coaching consists primarily of giving people feedback to reinforce what they do well while suggesting ways and means to improve their performance. Coaching implies that everybody can improve and hopefully everybody wants to get better at what they do. Many sales managers erroneously believe that they have to be better than the person they are coaching in the skill set they are discussing in order to be a useful coaching resource to that person. To be a good coach requires an understanding of the skills being discussed and a desire to help someone improve one's performance. Organizations that know how to provide that feedback will have more productive, effective, satisfied, and motivated employees. Effective sales management coaching can provide sales managers with the skills to help salespeople grow and develop professionally (Carter, 2006).

Result-oriented learning and market behavior are positively related to firms operating in a competitive business environment. The learning performance in business firms should be stronger where outcomes-based control is used. It has been observed that employees who simultaneously exhibit commitment and effort achieve higher levels of the unlearning process. An organization should allow an adequate flow of consistent information in work ambience to support the learning process and performance (Jones, 2007). In view of the growing competition among firms in the global marketplace, the measurement of employee learning has become critical to sustain competitive advantage. Customers and the competitive environment in a sales organization are the external factors that affect the learning process and the type of operating skills required. The central focus of external factors affecting learning performance is the enhancement of the skills and knowledge of employees, and it encourages the use of acquired knowledge and skills in business operations and decisions (Farrell, 2005).

Most firms find doing business in a dynamic market competition to be unpredictable as hyper-connectivity is increasing among market players and consumers. Meeting market requirements is becoming less complex for firms with adequate resources. Creativity in management, marketing, finance, and customer relations is intertwined and interdependent with the emergence of information technology and changing bottom-up organizational culture (Sargut and McGrath, 2011). Social networks have emerged as learning organizations through building and sharing users' experiences. New enterprise systems are linking the organizational learning process for peer conversations using social networks among various market players. Some early enterprise systems lived up to the expectations of growing organizations. However, companies can meet their expectations for enterprise systems through a slow and diligent learning process. This approach emphasizes the need for organizations to focus less on the technical and temporal aspects as a process of organizational learning.

The true role of performance measurement is to provide a means of management learning. It is widely believed that continuous management learning is essential for managers to keep up with market developments and take the right decisions to drive the organization in the desired direction. Applied organizational learning is the basic philosophy that underpins ideas of achieving competencies and capabilities in the management of corporate and functional issues. However, strong involvement of organizations in employees' learning helps managerial performance to improve on the following lines (Neely and Al Najjar, 2006):

- Understanding market trends and developing insights into organizational strategy.
- Underpinning implicit and explicit ideas of employees on how to make the company's business competitive and sustainable.
- Continuous learning in an organization helps employees in integrating organizational and market communication to achieve corporate business goals.
- Making right use of communication to diffuse knowledge and skills.

The concept of team learning is becoming popular to develop opportunities for co-creativity within the organization. Team learning helps organizations in implementing knowledge-led entrepreneurial thinking in a methodical way and adopting new business concepts for the entire industry in general. It has been observed that most successful teams had leaders who actively manage the groups' learning efforts. Teams that most successfully learn and diffuse knowledge on innovation and new technology exhibit the following attributes:

- Teams are designed for homogenous learning.
- Team leaders frame the challenges so that members can get motivated and involved to learn.
- Team learning creates an environment of cognitive care and fosters communication on innovation and technology.

A study finds that teams learn faster provided they are explicitly managed for adapting to a challenge in business. Team leaders in the business learning process tend to be chosen more for their technical expertise than for their management skills. Leaders of learning teams should become proficient in creating learning environments and technical competence. Organizations must identify leaders to serve specific learning teams who can motivate and manage teams with the objective of improving the competencies and capabilities of managers (Edmondson et al., 2001). Managerial learning communities in an organization are able to drive strategy, generate new lines of business, solve problems, spread best practices, develop managerial skills, and augment the intellectual capital of the company. However, such learning communities in a company tend to develop a self-proclaimed power of knowledge over a period of time and can become resistant to monitoring and evaluation. Such teams require specific managerial efforts to develop and integrate them into an organization and gain full leverage. Managers in an increasingly globalized and competitive market environment recognize the competitive advantage of organizational knowledge. Hence, firms with potential to sustain market competition and become market leaders should foster learning teams and build communities of practice to apply their knowledge. Learning teams need to monitor the market improvements to ensure that what is discussed and shared within these learning ecologies is being used in innovation and improving the business strategy. A community of practice comprises of enthusiastic managers and entrepreneurs informally bound together in a team by shared expertise and passion for innovation of the products, services, and management strategy of an enterprise. People in multinational companies form such learning communities for a variety of reasons including to develop socio-professional networks with peers, to respond to shifts in market behavior, and to meet new challenges within the company (Wenger and Snyder, 2000).

Organizations tend to focus on learning to sustain their competitive advantage. However, the learning process also deteriorates if not properly diffused and adapted. People with high innovative talents in the company struggle to remain within their comfort zones when the application of learning fails in various business situations and demonstrates incompetence. Hence, organizations should acquire skills to stimulate learning ability and facilitate application of learning in organizational growth and change. The taxonomy of learning ability consists of agile or active learners, passive learners, and blocked learners. Every growing organization has a challenge to increase the number of agile or active learners who are unusually effective in new or challenging situations and have the potential to drive a disproportionate impact in the business of the firm. However, a majority of employees in an organization are passive learners as they tend to learn as a matter of chance rather than showing a learning aptitude, innate behavior, or desire. Generally such learners are not promising in applying their knowledge and skills voluntarily in the growth of the business or the firm. Blocked learners are those people in an organization who have the least interest in learning and are dissatisfied in the organization or with their work where creativity is not required (Willams, 1997). However, organizations must develop strategies on how to learn and to analyze their own work culture and develop enough mutual understanding to evolve solutions where all employees would gain interest and remain dynamic as an organizational team (Schein, 1996).

Innovation transformation

Innovation in the market follows Darwinian principles of evolution as it undergoes two lifecycle axioms – survival of the fittest and the struggle for existence. Most innovative products launched in the market soon attract competition and face the challenge of substitution, while some products compete with low-end and disruptive technology products. In both situations innovative products struggle for their existence in the market and attempt to fit into consumer perceptions positively. Yet most organizations naturally resist change and pull out from investing in brand-building and communication to support the survival of innovative products. Most resourceful companies support change to innovate and succeed by meticulously distinguishing between their core and contextual activities and integrating the right innovation model in their business strategy.

Transforming markets for adapting product and services innovations is a major challenge for most companies engaged in doing business in consumer products. Innovative products need to be transformed to the perceived suitability of consumers for optimal use by way of total customization. Most innovative products have the limitation for 360° transformation owing to standardized functionality and built-in structural restrictions. Driving change in marketplace demand and consumer behavior has traditionally come through top-down initiatives such as corporate endorsements toward manufacturing design, quality, technology, and innovation for new products, and developing marketing best practices to inculcate perceived changes in consumer behavior. Critical innovations in consumer products such as light-emitting diode (LED) screens and lighting devices transformed consumer behavior and market demand to achieve more value at less price. Transforming buying behavior for such innovations is relatively easy when compared with educating consumers toward use of innovation in educational products and services. But within every organization, there are a few product innovations that encounter unique marketing problems that seem impossible to solve. Although these change agent products in a company roll out in the market with effective communication tools to drive awareness, attractiveness, trial, availability, and repeat buying stimulus, they often fail to gain consumer confidence in usability and so fail to generate the desired response in the market.

Companies can launch innovations and meet consumer need strategies by considering the following attributes:

- Co-create community orientation and engage in the process of self-appraisal of innovative products and services in terms of competitive benefits and value for money.
- Reframe innovation through facts and prepare for innovation transformation according to customer needs and market demand.
- Entail marketing of innovative products in the existing network channels and use direct marketing to create customer value.
- Make innovation safe to learn among consumers and market players by creating an environment that builds constructive opinions.
- Grow a communication grapevine through digital networks and physical community infrastructure for the innovations and competitive advantage.
- Make the innovations into problem-solvers and drive them in the market as a key to community satisfaction.
- Leverage social evidence for the innovation considering its applications to a larger community-led consumer awareness, such as ecofriendly detergents that minimize cesspool and soil pollution.
- Build immunity to innovations in the market against disruptions and misevaluations that could lead to low trust and commitment among consumers and market players.

Companies should ensure that throughout following the above steps they adopt a facilitating role without overpowering consumers or raising conflicts with competitors. Such a corporate attitude may cause damage to the brand image of the company. A customer-centric innovation transformation methodology can help solving even the most extreme dilemmas on innovation acceptability in the market and its socialization for sustained growth (Pascale and Sternin, 2005).

Companies that organize their innovation transformation efforts in systematic, well-managed ways are those whose efforts will be rewarded in terms of a high rate of acceptance among consumers, distribution harmony, and retailing diligence. The systematic model of innovation management of companies should link to strategy, problem-solving and cultural change, and be tailored to the needs of consumers. An innovation transformation model is illustrated in Figure 3.2.

Implementing the model in the phases exhibited in the figure allows for the progressive development of an innovation culture. The goal of the company should be to change the way in which innovation is led and managed to cater for the needs of consumers and the market. Accordingly, the company can establish a set of values, principles, and practices to strengthen and nurture the innovation through appropriate transformation on an ongoing basis considering the consumption culture, market requirements, and competitive dynamics to survive in the marketplace. This process could help the company in transforming not only the consumer culture but the entire company through innovative products and services that are robustly competitive (Vila, 2012).

Cultivating continual innovation and creating new business models have become essential success parameters for any business. Vertical and horizontal integrations are imperative to the success of a corporation, resulting in models that provide tremendous business

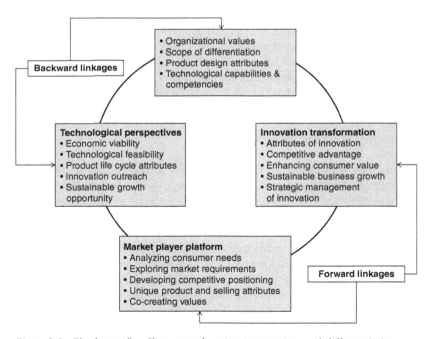

Figure 3.2   The butterfly effect: transforming innovation and differentiation

opportunities. This approach also brings great execution challenges. In addition to creating innovation through internal research and development, two significant areas where enterprises constantly strive to create innovative capabilities are mergers and acquisitions and partner strategies. Innovation and new business models can be successfully enabled through connecting specific products and solutions. A robust network foundation is essential for building higher-level infrastructure services. This foundation includes intelligent network capabilities at different network locations including branch offices, campuses, external connectivity, and home and partner environments. A converged network infrastructure can result in major savings when collaboration and video are enabled along with the right productivity solutions, for instance, through the use of unified communications and collaboration technologies, immersive video and videophones. A key technical requirement to scale business models is faster service provisioning. Through the use of a private cloud and intelligent automation solutions, corporations can reduce the time taken to provision a new service. Embracing virtual desktop technologies can also result in considerable advantages.

Broadly innovation is considered as an intellectual accomplishment at the grassroots of humanity, but commercializing it is a business skill compounded with capabilities, competencies, and resources of the organizations. Thus most business innovations are either developed by entrepreneurs or small and medium enterprises, but they lead to mergers or acquisitions with a larger business organization to gain enough resources to grow in the marketplace. Most of the innovations driving potential businesses are acquired by large companies and carried forward to develop commercially and position them sustainably in the marketplace. For example, in small information technology companies, young software developers have worked on developing interactive shopper software to support consumers in selecting clothing online that is suitable to their appearance and taste. This software was later made available for personal computers, local area networks, android phones and many more devices. The virtual dressing room can be installed in any place that has electricity and broadband Internet access, and the developers hope to eventually see the unit installed in areas like train stations and airport terminals. The technology, called *tryvertising*, is already popular in Japan, where some of the early trials have taken place. The system works by using a Kinect sensor along with a 60-inch LCD display and an iPad. It is able to respond instantly to the user's movements as they try on the clothing, and the developers claim that the system can even provide a virtual experience of the clothing's texture. Once an item has been selected, the shopper can use a printed QR code to access the item at the online store and complete the purchase. Mergers and acquisitions for product and services innovations require a combination of solutions that work to seamlessly integrate the marketing-mix, and this process also brings challenges in varied information and technology-related market environments. Most companies struggle with the process of integrating the physical and intellectual capital of a new acquisition into the parent environment.

Innovations of certain small companies that emerge in a niche are able to radically change their entrenched ways of serving large markets and claim a position of leading transformation in the market. Less common are companies that are able to anticipate a new set of requirements and mobilize the internal and external resources necessary to meet the innovation transformation process. Few companies make the transformation from their market-oriented business innovation model to a customer-centric innovation management model, which delivers the innovation to consumers in a sustainable way with high levels of satisfaction. Innovation transformation typically begins with a niche market searching a way forward to create a new consumer segment to sustain by developing a temporary monopoly situation. This seeks the following clarifications for companies to manage the transformation of innovation of products and services from premium consumer segment to mass segment, and finally down to the bottom of the pyramid:

- Is differentiating innovations by consumer or market segment a profitable strategy?
- Do companies really need to develop a differentiated marketing strategy to transform innovations and galvanize change?
- How is it be possible for companies to adopt new ways of managing transformed innovation in view of the preferences of consumer and market pressure?

Most companies develop new dynamic capabilities deliberately to manage the innovation transformation and market management processes. Companies that transform innovations toward consumer preferences gain fundamental advantages over their competitors in building marketing alliances for branding and distribution, creating experiential marketing challenging in business against conventionally operating competitors, and nurturing strategic changes in consumer behavior (Johnson et al., 2012).

Innovations in uncertain markets

Rapid shifts in consumer behavior, a rush of low-cost new products, short product lifecycles, and weak intellectual property rights execution in the marketplace causing the growth of imitated products, a flow of disruptive products, and alluring consumer communications, trigger uncertainties in the market. Innovative products launched in the market often suffer from the above uncertainties in the early stages of the lifecycle. Most companies attempt to differentiate their products and services and invest resources in building the brand in the introductory stage of their lifecycles but are not able to push them prolifically owing to the uncertainties of market responsiveness and the process of building trust.

The evolution of market space for innovative products or change drivers that have potential to drive the strategic butterfly effect depends on forces that are beyond the control of any company. Often market uncertainties are prompted by government policies, availability of capital, and competition wild cards leading to price wars and third party manufacturing. Historically the growth of innovation and technology largely falls into a boom and bust cycle and creeping market uncertainties. Such phenomena are most common in the consumer products and services sector. For example, the market for portable personal audio machines during the 1980s boomed but within a decade it faced uncertainties in the market from growth in technology and changes in consumer behavior toward Apple's i-pod, which was positioned as a lifestyle product in the mass market. Similarly, between 2005 and 2007, runaway enthusiasm led to the proliferation of hundreds of new green technology ventures, many of which ran into trouble during the following recession. Most innovative products fail in the market as they cannot establish a unique product and sales attributes and stay ahead of competitors (Schoemaker and Day, 2011).

The contemporary ideology on competition emphasizes the competitive environment, which contributes to various dimensions of rivalries. It has been observed that low-end competitors offering much lower prices for a seemingly similar product suffer with the common fear of uncertainty in business among competitors. The vast majority of such low-end companies fall into one of the four broad categories, as strippers, predators, reformers, or transformers (Potter, 2004). Global companies often try to promote competition among their salespeople by offering incentives to the best performer. Marketing planners develop strategies to defeat competitors as a way to ensure their company's success. Hence it may be stated that in corporate business management practices, competition is largely accepted as a desirable and effective way to improve performance (Armstrong, 1988). Certainly one would expect competition to be more effective under some circumstances. It is surprising to learn how difficult it was to find empirical evidence about situations in which competition proved superior, especially when one may look at the range of evidence examined by Alfie Kohn (1988). However, Kohn emphasizes that the competition leads to a less positive regard for people of different ethnic backgrounds. Many organizations feel that in growing competition, establishing strategic alliances would better check a competitor's penetration than an own brand or technology-driven company. They recognize that alliances and relationships with other companies of repute are fundamental to outwit, outmaneuver, and outperform competitors by way of better branding, better service, and tagging global brands for assuring the quality of goods and services. Alliances and relationships thus transform the concept of the competitor.

Market complexities are growing in tune with the competition in emerging markets. As uncertainty in the marketplace is rising, firms lean toward making important strategic decisions through judgmental tools rather than applying quantitative methods to forecast market trends. Factors including the effects of globalization, the prospects for regional conflicts, and the advancement of technology pose major threats in determining firms' forecasts (Borison and Hamm, 2010). Nevertheless future markets are often predicted by judgment-driven decisions, and companies need to improve their strategic decision-making process by understanding market competition. In a prediction market, payoffs are tied to the outcomes of future events. The design of how the payoff is linked to the future event can elicit the market's expectations in reference to a range of different parameters.

Marketplace strategy includes elements of product and customer segments, competitive posture, goals and moves, and directions of the firm. Products and customers are categorized in different ways. Customers are segmented on the basis of the products and services they use at any point of time. Customer demographics are also considered to a large extent in segmenting customers. The competitor's position and policy direction are better known to the distribution channels than any other external agency. Tapping of the right information by taking the distribution channels into confidence would be more appropriate than any other means open to the company. Rival business firms often choose distinctly different channels to reach end users.

Competitive posture reveals how a competitor competes in the marketplace to attract, win, and retain customers. The customer is the kingpin in determining competitive posture. The competitive posture of the company consists of product line, attributes of the product, functionality, service, availability, image, sales relationship, and pricing pattern. The product line broadly refers to the range of products available to the competitor. The distributors and retailers are more concerned with the width (item under product range) of the product-mix. Some companies focus on a narrow range of products and build a strong image among customers. The product attributes vary in terms of shape, design, style, color, and added advantages. Further, the customers may view the functionality of the product as the satisfaction derived from the products. The dimensions of the functionality are highly product-specific. In competitive markets, the efficiency of the services discharged and extended to buyers also contributes in building or breaking the marketplace strategy. Products, in the same market or competitive domain, largely vary in their availability, which may be due to weak or faulty supply chain management. Competing firms must study this situation and develop strategies accordingly. The pricing strategy of mercantile and service sector companies is very sensitive and may carry enough strength to destroy the rivals' business. Such market tactics among companies dealing with fast-moving consumer goods (FMCGs) and services have been observed time and again. An example of price war is the low-cost airlines in India. Jet Airways, Kingfisher Airlines, and Indian Airlines drive campaigns to attract potential customers as well as to prevent the switching of existing customers by slashing prices on domestic trunk routes. The position of products and services, and the level of competition in the marketplace may be assessed by measuring the dynamic moves (strategic and tactical) in the given product-customer segments in a competitive marketplace.

Many technology-driven firms consider establishing strategic alliances as an effective strategy to sustain market competition. They recognize that alliances and relationships with other companies of repute are fundamental to outwit, outmaneuver, and outperform competitors by better branding, better service, and tagging global brands for assuring the quality of goods and services. Alliances and relationships thus transform the concept of the competitor. The strategic alliances may be in various forms such as branding, logistics, research and development, production and operations management, packaging, services, sales, and customers. The company has to list all alliances that it is planning to have to outperform the competitor, categorize all available alliances by activity, value chain, and resources, and identify the key alliances, which will be decisive on the marketplace strategy of the competitor. It is essential to identify alliance partners and know about their marketplace strategies. The purpose of the alliance has to be made transparent at the very beginning of the deal. The company has to draft the terms of the alliance clearly for striking the final deal. The terms of alliance must delineate the resources contribution of each partner, the roles and responsibilities of the alliance partners, duration of the alliance and its benchmarks. The company proposing to have alliances must assess the evolution date of the alliance, alliance attributes, marketplace signals, and consequences for the competitor in terms of changes in marketplace strategy. The company should also identify the indicators to monitor the terms of alliance with a view to reorient business needs, mutual interest, and commitment. Marketing environment for a competitive environment is a combination of factors that customers use as tools for pursuing marketing objectives in the identified markets for achieving targets. These factors have to be strategically mixed in marketing planning for offering quality services and optimizing customer value. It is an integrated approach for promoting services with a view to expand the area of the services market. The traditional components of marketing-mix, the "4Ps" of product, pricing, place, and promotion are further supplemented by another set of "Ps" to make the "11Ps" of product, price, place, promotion, packaging, pace, people, performance, psychodynamics, posture, and proliferation.

Market environment for butterfly effects

Butterfly effects are sensitive to the market environment as they grow and make impact. Companies that enjoy monopoly or near-monopoly market conditions have better opportunities to trigger small changes to gain profits in the market at a larger scale. However, in oligopolistic market conditions small changes in products, services, processes, and strategies largely drive tactical gains to a company and call for quick consumer responses. In order to make the butterfly effect sustainable companies need to introduce changes in phases in the market backed by effective communication to stimulate consumers to accept the changes in products and services.

Companies should introduce changes that are sustainable and deliver higher advantages to consumers in contemporary market competition. Competitive firms intend to engage in a continuous organizational learning process with respect to the value creation chain and measure performance of the new products introduced in the market. In growing competitive markets large and reputed firms are developing differentiation strategies to move into mass markets by combining innovation and changes in their products and services as "high-value integrated solutions" tailored to each customer's needs rather than simply "moving downstream" into services. Such firms are developing innovative combinations of service capabilities such as operations, business consultancy, and finance required to drive the butterfly effect in business by provide complete solutions to each customer's needs in order to augment customer value toward innovative or new products. It has been argued that the provision of integrated solutions is attracting firms traditionally based in manufacturing and services to occupy a new base in the value stream centered on *systems integration* using internal or external sources of product designing, supply, and customer-focused promotion (Davies, 2004). Besides the organizational perspectives of enhancing customer value for any change introduced by the company, functional variables like pricing play a significant role in developing customer perceptions toward the new products. The attributes and path of environmental factors to drive the butterfly effect for products and services in the competitive marketplace is exhibited in Figure 3.3.

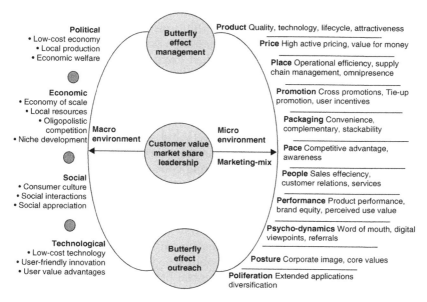

Figure 3.3 Market environment for the butterfly effect

The market environment for butterfly effects is largely driven by the micro business environment of a company, integrating the 11Ps model of marketing-mix and macro environment comprising political, economic, social, and technological factors as exhibited in Figure 3.3. A strong butterfly effect with small changes in the micro environment of a company could lead to larger benefits in reference to customer value, high market share, and sustainable leadership. Companies should manage both macro and micro business environments to drive the extensive outreach of the butterfly effect in the marketplace.

Most product differentiations exhibit some form of risk in competition. There are some firms that can drive consumer attention in competitive markets and can create competitive advantage. Operating on economies of scale for a large firm may also have a significant competitive advantage to drive changes as it may enjoy a large volume of production at lower costs, which may further lead to price leadership with low retail prices. Such a strategy would also prevent potential competitors from entering the business. An incumbent firm may make it hard for a would-be entrant by incurring huge sunk costs with high budget advertising. In view of such strategy any new differentiation may compete effectively in the market but have low market share during the initial period. However, it can be alarming for companies to worry about sunk costs incurred on advertising or researching a product idea. Another radical strategy may be used by powerful firms to discourage consumer switching behavior by raising exit costs, such as product insurance, warranty and guarantee terms, and product exchange policies. Thus firms can earn excess profits by making the differentiated products compete with those of rival companies, by bringing down prices.

High-performing companies like Barclays, Cisco, Dow Chemical, 3M, and Roche work to establish basic rules for setting and delivering differentiation strategy in products and services, which are easy to implement, realistic, and short-run result-oriented, and transparent in driving the change transition among consumers. These companies work on discussing within the company the most attractive differentiation in products, services, or marketing strategy to gain advantage in the competitive marketplace. High-performing companies create cross-functional teams drawn from strategy, marketing, and finance to launch innovative products or make competitive differentiation in existing products to enhance their outreach. Successful differentiation in the market would reflect both the real profits of the company and augment the performance of products, services, and brands relative to competitors. It has been observed that a rigorous analytic framework is used by high-performing companies to develop and implement differentiation in their manufacturing and marketing strategies. Such companies develop their differentiation plans in tune with market trends and assign strategic business units to implement new marketing strategies. These companies manage resource deployments early to support scheduled production and marketing activities. Proper resources management would in turn help the company create more realistic forecasts and more executable plans. By discussing up-front the level and timing of critical deployments for differentiation and innovation strategies, it should be possible for companies to gain larger outreach and higher market share. Companies like Barclays, Cisco, Dow Chemical, 3M, and Roche clearly identify priorities and prioritize tactics so that mangers have a clear sense of how to direct butterfly strategies and monitor their performance. Tracking resource deployment, monitoring, and evaluating results against plans, using continuous feedback to reset assumptions, and reallocate resources have been the principal activities performed by the business monitoring centers of these companies.[1]

Multinational companies develop the most profitable strategies on differentiation by offering customers something they value that competitors do not offer. A company can differentiate its products and services at every point where it comes in contact with its customers through cosmetic customization from the moment the company realizes the changing preferences of consumers. Most companies adopt liberal thinking to their customers' entire experience and uncover opportunities to position their competitive offerings in various attractive ways against competitors' products. Large companies successfully differentiate even a common product such as candles through differentiation against competitions (MacMillan and McGrath, 1997). For instance, by analyzing its customers' experiences and exploring various options, Blyth Industries, an American candle manufacturer, has grown from $0.5 million sales in 1997 into a global candle and accessory business with nearly $635.2 million in sales in 2010.

A careful analysis of a microenvironment indicates whether a company can successfully enter a specific market with product differentiation to gain competitive advantage. It may be hypothesized

---

[1] Euro Monitor online, www.euromonitor.com. For more information on the functional efficiencies of high-performing companies, see Michael C. Mankins and Steele Richmond, Turning great strategies into great performance, *Harvard Business Review* (July 2005).

that business growth of a company depends on the level of product differentiation and delivering customer value. This is manifested in the way in which a company plans to compete in the market and so also within the industry. Differentiation, in turn, is a function of the interplay of many factors including political, legal, and macroeconomic context; the quality of the microeconomic business environment; and the sophistication of company operations and strategy. Together they determine the capacity, the strength of competitive firms, and market leadership. A context that creates pressure for firms continuously to upgrade the source and sophistication of their advantage and at the same time supports the upgrading process is a favorable microeconomic context. Pressure for upgrading is supplied by *demand conditions* featuring differentiated products and experimenting customers, whose demands spur across the segments to innovate in order to upgrade their product/service offerings, driving competitive advantage to the company. Particularly valuable is the pressure from local customers who anticipate the nature of demand elsewhere in the world. Different competitors, however, might aim to satisfy different types of demand: existing, latent, or incipient. *Existing demand* refers to a product bought to satisfy a recognized need. *Latent demand* applies in a situation where a particular need has been recognized, but no products have been offered. *Incipient demand* describes a projected need that will emerge when customers become aware of it sometime in the future. In all three demand conditions strategic differentiation of products and services may trigger the butterfly effect for the company by enhancing large benefits and market leadership.

The contemporary ideology on competition emphasizes the competitive environment, which contributes to various dimensions of rivalries. It has been observed that low-end competitors offering much lower prices for a seemingly similar product has been the common fear of industry leaders managing their business among competitors. The vast majority of such low-end companies fall into one of the four broad categories of strippers, predators, reformers, or transformers (Potter, 2004). Each of these is defined by functionality of product and convenience of purchase. Industry leaders have significant advantages for combating low-end competition, but they often hesitate because they are afraid their actions will adversely affect their current profit margins. The solution then may be to find the response that is most likely to restore market calm in the least disruptive way, and a differentiation or value addition in existing products may cause disruption in the marketplace. An industry leader could choose to ride out the challenge by ignoring, blocking, or acquiring the low-end competitor or could decide to strengthen its own value proposition by adding value, high- and low-end product differentiations, new price points, changing the levels of benefits, and developing sustainable competitive products and services innovations. Such strategies or tactics can be effective in the long or short term, but change leaders need to consider strategic moves to penetrate with competitive differentiation in the bottom-of-the-pyramid market segment.

Firms enjoying the butterfly effect also maneuver the arena of customers, channels, institutions, and geographical coverage in order to reconfigure their competitive strategy. Software companies like Intel, Microsoft, and 3M always keep extending their product line, implementing research and development results and never let the competition rest in the end-customer arena. Healthy companies feel that the greater the competition the higher will be the challenge to establish the brand in the market. The collaboration of Suzuki with Maruti Udyog Limited in India has changed the dominance of the popular brand holder Premier Automobiles Ltd and created a new competitive context of small city cars. The channels of supply for any company are always vulnerable to the butterfly effect as channels view market changes as a potential risk. The common practice followed by competitors is to break the supply chain by offering more perks and margins than the leading brand. However, if the channels are favorably treated with long-term advantages, the endeavor to build the linkages with them would withstand any competitive rivalry. The collaboration between the Procter & Gamble and Wal-Mart involving strong integration of product ordering, inventory control, and logistics may be a classic example in this context (Fahey, 1999). The factor advantage in competition may be defined as the differentiation in manufacturing and marketing that could exhibit a unique selling proposition.

The stakes of companies in business competition may be understood as the benefits of winning the game and the cost of losing the business in the market. Many companies in the marketplace intend to escalate the stakes through product differentiation, market attractiveness, and corporate posture as some of their competitive strategies. Fast-growing companies also redefine their marketplace strategies for gaining a win/win situation in the market by making continuous differentiations and changes to show the posture of an innovative company. For instance, multi-domestic consumer products companies like Nestlé, Colgate Palmolive, Unilever, and Procter & Gamble are engaged in continuously differentiating product lines within and across product categories. There are many competitive strategies used by companies to get and retain customers and channels. Companies desiring to strengthen themselves against competitive threats in the market need to develop different modes of entering the market. Companies also need to refocus their strategies to attract customers and retain them for long-term benefits. Many organizations are driven by one or a few predominant, long-run goals that imbue the organization with a collective challenge, shared vision, and sense of mission or purpose. Such goals have been designated by others as strategic intent or vision and superordinate goals. Among goals set by companies, a few may include reorientation toward research and development to products that are new to the marketplace and extending product lines to attract new segments of customers. Companies engaged in continuous differentiation also use alliances to build a significant posture in the marketplace by achieving competitive leadership.

Change dynamics and the butterfly effect

Companies choose from many tools when they want to encourage employees to work together toward a new corporate goal. One of the rarest skills in managing market competition is the ability to understand which tools will work in a given situation and which will cause damage to the business growth of the company. Change management tools leading to the butterfly effect in the market fall into four major categories, namely market share, stakeholder value, leadership, and culture. In choosing the right tool to manage market change companies should look at two critical dimensions: the extent to which consumers agree with differentiation and match the change with what the customers want, and the extent to which the differentiation contributes to competitive advantage. Companies like Microsoft established market leadership and acquired a larger market share by continuous differentiation and making consumers adapt to the changes brought about by the company in each new version of the Windows operating system and Microsoft Office workstations over the years. Some company leaders, like Continental Airlines' Gordon Bethune, General Electric's Jack Welch, and IBM's Lou Gerstner, are tactical in choosing the right tools for product differentiation to gain immediate advantage over competitors (Christensen et al., 2006).

Different companies within the same industry, such as computer manufacturing, independently design and produce components, for example, disk drives or operating software, and these modules change

existing consumers' attitude toward adaptation of newer differentiations. Companies with diverse businesses move toward differential
product offers in tune with competitive market dynamics and drive
consumers to adapt to the new differentiated products and services.
Leaders penetrating the butterfly effect with continuous differentiation
control the market more effectively than static or less dynamic companies. Companies engaged in driving changes in consumer markets
watch the competitive environment closely for opportunities to link
innovations and new ideas as competitive tactics to lead the market.
Companies as change leaders will also become knowledge managers in
the industry to keep focused on innovation strategies pursue continuous growth (Baldwin and Clark, 1997).

Irrespective of the industry and market segments, most companies
operate on rapid evolutionary tracks at greater risk. A company's core
capability to redesign its value chain continually lies in gaining the full
extent of competitive advantage. The ultimate goal of strategic value
chain analysis to absorb product differentiation and changes is building
an organizational capability for a fast response toward evolving industry
dynamics. Organizations driving the butterfly effect through competitive differentiation need to learn in which consumer or market segment
value needs to be created and which areas of the business should remain
in-house or be outsourced for optimizing profit and market advantage
(Fine et al., 2002). Most companies invest resources in developing
changes in consumer behavior by creating sustainable values and new
lifestyle practices. Managers of customer-centric companies agree that
their efforts should be focused on growing the lifetime value of their
customers. In order to induct change management in organizations
most companies outsource critical business processes and drive change
internally in phases.

Section II
Building Global–Local Marketing Effects

4
Market Trend Analysis

Most firms making efforts to gain competitive advantage build their marketing strategies on product improvements as impulsive changes to attract consumers and the market. Changes in existing products, services, or marketing strategies often face consumer resistance. This chapter defines market resistance as an opposition to traditions in the marketplace to create new behavior among consumers. Market shifts explore purposive behavior of consumers and attempt to recreate the modern social conventions that manifest positive impact on competitive differentiations in the marketplace. Many companies recognize that their dispersed global operations drive innovative ideas and build capabilities for introducing competitive market changes. This chapter explains the role of managers in successfully bringing innovations to an enterprise and expanding at the global scale. Arguments are illustrated with examples in reference to phases of innovations, behavioral metrics, the change-resistance cycle, critical success factors, opportunities, threats and disruptions, and chain reactions of innovation. The chapter also addresses the concept and practice of conceiving ideas and nurturing strategic business shifts in a competitive marketplace and suggests ways to increase effectiveness in managing innovations and corporate goals.

Globalization has opened many routes to marketing including marketing opportunities through the Internet and virtual shops. However, amidst increasing market competition, the rules of the game are subject to change without notice. In this process a company must understand thoroughly all the moves of rival firms from various sources. The locales of business rivalry have to be spotted to assess their strengths. An intriguing aspect of the marketplace is that the nature of competition can change over time. A technology, company, or product does not need to remain prey to another forever. Competitive roles can be radically altered with technological advances or with the right marketing decisions. For example, external light meters, used for accurate diaphragm and speed setting on photographic cameras, enjoyed a stable, symbiotic (win/win) relationship with cameras for decades. As camera sales grew, so did light meter sales. But eventually, technological developments enabled camera companies to incorporate light meters into their own boxes. Soon, the whole light meter industry became prey to the camera industry. Globalization has not only accelerated the growth of companies from developed countries that are striving to gain exponential growth in business across market territories, but has also benefitted regional firms by competition in various sectors of business. Hence, market competition in the twenty-first century appears to be random, multi-directional, and omnipresent irrespective of the region, products, and services.

The emerging markets of developing countries have received signals from global competition and are rising fast. However, there are many hidden risks in the rise of potential firms to the global marketplace and the changing intensity of existing market competition. For example, observations in various research studies reveal that there were four factors that drove Japanese firms' early export growth, namely strong corporate models and cultures, a domestic market isolated from competition, a compliant labor force, and cohesive, homogeneous leadership. But when the firms moved into foreign markets, those strengths became downfalls. Entrenched in their corporate ways, Japanese firms were too narrow-minded to look for local insights, and they lacked leaders who had international knowledge. They were also unprepared for contentious overseas labor relations and the sophistication and expertise of their global competitors. Thus, to avoid Japan's fate, emerging giants must change their business models, reduce their reliance on protected domestic markets, learn to cope with diverse labor, and shake up their leadership (Black and Morrison, 2010).

Contemporary global business models explain that firms tend to structure themselves as one of four organizational types: international, multi-domestic, global, and transnational. Depending on the type, a company's assets and capabilities are either centralized or decentralized, knowledge is developed and diffused in either one direction or in many, and the importance of the overseas office to the home office varies. International marketing refers to exchanges across national boundaries for the satisfaction of human needs and wants. The various marketing functions coordinated and integrated across multiple country markets may be referred to as global marketing. The process of such integration may involve product standardization, uniform packaging, homogeneity in brand architecture, identical brand names, synchronized product positioning, commonality in communication strategies or well-coordinated sales campaigns across the markets of different countries. The term "global" does not convey the literal meaning of penetration into all countries of the world.

Many factors determine the nature of competition, including not only rivals, but also the economics of particular industries, new entrants, the bargaining power of customers and suppliers, and the threat of substitute services or products. A strategic plan of action based on this multiplicity might include positioning the company so that its capabilities provide the best defence against competitive forces, influencing the balance of forces through strategic moves, and anticipating shifts in the factors underlying competitive forces. In outwitting competitors companies must detect changes in the strategy game in reference to the market players' status in gaining more knowledge, networking, entrepreneurship, and increasing ambitions. The driving forces of competing firms, their organization, and micro-economic environment need to be studied carefully by the company planning to overtake competitors in the business. Further in the process of winning the battle of rivals it would be helpful for a company to understand the changing stakes of competitors and the forces after such developments. A company can outmaneuver a rival by being more skillful in particular tasks and reshaping the stakes in one or more business arenas. Outmaneuvering rivals is the core of changing the rules of the marketplace. Strategy for outperforming a competitor is largely based on two issues – performance parameters and the assessment criteria of the performance. However, the critical parameters may include research for the following information as to who is:

- Creating new customer needs that do not exist.
- Developing and establishing the new attributes of the product.
- Establishing new channels to reach all existing and potential customers.
- Reinventing stakes to condemn others to play catch-up roles.
- Creating new capabilities as the source of new products and customer needs.
- Creating a knowledge base for driving the capabilities for the new goods and services.
- Establishing new relationships with channels, institutions, and customers.
- Winning or losing in the business battle.

- Establishing new chains of customer delight.
- Leading the product.
- Dominating the price–value relationship.

The parameters and assessments of the above actions would help in focusing both the thinking and strategy-building process for sailing through the competition successfully. The current and future strategy of competitors must be considered by any company planning to outwit, outmaneuver, and outperform them.

Global retailing firms build their strategies to resolve the regional disparities in their strategies by coordinating and integrating the strategy implementation activities that involve centralization, standardization, delegation of authority, and local responsiveness. In the global marketplace India and China have made significant progress in economic and commercial sectors. China has emerged as a manufacturing base for the world in providing quality products at low prices and also leading the retailing operations in domestic and international markets. As more firms turn their attention to compete in emerging markets, they strive toward developing a viable alternative to sustain competition. Market orientation requires a different competitive mind-set and a systematic way of looking for opportunities, instead of looking within the conventional boundaries that define how an industry competes; managers can rather look methodically across them. In the process of market orientation firms can find scope for real value enhancement rather than looking at competitors within their own industry. Accordingly, firms with a customer-oriented business culture have been shown to facilitate innovativeness in customer services to improve their overall business system and develop a positive perception among customers, which is expected to yield long-term loyalty. Customer-focused firms that also have market orientation rely on developing strategies toward increasing customer satisfaction and loyalty through improved service quality. It is commonly perceived by marketing managers that market-oriented campaigns are expensive but actually can lower operating costs and increase market share by yielding high sales. It is more profitable for a retailing firm to establish long-term customer relationships than to adopt a short-term transaction-oriented approach. The customer-centric strategies of a firm should go beyond customer relationships and incorporate cross-functional integration of processes, people, operations, and marketing capabilities enabled through information, technology, and applications.

Globalization has increased access to markets as remote markets have been reduced following political and economic changes world-wide.

Market access has also been improved by growing trade blocs at the regional level. Such access to markets is further reinforced by reducing trade barriers through far-reaching business communication strategies, product and market development programs, and customer relations. This situation has given a boost in market opportunities as narrowing trade barriers helped in deregulating certain sectors of trade such as financial services. Technical operating standards and protocols are being widely adapted to synchronize with global industry standards. Resources are managed externally to a large extent as the best and low-cost materials are procured locally by multinational companies. The benefits of global sourcing for such companies include low-cost labor, uniform quality, innovative ideas, access to local markets, economies of scale, lower taxes and duties, lower logistics costs, and more consistent supply. However, there are also some risks in global sourcing, which might be political, economic, exchange, or supplier risks. In globalization, product lifecycles are getting shorter as new products are penetrating with higher speed in markets due to technological development and scale of operations. In this process many products are dropped off the product lifecycle either at the stage of introduction or growth. There are few products that sustain till the mature stage is passed. The growth of technology and its dynamic synchronization with industry are converging fast and leading toward quick adaptation of global products. The globalization of customer requirements is resulting from the identification of worldwide customer segments of homogeneous preferences across territorial boundaries. Business-to-consumers and business-to-business markets are powered by consumer demands from global companies as they are perceived to be more value-oriented and offer added benefits.

The globalization process reinforces the concept of locality, for a very simple reason: what is traded in a global context must be produced somewhere; global networks must begin and end somewhere. So the emergence of the global dimension in our societies does not mean the disappearance of locality, but rather the strengthening of a concept that is at the very source of globalization. Cities are anchorage points for globalization par excellence because few human territories can offer such complex facilities built up over time, offering so many facets, material and conceptual, inherited and innovative. The process of going global has enabled individuals, corporations, and nation-states to influence actions and events around the world faster, deeper, and cheaper than ever before, and equally to derive benefits from them. Globalization has led to the opening, the vanishing of many barriers and walls, and has the potential for expanding freedom, democracy, innovation, and social and cultural exchanges while offering outstanding opportunities for dialog and understanding.

Global competition is observed in both aggressive and defensive dimensions in the market. Companies that are capable of managing appropriate diffusion of technology and an adaptation process among customer segments are found to be highly successful. Competition among multinationals these days is likely to be a three-dimensional strategic game wherein the moves of an organization in one market are designed to achieve goals in another market in ways that are not immediately apparent to rivals. There is growing consensus among international trade negotiators and policymakers that a prime area for future multilateral discussion is competition policy. Competition policy includes antitrust policy (with merger regulation and control) but is often extended to embrace international trade measures and other policies that affect the structure, conduct, and performance of individual industries. The leading alliances between major multinational enterprises may be seen in reference to production, finance, technology, and supply chain along with other complementary activities. To compete in major global markets multinational companies deliver substantial financial resources. Logistics and supply chain management is an art of management of the flow of materials and products from the source of production to the end user. This system in terms of multinational companies includes the total flow of material right from the acquisition of raw materials to the delivery of finished products to customers. The function of distribution is the combination of activities associated with advertising, sales, and physical transfer of goods and services to retail and wholesale delivery points, as is being observed by global companies in order to establish their competitive strength in the market. Logistics management is an important function handled by such business companies in the marketing process, and effective logistics management improves both cost and customer service performance of the company. Globalization of distribution is particularly important for companies using the Iinternet for e-commerce as they can operate economies of scale with a wider reach of customers.

Behavioral resistance to change

The common cognitive behavior of consumers delineates that most consumers are resistant to change in products and services they are used to. Thus, improvements in products do not always encourage consumers to respond favorably and restrict the growth of changes introduced by companies to mark their differentiation and gain competitive advantage. Many consumer products grow as sustainable brands in the family context; for instance, use of a particular brand of dental cream may be adopted in a family over generations. Consumers resist accepting changes in such brands grown over generations in the family despite competitive differentiations introduced by the company.

While introducing product differentiation, companies should consider the seamless effects of change, the lifecycle of change, integrity of performance, commitment of the company, and empathy of consumers (SLICE) in managing consumer attitudes toward changes in reference to the following concerns:

- the time span to adapt to a change initiative;
- required psychodynamics among consumers in driving the change; and
- developing consciousness across consumer segments toward recognizing the differentiation, change, or competitive gains.

Some research studies indicate that there appears to be a consistent correlation between the outcomes of competitive differentiation and SLICE factors. This framework has a simple combination of elements for companies to manage differentiated products in the marketplace for gaining competitive advantage (Sirkin et al., 2005). Conventional differentiation models, in which a company plans for change, implements change, and tries to gain stability in the marketplace, are no longer workable in an environment of market uncertainty and behavioral vulnerability of consumers, when most companies see customization as a tool to acquire and retain consumers in a competitive marketplace. The changes associated with technology implementation, enhancement of use value of products through design and applications improvements, and delivering competitive advantages to the consumers are the key drivers to develop the butterfly effect in global markets. Companies cannot anticipate all the changes that would yield a one-time impact, but adaptation to change in the marketplace is a slow process that is often discouraging. Hence, butterfly effects in the markets responding to changes are not spontaneous or rapid, but rather sluggish and complex, and indeed often disappear during the consumer ice-breaking exercise of learning about the product and service differentiations. The butterfly effect on competitive differentiation may be best observed when companies develop customer-centric changes and customer segment-based launching of new products. However, there exist two necessary conditions to drive the butterfly effect in the global marketplace, namely, aligning the competitive differentiation model with corporate goals and minimizing the possibility of failure. Companies should understand that developing competitive differentiation and launching improved products is not part of radical innovation or experimentation but should serve as a confident strategy to revive product attractiveness, rebuild consumer confidence toward the brand, and strengthen market share and corporate posture against competitors (Hofman and Orlikowski, 1997). Consumers are resistant to changes and differentiations proposed by companies to gain competitive advantage because of several self-reference and socially driven factors, as exhibited in Figure 4.1.

In order to understand the reasons for consumers' resistance in adapting to the competitive differentiation strategies of the company toward products and services, it is necessary to review the market and customer challenges a company faces, as exhibited in Figure 4.1. One of the fiercest challenges, which every company has in developing competitive differentiation, is the difficulty in outmaneuvering existing competitors. In doing so, a company needs to trigger consumer defection from competitors by creating enhanced value through differentiation in its own products or services and inculcating attitudinal changes among

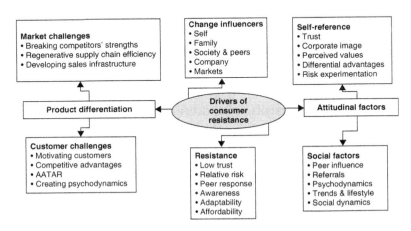

Figure 4.1   Attitudinal resistances of consumers toward competitively differentiated products

consumers. Most companies practice differentiation as a continuum strategy, but often suppliers resist getting involved in the product distribution process because of uncertainty of consumer preferences. As companies persist in implementing perennial changes in their products and services, they need to invest resources increasingly in marketing and sales infrastructure to exhibit competitive attractiveness. Companies also need to invest in acquainting consumers about differentiation through the AATAR paradigm, that is, attributes, awareness, trial, availability, and inducing consumer to repeat buying.

Understanding the attitudinal factors of consumers is more complex for companies than the organizational issues in managing competitive differentiation shown in Figure 4.1. Most consumers develop their perceptions and attitudes with self-reference criteria set by themselves, including trust, corporate image, perceived values, differential advantages, risk factors, and pros and cons of experimentation. On the other hand, social factors comprising peer influence, referrals, trends, lifestyles, and social dynamics help consumers in developing attitudes toward adapting to changes. However, despite the product differentiations brought about by a company in markets offering consumer value, most consumers show initial resistance because of low trust, relative risk, value for money, and low knowledge on the "4As" of awareness, attributes, adaptability, and affordability prospects.

Most companies engage in developing product differentiation for competitive benefit, which moves through an evolutionary process in initial days in the test market and can become revolutionary as a trendsetter in the market. For instance, the iPod was introduced by Apple Inc. in 2001 as a technologically differentiated personal audio device against the existing competition of Walkman, a similar gadget made by Sony Corporation. In the evolutionary process, by 2013 Apple had developed various versions of the iPod such as iPod Shuffle, iPod Nano, iPod Classic, and iPod Touch. This product has driven technology differentiation with glamor and has sustained its presence in the market as a trendsetter that outperforms conventional gadgets from the market competition.

The differentiation process in products or market segments moves through a series of developmental phases that include creativity and innovation, building consumer attitudes, preparing the market, supply chain coordination, and services management. Each phase evolves with unique strategies and commitments, steady growth, and stability, and ends with a revolutionary period of product and market attractiveness and change. The critical task for market management in each revolutionary period is to find a new set of organizational practices that will become the basis for managing the next stage of product differentiation. Fast-growing consumer companies therefore experience the irony of introducing major change as an advanced solution to consumer issues and competitive advantage to drive sustainable business growth (Griener, 1998).

All products with differentiated competitive advantages launched in the market face initial resistance from consumers, and attitudinal change toward new products or services develops slowly. During the period of transition of consumer behavior there always remains a threat of the competitors using defensive tactics to retain consumers of their brands. Hence, companies aiming at introducing competitive differentiation should also develop strong customer focus in implementing change-marketing strategies. However, preparing the company for implementing change management is not an easy proposition. For instance, Abbot Healthcare, IBM, and Samsung are engaged in learning the kind of customer focus that creates an advantage over competitors, and have experienced great difficulty in creating strategies for companywide transformation to introduce differentiation marketing.

Product differentiation opportunities and threats

Recent trends in the marketing of consumer products suggest that multiple-benefit products are becoming more common, and frequent introduction of new processed consumer products in the market is being encouraged. Companies stimulate consumer preferences for such new product introduction – for example, tomato juice with soy has been a recent new product in the processed consumer products segment that is positioned on organic and nutritional attributes. Health benefits and ingredient naturalness are positively valued, but such preferences and valuations depend on an individual's education, income, and consumer product purchase behavior, though naturally occurring nutrients are preferred by the consumers over fortification (Teratanavat and Hooker, 2007). The key trends fostering growth in consumer products markets are convenience, functionality, and indulgence. Packaging has become an integral constituent of processed consumer products, which contributes to consumer value and market demand. Besides, consumer products frequently require the general marketing approaches and techniques applied to the marketing of other kinds of products and services. Moreover, while going for product innovation, critical success factors must be taken into account (Ahmed et al., 2005). Identifying the impact of the decision on the attributes on a product's lifecycle in the consumer products sector is often difficult. Developing relationship between attributes of new products and consumer response is more challenging in the early phases of design, since the consequences of the decisions are far away and little is known about the product's lifecycle. Nevertheless, decisions on new product development have a marked influence on the lifecycle characteristics of a product during the early phases (Salonen et al., 2007).

Managerially, multi-brand testing process allows a firm to forecast the impact of its new product introduction on the market shares of competing brands (including those marketed by the firm) at both aggregate and segment levels. Hence, the firm can use the results to measure segment-specific cannibalization and switching effects; in addition, it can identify segment-specific adoption patterns following the introduction of the new product. The multi-brand testing process allows the firm to choose customized marketing-mix strategies for different segments after allowing for the effects of competitive retaliation following the new product introduction (Sharan et al., 2007). There are many key marketing concepts, including market orientation, marketing competencies and resources, and competitive marketing strategies that explain the success of small agro-consumer products companies in the international market. Some research studies indicate that the influential impact of adopting a market orientation, developing competencies in advantage-generating consumer products, channel and relationship management areas, leveraging strategically relevant managerial, production and brand resources, and deploying appropriate competitive marketing strategies significantly affect the process of new product introductions and variability in their cyclicality (Ibeh et al., 2006). Consumer-oriented innovation is an increasingly important source of new product development and competitive advantage in reference to the speed with which product innovations are brought to the market (Davenport et al., 2003).

In many cases, aesthetic properties are as important as technical functions. When one considers the subjective part of the requirements, the feelings, impressions, sensations or preferences of consumers must be quantified and modeled in advance. This is a major challenge in new consumer products design (Petiot and Grognet, 2006). There are many externalities in a market that influence companies to decide on the appropriate time to launch new consumer products in view of high–low demand seasons. A consumer product with an anticipated long life would also suggest a quick launch in the market as the high season for the product might be approaching shortly in a given market (Radas and Shugan, 1998). Business enterprises are always seeking robust and innovative approaches for new product development as part of their competitive strategy, which may include phase reviews during the process of product development. A number of researchers offer a different view of product development, however, and suggest that phase reviews can slow down product development. Hence, a critical path should be determined to effectively introduce new products in a marketplace (Kumar and Krob, 2007). It has been observed that new products reveal an indirect effect on consumer value and financial performance. In contrast, those in pursuit of positive financial performance and consumer value should simultaneously focus on the development of market orientation with the introduction of a new product. Even though this will not necessarily lead to the development of innovative processes and new product success according to the present study, this approach may lead to a greater market share in the long term (Paladino, 2007).

The timing of new product introductions has drawn significant research interest, and many studies have traditionally analyzed the introduction of new products within the context of product line expansions at a given time. It has been observed that optimal timing for introducing two new products depends on the degree of substitutability between an extension of an existing product line and the introduction of an improved product (Wilson and Norton, 1989). A sequential introduction of two new products in the market comprising one of a high quality and the other of low quality alleviates cannibalization by forcing consumers of the lower-end product to wait before they make a purchase. With this strategy, the company balances the benefits of weaker cannibalization against the deferring of profits from the low-end product. Consumer products might be delayed in being introduced to the market until the need for growth is found greater than the fear of cannibalizing existing products. Further, emphasis on the drawbacks from mistiming in the introduction of a new product has been studied by some researchers. The research has tested empirically the relation between timing of a new product introduction and its market success (Lilien and Yoon, 1990). It is observed in the retail consumer products sector that entry-based advantages for new products are due to the relationships between market demand and consumer perceptions. The perceptual measures of overall preferences and attribute-level beliefs contribute to the success of a new product. However, early entrants are perceived to be significantly superior to later entrants by customers (Denstadli et al., 2005).

The introduction of new products in the marketplace seems critical for many companies to check the decline in overall sales volume of their products and prevent consumers from switching to other brands. However, the timing of launching new products is crucial for their success in the market, and companies need to analyze carefully market conditions before introducing the new products (Axarloglou, 2003). Introduction of new consumer products often faces operational problems in the management of proper supplies. Manufacturers of consumer goods need to see the market situation and end consumer demand in order to efficiently allocate production capacity and procure materials. However, the difficulty of obtaining timely and accurate demand data from point-of-sales (POS) calls for alternative solutions to be developed. A research study offers a solution that is based on readily available sell-through data from channel partners, such as distributors, to monitor what happens in the market in product introduction situations. The difficulty with using demand information from distributors rather than POS is a "bullwhip effect" that distorts demand while moving upstream in the supply chain (Salmi and Holmström, 2004). Physical factors such as time and place involved in buying new products also affect consumer decisions on new products. Confidence and trust in production systems, integrity of regulatory systems, and reliability of suppliers appear to be the major determinants of product-market image as viewed by the gatekeepers of the consumer products distribution channel. Understanding of the determinants of consumer confidence in the safety of consumer products is important if effective risk management and communication are to be developed. Consumer perceptions regarding the safety of particular product groups, personality characteristics, and socio-demographics, are potential determinants of consumer confidence on leaning toward new consumer products introduced in the market (de Jonge et al., 2007).

Three distinct dimensions of emotions, namely, pleasantness, arousal, and dominance, have been identified as major drivers in making buying decisions among consumers. The convergence of sales promotion, consumer perceptions, value for money, and product features drive arousal among consumers. Consumer values are created toward the new product through individual perceptions, and organizational and relational competence. Firms need to ascertain a continuous organizational learning process with respect to the value-creation chain and measure performance of new products introduced into the market

(Rajagopal, 2007). Product attractiveness consists of product features of improved attributes, use of advanced technology, innovativeness, extended product applications, brand augmentation, perceived use value, competitive advantages, corporate image, product advertisements, and sales and services policies associated therewith. These features contribute in building sustainable consumer values toward making buying decisions on new products. The attractiveness of new products is one of the key factors affecting the decision-making of consumers, and in turn is related to market growth and sales. The higher the positive reactions of consumers toward the new products in view of their attractiveness, the higher the growth in sales (Rajagopal, 2006).

Disruptive tendencies in markets

A disruptive innovation initially grows in a niche market and gradually penetrates into the existing market by cultivating its demand among consumers. Over a period of time the new product or idea completely redefines the industry. A disruptive innovation helps in developing a new market and value network, but drives disruption in the longstanding market demand and value network by displacing an earlier technology. Disruptive innovation may be described as the process that improves a product or service in a different way against the normal market drivers, typically first by developing a new consumer segment in a new market or by inducing consumers to defect from the existing market. Most disruptive innovations are radical as they skip some stages of the growth process of existing products and technologies to gain competitive advantage in the market quickly. In contrast to disruptive innovation, a sustaining innovation does not create new markets or value networks but only evolves existing ones with better value, allowing firms within to compete against each other's sustaining improvements. In view of the globalization and marketing practices of emerging companies it has been observed that market disruption has become a growth function for technology and its application.

Clayton M. Christensen has revolutionized the concept of disruptive innovation with his "technology mudslide hypothesis" (Christensen and Overdorf, 2000). This is the simple notion that an established firm fails because it is unable to cope with the changing technological advances of competing firms. In this hypothesis, the attributes of a firm can be explained by the analogy of creepers – one that finds its own path to climb and the other that survives as a parasite to climb.

Products emerging out of disruptive technology are like parasites, which are built on the products available in the market with popular technologies. Disruptive innovation products largely focus on the low-cost and utilitarian values of consumers. Good firms are usually aware of emerging innovations underneath the market, but their business environment does not allow them to head off disruptive innovations as this is risky to pursue owing to low profit, and may drain the resources of the firm. Generally, a firm's existing value networks place insufficient value on disruptive innovations to allow pursuit by another firm. Start-up firms live with different value networks until a disruptive innovation is able to invade their value networks, grow parallel in the market, create a me-too entry, and strengthen its chances of co-survival in the existing market.

Disruptive innovation may be a product or a service designed for a new set of customers by inducing them to defect from an existing buying stream. Generally, disruptive innovations are technologically straightforward, convincing to consumers, and generate value for money. Some disruptive innovations offer more for less to customers through a different package of attributes that may have higher significance to the consumers in the bottom-of-the-pyramid market segment than to those of the mainstream market. Christensen argues that disruptive innovations can damage successful brands and well-managed products of reputed companies that are responsive to their customers, and have invested resources in conducting excellent research and development to support innovation. These companies tend to bypass markets that are most susceptible to disruptive innovations as there appears the risk of low profit and limited scope for business growth. Thus disruptive technology provides products and services with focus on the customer and drives a strategically counterproductive impact on existing products in a market. However, in a positive sense the disruptive innovation may be considered as the constructive integration of attributes of the existing technology. Disruptive innovations generate radical insights that could help in improving the economic benefits to consumers and provide better opportunities for firms to grow in the mass market.

As companies tend to innovate faster, customers' needs evolve over the period and set the demand for products with new technologies in the market. However, most organizations develop complicated, high-technology, and expensive products for customers. High-technology/high-value products help companies to succeed in the premium market segment by maintaining a high price/high profit ratio. Such a strategy encourages disruptive innovations at the bottom of the market and allows consumers there to access products. Major attributes of disruptive innovations include:

- low price profile;
- high perceived use value;
- low gross margins;
- small target markets;
- simple products and services;
- attractive solutions.

The bottom-of-the-pyramid market offers lower gross margins and is non-competitive to other firms to develop strategies to move upward in the market and create space at the bottom for new disruptive competitors to emerge.

Disruptive market behavior and streamlined differentiations in products and services by companies survive simultaneously in the competitive marketplace. As companies introduce differentiated products in their markets, disruptive products grow underneath the mainstream retailing in the mass market as well as in the bottom-of-the-pyramid market segment. The prominence of disruption of products and services in the market causes serious threats to the mainstream marketing strategies of companies and might also lead to failure of business in specific markets or consumer segments. One of the most consistent patterns in business is the failure of leading companies to combat unnoticed disruptions emerging in the market whenever new technologies or product differentiations are introduced. The reason at the grassroots why companies succumb to disruptive products is the defection of their customers to the low-end disruption. However, to stay sustainable within the industries and competitive marketplace, companies must be able to spot disruptive technologies and protect their market and consumer segments that are serving mainstream customers (Bower and Christensen, 1995). Figure 4.2 exhibits high- and low-end differentiation strategies for developing sustainable competitive advantage.

Figure 4.2 illustrates that most companies position their differentiated and new competitive products in high-end markets by promoting high-cost technology, high price, and developing high brand equity for gaining sustainable competitive advantage. However, as new products are positioned in high-end markets the threat of new entrants increases. Sometimes companies choose to launch their differentiated products in a market niche, catering to the consumer needs in a limited territory. Companies gain first mover advantage in low-end markets by

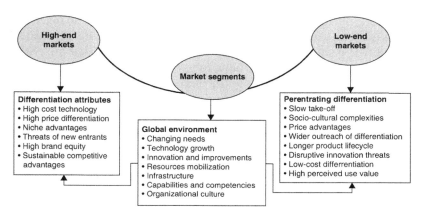

Figure 4.2 Differentiation strategies across market segments

positioning their differentiated and new competitive products through low price offers and creating high perceived use value for their products among consumers. However, new products take off in the low-end markets slowly but attract wider outreach among consumers. Companies need to play safe in this market segment as disruptive innovations might grow here and cause damage to any new differentiated products brought to this segment. Hence most companies introduce low-cost differentiations in low-end markets.

Low-end disruptive innovation products are targeted to customers who are satisfied even with the partial performance of the product but derive high emotional satisfaction, while new-market disruption aims at the new consumer segment to cater both for high product performance as well as emotional satisfaction. Low-end disruption in the market takes place when demand for the product exists but products are unavailable. Consumers have the latent desire to experience the high-end products but often these products are not affordable. Consequently, at some point the performance of the disruptive products overshoots the needs of certain customer segments, and at this point, a disruptive technology may enter the market and provide a product with high perceived use value, gaining a reasonable market share. In low-end disruption, the disruptive product is focused initially on serving the least profitable customer, who is happy with the partial performance of the product. Such customers will be willing to pay a lower price than others and have greater satisfaction on acquiring the product than over its performance.

Once the disruptive products gain a sustainable market share, their manufacturers seek to improve their profit margin over the established brands; the disruptive products now enter the differentiated price segment where the customer is willing to pay a little more for higher quality. Hence, the disruptor firms set the pace of the innovation process for products to meet the desired quality and establish themselves as a back market product. Over time the disruptive products will move up-market and focus on penetrating more attractive consumer segments. This business situation takes the disruptive products out of the niche. New market disruption occurs when a product fits a new or emerging market segment that is not being served by existing incumbents in the industry.

Sustaining innovation, pioneered by established companies, ensures these companies' competitive status in a market by enhancing and improving existing products' performance in an expected way that customers value (Christensen and Overdorf, 2000). However, disruptive innovation usually originates from newcomers and upsets the market status by fundamentally altering the way customers think about product performance because it exceeds their expectations in an unexpected way. In comparing both innovation types, it can be seen that sustaining innovations are the type of technological outcomes that can be outperformed by large and established competitors within a short period of time, while disruptive innovations cannot be imitated or outdone by other companies due to the number of difficulties they face. Some of the difficulties that established companies face are their flexibility in political, operational, and cultural positions (Kim and Mauborgne, 2005). With disruptive innovation, the vital concern is to make such a leap that the relevant offering provides a better product/service than anything that existed beforehand. It is almost impossible for established companies to cope with this change as they are focusing on their sustained innovation, which helps to maximize profits and keeps making their products more desirable. However, established companies can be disruptive by attracting low-end customers as in the case of the portable digital music player. Many companies are in search of an innovative strategy to move on to a market where there is no competition yet. In view of that, many academics and managers are trying to find a systematic framework for a strategic innovative business model. Disruptive technology largely serves the low-end or new niche market customers and upon establishing a strong market foothold; it enters the market competition and engages in continuous research and development to improve performance of products and services. Research and development strategy comprising simplification of usage of technology and application of new products drives disruptive innovations (Yu and Hang, 2010).

Market differentiation and the butterfly effect

Most multinational companies targeting gaining sustainable growth in business vigorously promote their product, process, and services differentiation through various ways in order to convince consumers and to develop a positive attitude toward changes. Thus, companies push intellectual and financial resources into creating differentiated products or services for their consumers. However, in many situations, differentiation may not be a profitable strategy. Sometimes negative word of mouth, cultural ambiguity, and lack of customer relationship efforts by the company might raise questions on the success of product differentiation and the chain reaction to drive the butterfly effect effectively. Some consumers learn about alternative products, innovations, and technologies through advertising, while some do not see advertising for all relevant alternatives. As a result, a significant fraction of consumers make decisions with limited information and experience about the available alternatives but these consumers could have a high outreach to influence the consumer community, triggering a chain butterfly effect. The value of creating differentiated products is ambiguous when awareness of products and their characteristics is the key determinant of consumer behavior (Soberman, 2003).

Cross-cultural product differentiation tends to favor diversity within a society but not across societies. Competition in global markets tends to increase diversity over time by accelerating the pace of change and bringing new cultural goods with each era or generation. However, cultural similarities tend to come together over time across regions. That is, although chain restaurants take an increasing percentage of restaurant sales, growth in dining out has led to an expansion of specialty food opportunities. While cross-cultural differentiation alters and disrupts each society and its consumer segments, it also supports innovation and creative human energies. Extreme differentiations – like the manufacturing and marketing of high speed motorcycles – might cause a plethora of innovative and high-quality creations in many different genres, styles, and media cross-cultural exchange to drive the butterfly effect in the global marketplace (Cowen, 2002).

Competing firms pay more attention to the sources of competitive factors, their quality, cost, and management in order to gain advantage over each other. The customer, the end user, is the ultimate target of competitors in building aggressive and defensive strategies in business. Competing firms try to attract customers by various means to polarize business and earn confidence in the marketplace. It is necessary for successful business companies to look for such a place of business that provides them with location advantage and holds customers for their goods and services. Business cordoning or securing trade boundaries is an essential decision to be taken in building competitive strategies to attack rivals across regions. Even the small business company can compete globally with firms of all sizes through the Internet. The distribution channels, franchisees, carrying and forwarding agents, retailers and mailers with value-added services represent an increasingly intense business rivalry or competition in all markets or competitive domains. Firms such as Godrej (diversified products), Procter & Gamble (consumer goods), and Compaq (computers) reward their managers handsomely for winning business battles in their channel wars. In succeeding in market competition, institutional and political patronage provides long-run support to winning companies.

A differentiation strategy in products and markets has not only shown many advantages for business growth in global markets but has also posed threats to the regional business environment. Competition among firms is increasingly shifting from company vs. company to supply chain vs. supply chain. Benefits can be grouped as customer-oriented benefits, productivity benefits, and innovation-related benefits. Factors supporting collaboration are observed as trust, common goals for cooperation, and existence of cooperation mechanisms, while barriers are related to the three factors of lack of trust, unfavorable risk–benefit evaluation, and lack of common goals for cooperation (Dilek et al., 2005). Collaboration with regional companies for differentiating corporate posture and operational strategies is growing rapidly in the global marketplace.

On the contrary, heavy competition in India in almost all product categories has been experienced due to diversification by large and medium companies and the increased entry of multinationals, which has restricted the growth of domestic Indian companies. Previously, large companies enjoyed high profit margins by targeting premium-priced products in the upper strata of Indian society. High levels of competition from equally reputed brands have not only decreased the companies' market share but also created price wars, reducing profit margins, and limiting market growth. This has motivated companies to consider the lower classes and rural segments, which they had previously ignored (Dubey and Patel, 2004). In growing competitive markets large and reputed firms are developing strategies to move into the provision of innovative combinations of products and services as "high-value integrated solutions" tailored to each customer's needs rather than simply "moving downstream" into services. Such firms are developing innovative combinations of service capabilities such as operations, business consultancy, and finance required to provide complete solutions to customer's needs in order to augment the customer value toward the innovative or new products (Rajagopal and Rajagopal, 2007).

Competition may be characterized as striving together to win the race, not to destroy the other competitors from the point of view of the supporters of globalization. Local market competition is targeted toward the customers, and competitors strive to win the customer, temporarily or permanently. However, in the business-to-business process, competition may become more tactical and strategic in order to outperform rival firms. In this way, competition can be seen as regulated struggle. Competitive roles can be radically altered with technological advances or with the right marketing decisions (Rajagopal, 2006).

The differentiation and growth of products of multinational companies is mostly centralized in the country of origin and the products that emerge tend to have FABs (features, advantages, benefits) specified by the central marketing system of the company. Hence, key technologies and major product introductions cater primarily to customers in that geographical region. Marketing and customers in other regions are relegated to acceptance of custom modifications or they have the choice to buy from other local suppliers. Product targeting goes beyond the perceived use values of the customers, local preferences, and local language. Expectations regarding size, shape, customized items, price, and availability vary widely. Hence, regional markets tend to be dominated by local companies. Often the companies offer locally engineered or customized products at a differential price to win market share. For growth and success in the new global economy, the guiding principle must be "Go Global – think Local!" Automation suppliers must become truly global by allowing local development of products for local markets. The best approach is to develop technology through global alliances, preferably with relatively small, fast-moving local companies, to increase the outreach of product differentiation, innovation, and technology.

Firms face profound challenges to manage business in future. The first challenge is to keep pace with the rapid growth and greater involvement of firms in global business activities. Social media has emerged as one of the new and powerful platforms for firms to stay abreast of the consumer dynamics in the global marketplace. In particular, the tremendous growth in interactive marketing activities has necessarily engaged new entrants in global business-to-business activities, to which much greater attention should be paid. The second challenge for firms is toward the process of business transition, which demands managing supply chain systems through greater coordination of entire distribution channels, alliances, and relational exchanges. Most companies are relying on social network platforms for faster exchange of communication, on one hand, and implementing sophisticated technology of market communication through the radio frequency identification (RFID) platform, on the other. Finally, another challenge fostering a major change in how firms conduct business and compete is the transition to electronic forms of exchange, particularly with respect to information access, storage, and retrieval (Samiee, 2008).

Market access has also been improved by the growing trade blocs at the regional level. Such accessibility to markets is further reinforced by reducing trade barriers through far-reaching business communication strategies, product and market development programs, and customer relations. This situation has given a boost in determining market opportunities as narrowing trade barriers has helped in deregulating certain sectors of trade, such as financial services. However, there may be some exceptions to this common pattern. The global marketplace equipped with the application of global communications has become the focus of the global business arena, which keeps world markets remain open and involved in fair competitive practices. At the same time anti-globalization moves also exist in the process of development that protest against the hazards of suppressive strategies of the global companies as affecting regional trade entities. Globalization moves have opened up high comparative advantages in many manufactured goods through partnership deals to explore business in emerging economies. They generally display an increasing specialization trend and high consumer values. The leading alliances between the major multinational enterprises may be seen in reference to production, finance, technology, and the supply chain along with other complementary activities.

The markets today not only provide multiple goods and services to customers but also expose their behavior to cross-cultural differences and innovations. The specialization of the production process has also brought such cultural changes by business penetration into low-production skills regions. Apparel from Asian countries like Indonesia and South Korea and all types of consumer goods from China, electronics from Japan and perfumery from France are good examples to explain the specialization and cross-cultural sharing of consumer behavior. Conducting business is a creative enterprise and doing it out of one's own country is more demanding. Industry structure varies dramatically across countries in the world, and for a global enterprise to strive against the odds requires strong adaptation behavior. In international business a company needs to best prepare itself to achieve competitive advantage in the marketplace. International partnering in reference to production technology, co-branding, distribution, and retailing may bring high success to the companies of the home country in increasing market share in the region as well as augmenting customer value for mutual benefit.

With the emergence of virtual shopping and liberalization of economic policies in developing countries all over the world competition has become like a traditional horse derby in which many companies participate in a neck-to-neck race. In this business game the rules are subject to change without notice, the prize money may change at short notice, the route and finish line are also likely to change after the race begins, new entrants may join at any time during the race, the racers may form strong alliances, all creative strategies are allowed in the game and the state legislation may change without notice and sometimes with retrospective effect. Hence to win the race any company should acquire the strategies of outwitting, outmaneuvering, and outperforming their competitors. In this process a company must understand thoroughly all the moves of rival firms from various sources. The locales of business rivalry have to be identified to assess their strengths. In a given situation it may be necessary for a firm to ally with a strong brand to survive the competition and safely enhance its reach to the markets.

Social media today is an agglomeration of various online tools that are designed for and centered on social interaction. Social media serves as a conglomeration of web-based technologies and services such as blogs, micro-blogs (i.e., Twitter), social sharing services (e.g., YouTube, Flickr), text messaging, discussion forums, collaborative editing tools (e.g., wikis), virtual worlds (e.g., Second Life), and social networking services. Unlike traditional media, social media relies on user-generated content, which refers to any content that has been created by the users of any demographic or professional category. Traditional media such as radio, books, and network television is primarily designed to be a broadcast platform (one-to-many), whereas social media is designed to continue dialogs among peers and organizations. Social media has not only been sourced by companies for promoting their business, but also much government activity is now focused on social media. So, there emerges a new challenge for governments that want to regulate the communication flow through social media (Bertot et al., 2012).

Social institutions play a significant role in nurturing cultural heritage, which is reflected in individual behavior. Such institutions include family, education, and political structures, and the media affects the ways in which people relate to one another, organize their activities to live in harmony with one another, teach acceptable behavior to succeeding generations, and govern themselves. The status of gender in society, the family, social classes, group behavior, age groups, and how societies define decency and civility are interpreted differently within every culture. Social institutions are a system of regulatory norms and rules of governing actions in pursuit of immediate ends in terms of their conformity with the ultimate common value system of a community. They constitute underlying norms and values making up the common value system of a society. Institutions are intimately related to and derived from the value attitudes common to members of a community. This establishes institutions as primarily moral phenomena, which leads to enforce individual decisions on all human needs including economic and business-related issues.

5
Consumer Value Management

Often companies drive innovation to bring change in the market for competitive advantage and reduce the cost and time of manufacturing a product or delivering a service with the desired quality and competitive advantage. Most challenging issues in the market, such as change management, improvement in products and services, and enhancing customer value, are on the axis of identifying redundancies in existing market competition and eliminating them to reduce cost and time involved in the process of generating end values. This chapter addresses the critical issues on delivering customer value and enhancing organizational competency in managing customer values. The chapter illustrates attitudinal models for adapting to competitive differentiation, suggesting that co-creation of new product development and competitive differentiation are two efficient strategies that companies intend to follow. The chapter also addresses various issues referring to managing process improvements and developing an innovations value chain within the value chain triangles of QCT (quality, cost, and time) and TBC (technical, behavioral, and cultural factors).

Increasing market competition induces companies to invest physical, financial, and human resources in developing differentiation continuously to stay abreast of changes in consumer preferences and market requirements. Intellectual capital contributes enormously to the innovation, differentiation, and change behavior of consumers and markets. Most companies develop meticulously their innovation and competitive differentiation strategies to gain sustainable advantage in the competitive marketplace. However, one of the principal challenges among companies is to develop internal competencies in managing the differentiation, and building capabilities to diffuse the competitive differentiation for wider outreach and acceptability among consumer segments. The market competitiveness of a company is derived from its core competencies within its products, services, and operations. Core competency of a company is commonly developed through knowledge sharing and collective learning in the organization. This is built especially through the capacity to coordinate diverse production skills and integrate streams of technologies. Companies engaged in establishing their leadership in the competitive market through differentiation must identify core competencies that provide potential access to a wide variety of strategies and make a contribution to the customer benefits of the product, while being difficult for competitors to imitate (Prahalad and Hamel, 1990).

Organizational capabilities and competencies

Competencies in marketing organizations can be broadly classified as organizational level, strategy level, and implementation level. Competencies to develop continuous innovation and differentiation should be pushed by the companies at the strategy level. The strategy-level competencies toward developing innovative and intervening strategies are embedded in the competencies at organizational level. The identification of the former is important for organizations interested in using competencies to achieve competitive advantage. Once the appropriate strategy-level competencies are identified, a competency-based market information system can be implemented to ensure that the strategies implemented actually do possess the identified competencies in a marketing organization (Cardy and Selvaraj, 2006). Besides the organizational-level, strategy-level, and implementation-level, successful marketing firms consider developing three types of competencies, namely superior technological know-how, reliable processes, and external relationships. Companies may not be able to achieve all types of competencies as different approaches are needed to develop each type of competency. While large and multinational firms have historically relied on technological know-how and reliable processes, they are planning to develop competencies in external relationships for sustainability in the competitive marketplace. External relationships help firms in strengthening and extending their organizational core competencies while responding to the demands of globalization, mass customization, enhanced quality, and rapid technological change (Mascarenhas et al., 1998).

Companies successfully differentiating their products and services and driving change in the market to attract consumers rely on superior technological know-how, reliable processes, and close external relationships in order to improve their organizational competencies. While these firms have historically relied on technological know-how and reliable processes, different approaches are used to develop each type of competency. In this process companies tend to plan more close external relationships by simultaneously improving their internal competencies for effective implementation and sustainable business growth. External relationships help firms in building capability to manage the consumer and market resistance toward product differentiation and change. Strong external relationships strengthen the vision of companies on globalization, mass customization, enhanced quality, and keeping pace with technological growth.

The degree of competition in a market is largely affected by the moves and countermoves of various companies participating in the market. Differentiation among products and services is intensified by companies in accordance with the increase in degree of market competition. Generally, the differentiation and change process begins with a company trying to achieve a favorable position in the competitive marketplace by pursuing appropriate strategies that are advantageous for the firm. Sometimes differentiation may turn into disruption and cause harm not only to rival firms but also restrict the entry of new firms temporarily. For example, innovation in digital photo and video camera devices created differentiation for the first mover company Kodak in 1995, but the market opportunities were highly exploited by the Asian companies Panasonic, Sony, and Samsung. One of the fallouts of this differentiation was observed as business growth in the consumer photographic film manufacturing industry declined, with no scope for revival.

Thus, companies engaged in developing differentiation strategies largely set trends in the markets and cause unprecedented changes. The competition attracts firms seeking to capitalize on an available business opportunity. As the number of firms involved in the process of sharing the pie grows, the degree of competition increases. When the entire market represents one large homogeneous unit, the intensity of competition is much greater than in a segmented market However, if a market is not appropriate for segmentation, firms may compete to serve it homogeneously, thus intensifying competition. Hence, in either of the market scenarios the intensity of competition is unavoidable for participating firms. Understanding the capabilities and competencies (C&C) of a rival and developing the company's own are the most important tasks in navigating the marketing competition. This is essential for sustaining the company, acquiring circumstantial leverage and winning the marketplace in future. Its capabilities in general address how well an organization performs or executes such vital activities as customer relationship management, services, supply chain management etc. Competency is what an organization does well across the region and subsidiary units or customer segments. In all, the C&C involve action, focus, and emphasis on what the competitor does in the market to outperform his business rival. The common competencies that can be judged in reference to a competitor are as follows:

• Quick movement of products to the marketplace from R&D unit.
• Faster response to market opportunities.
• Providing convincing and unique solutions to customer problems.
• Hire, train, and retain best personnel.
• Develop, nurture, and extend the best relationship with customers and alliance partners.

There are four key tasks in the management of core competency, namely, selecting core competency, building core competency, deploying core competency, and protecting core competency. Companies are likely to differ in terms of their abilities to select, build, deploy, and protect core competency. These differences are, in turn, likely to yield differences in corporate performance. Building core competency requires the accumulation and integration of knowledge inside and outside of the company. For example, the core competency of a telecom company in managing billing systems, an insurance company's core competency in claims processing, and Sony's core competency in miniaturization are each a tapestry of many individual technologies and skills. The core competencies of the companies are those that push down competitors' products in all business domains. These strategies are central to customers, channels, and alliance advantage:

• dynamism;
• span;
• robustness;
• security against imitations;
• ability to expand.

The dynamism of developing differentiation strategies refers to continuous change for the betterment of policies and execution of strategies. The organization must be able to identify new markets continuously and never be static at any point of time. An organization must have a wide span to discharge its competency without specifying the boundaries of time and area. Sometimes organizational competencies may vary in adaptability to the current and future business domains, and companies need to build internal strengths in tune with the market requirement to gain wider butterfly effects. A competitor cannot always leverage a competency for new products or services development in changing business domains. Companies must secure that their capabilities and competencies (C&C) strategies are not replicated by other firms or used in a distorted manner. Indeed, the C&C of any company should be able to be enhanced continuously so that they add to the firm's sustainable advantages. Large marketing firms foster implementation of competitive marketing strategies as an organizational learning path and provide employees with psychological safety. These companies also employ distinct approaches to day-to-day work that enhance the competencies of the firm to sustain itself in the competitive marketplace. These approaches include the application of available knowledge, encouragement of employee collaboration by information sharing on core functions, capturing data on processes on a regular basis to map the process, and analyzing data to find ways to improve the implementation of competitive strategies (Edmondson, 2008). The key attributes of capabilities and competencies of companies required for effective differentiation are exhibited in Figure 5.1.

In practice, today's global competition is more dynamic and multidimensional. The mature industry paradox is that leadership demands differentiation, yet differences are quickly copied. Single-factor innovations tap one competency, and capable competitors can usually match it. Multiple competencies strengthen several dimensions and in effect redefine the basis of competition. The "shadow strategy task force" is offered as a method to force managers to relinquish the comfort of the firm's accepted view of itself. This approach begins with the objective of identifying the strategies and competencies that, in the hands of competitors, might be used to attack the firm's competitive position successfully. Especially critical on the task force are individuals with insight into how customers, suppliers, and competitors view the firm's products and services. Developing new competency requires constant experimentation. The innovation–imitation–equilibrium cycle suggests that industry leaders teach customers what to demand by defining the current state-of-the-art in performance, price, service, and other dimensions; customers learn to judge competitive offerings against these standards, and the learning effect is cumulative (Werther and Kerr, 1995).

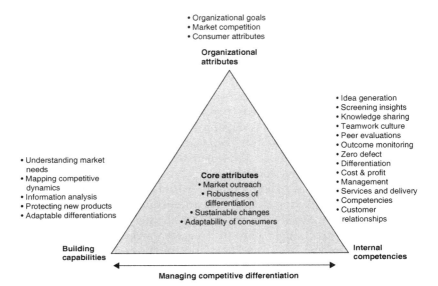

Figure 5.1   Attributes of organizational capabilities and competencies for managing competitive differentiations

There are many ways to categorize core competency, broadly distinguished as market-access competency, integrity-related competency and functionality-related competency. *Market-access competency* includes management of brand development, sales and marketing, distribution and logistics, technical support, etc. All these skills help to put a firm in close proximity to its customers. The attributes associated with competency, like quality, cycle time management, just-in-time inventory management and so on, which allow a company to do things more quickly, flexibly or with a higher degree of reliability than competitors, constitute the *integrity-related competency* of a firm. *Functionality-related competency* leads to the skills that enable the company to invest its services or products with unique functionality and invest the product with distinctive customer benefits, rather than merely making it incrementally better. This functionality-related competency is becoming more important as a source of competitive differentiation, relative to the other two types of competencies. In the growing competitive phenomenon, companies are converging towards universally high standards for product and service integrity, and are moving through alliances, acquisitions, and industry consolidation to build broadly matching global brand and distribution capabilities. Interestingly, the Japanese concept of quality has shifted from an idea centered on integrity ("zero defects") to one focused on functionality ("quality that surprises," in that the product yields a unique functionality benefit to the customer).

Comparative analysis examines the specific advantages of competitors within a given market and offers structural and response advantages. *Structural advantages* are those built into the business, for example, a manufacturing plant in Mexico may, because of low labor costs, have a built-in advantage over another firm. *Response advantages* refer to positions of comparative advantage that have accrued to a business over time as a result of certain decisions. This type of advantage is based on leveraging the strategic phenomena at work in the business. Besides, the examination of the business system operating in an industry is useful in analyzing competitors and in searching out innovative options for gaining a sustainable competitive advantage. The business-system framework enables a firm to discover the sources of greatest economic leverage, that is, stages in the system where it may build cost or investment barriers against competitors (Normann and Ramirez, 1993). The framework may also be used to analyze a competitor's costs and to gain insights into the sources of a competitor's current advantage in either cost or economic value to the customer.

In developed markets brands are perceived as low-profile and are paying a high cost for changing such a perception. However, the Indian market has opened up the opportunity for brands to position at a premium scale at relatively low cost. Firms play as high-profile rivals in the Indian market as their business strategies closely cut across each other to achieve their business goals. Most companies focus on matching and beating their rivals. As a result, their strategies tend to take on similar dimensions. What ensues is head-to-head competition based largely on incremental improvements in cost, quality, or both. The multinational companies, which are dynamic in strategy experimentation, and innovative companies break free from the competitive pack by staking out fundamentally new market space by creating products or services for which there are no direct competitors. This path to value innovation requires a different competitive mind-set and a systematic way of looking for opportunities. Instead of looking within the conventional boundaries that define how an industry competes, managers can look methodically across them. By doing so, they can find unoccupied territory that represents real value innovation. Rather than looking at competitors within their own industry, for example, managers can ask why customers make the trade-off between substitute products or services. Often consumers also look across the substitutes available to them in managing their choices. In both cases, powerful insights are derived from looking at familiar data from a new perspective (Chan and Mauborgne, 1999).

Managing improvements

Effective management of a firm typically requires both planning and control, establishing performance-measuring, rewarding systems to reinforce specific goals of the organization, and developing the mind-sets of managers by creating a sense of shared responsibility in performing tasks. Although companies invest considerable time and money to administer polices through managers, it is necessary to focus management strategies on how the structure of the sales force needs to be closely associated with the performance indicators of a firm's business. Firms must consider the relationship between the differing roles of managers in reference to intrinsic and extrinsic tasks, degree of specialization, and how to develop corporate image. These factors are critical in measuring efficacy of management because they determine how quickly a firm can respond to market opportunities, set competitive goals, and reflect on the revenues, costs, and profitability of the firm (Tsai et al., 1991).

The task of a manager changes over the course of the strategy administration process. Different abilities are required in each stage of management, including analysis of strengths, weaknesses, opportunities, and threats, creating solutions, and taking the lead. The success of managers depends on their knowledge, attitude, and practice, and they need to be SMART, comprising qualities of being strategic, measurable, aggressive, responsive, and time-driven (Rajagopal and Rajagopal, 2008). Managers often view their tasks as a set of stereotypical activities but in practice management is a diligent task that involves variety of conflicts and high risk. Hence, the performance of managers is demonstrated by effective administration skills not only in developing new ambiance to carry out tasks effectively but also to resolve conflicts and ambiguities during the task-handling process and dynamics. Result-oriented performance and control are positively related attributes of managers that lead to the success of the organization (Hultink and Atuahene, 2000).

Managers' goals arise out of necessities rather than desire; they excel at defusing conflicts between individuals or departments, conciliating all sides while ensuring that an organization's day-to-day business gets done. Managers should also possess the traits of a good leader to drive enthusiasm among employees of the organization as well as direct them in competitive dynamics. Leaders, on the other hand, adopt personal, active attitudes toward goals. They look for the opportunities and rewards that are available around them, inspiring subordinates and firing up the creative process with their own energy. Their relationships with employees and co-workers are intense, and their working environment is often chaotic (Abraham, 2004).

Managing improvements in existing products and developing differentiation are continuous processes for companies striving to establish competitive advantage. Most companies thus introduce the practice of empowering employees to inculcate innovative thinking behavior. Thinking on product differentiation is a continuous process, which should be linked to *kaizen* – a Japanese term for continuous improvement. Improvement or *change for the better* refers to philosophy or practices that focus upon continuous improvement of processes in manufacturing, engineering, and business management. *Kaizen* refers to activities that continuously improve all functions, and involves all employees from the CEO to assembly line workers. It also applies to processes, such as purchasing and logistics that cross organizational boundaries into the supply chain. In fact, *kaizen* is a social culture of innovation, adopted by Japanese organizations. However, *ad hoc* learning focused on tacit knowledge may serve as a tool for organizational survival against market risks and uncertainties. It is perceived by employees of some organizations that limiting diffusion of corporate strategies and market information often leaves them unaware of the developments affecting their performance (Carswell, 2005).

Most companies refrain from planning for long-term growth or looking for the next big change whenever market uncertainty increases and differentiation becomes risk averse. However, concentrating on small improvements to spread across the mass and bottom-of-the-market segments often appears to the best course of action. To be successful in bringing change to the market and delivering competitive advantage to consumers, a company must be capable of managing different innovation streams simultaneously. Incremental innovations help a company's bottom line while architectural innovations reconfigure differentiations to plan for sustainable competitive growth in the marketplace. By dealing with the above differentiation streams simultaneously, companies can hope to gain market leadership over time (Gary, 2003). It has been observed in the global marketplace that success in product differentiation and improvements are more likely to result from the systematic pursuit of opportunities. Within a company or industry, opportunities can be found in unexpected occurrences, incongruities of various kinds, process needs, or changes in an industry or market. Outside a company, opportunities arise from demographic changes, changes in perception, or new knowledge. Innovations based on new knowledge tend to have the greatest effect on the marketplace, but it often takes decades before the ideas are translated into actual products, processes, or services. The other sources of innovation are easier and simpler to handle, yet they still require managers to look beyond established practices (Drucker, 1998).

Value enhancement in innovative products may be achieved by improving performance, manufacturability, convergence of product attributes with customer demands, and improvement in the product process in reference to time, cost, and user benefits (Maylor, 2001). The introduction of most new products demands a communication campaign to diffuse the consumer benefits the products can provide. Communicating product improvements through social media channels involves low costs and higher reach among the audience. Manufacturers typically employ direct channels to communicate minor improvements. In order to create product and customer value, firms should work on improving the reliability of products soon after their new products are launched in the market. The reliability improvement of new products is the larger picture of improving product quality concerned with the performance of the product's function over a stated period of time. Most firms share with consumers the results of product performance under test conditions. However, quality is defined as conformance to requirements that assures fault-free product performance experienced by the customer. Compared to product quality, reliability has a more product-specific definition that relates to continuously improving the performance of the product's functionality. Product reliability management largely involves the following measures being taken by firms:

• Efficient management of the reliability function in all innovative products.
• Intensity and precision in evaluation of reliability value of new products during the design, concept testing, and development phases.
• User applications for the new products, application failure information, statistical analysis, and imposing standards and control on the uniformity of manufacture and assembly of these new products.

Recent research has shown that product reliability is positively correlated with customer confidence and profit margins. Online quality control techniques are relatively appreciated in many sectors of manufacturing industry, and recent single-industry investigations show that most of online quality control techniques, which should be useful in assessing and resolving quality during the manufacture of the product, remain insufficiently used (Ahmed, 1996).

Product innovation and improvement move through generations and reach the hybrid generation by optimizing technology and co-creating innovation and improvement in association with consumers and market players. First-generation products are largely technology-driven, and firms tend to push them following a market-oriented approach, assuming that a product offered in the market creates demand by its own attributes. Firms developing products of this generation invest substantial resources in research and development activities, and follow simple, linear, and sequential process. As the new products move to the second generation, firms adopt open market innovations that are derived through various marketing initiatives. The innovative products of this generation are customer-centric based on need and demand pull. Hence, second-generation products move faster in the market at relatively lower investment as compared to those of the first generation. Some large firms employ substantial resources to conduct market research and analyze information to establish consumer needs and invite ideas to develop new products from consumers and market players. Firms with applied market research often skip the conventional first-generation process and begin innovation with the attributes of the second generation.

Most firms tend to work with strategic alliances, process integration, and operational networking toward developing new products in further generations. Integration takes place between design, engineering, manufacturing, and servicing functions, and the role of both customers and suppliers in the new product development process. Firms constitute parallel functional teams, develop operations integration, and develop customer-centric strategies during these product generations. The hybrid generation of new products is largely driven by co-creation with the help of consumers and market players as well as by co-hosting the product jointly with alliance companies. Firms follow a technology-led marketing process to position hybrid products and drive their manufacturing through six sigma or lean processes to achieve zero defect in their products. As the new products move to new generations, increases in the current sales price can bring about resistance from customers, which may affect the performance of the products. Customers' feelings about continuous price rises is always the problem. Increasing the price would result in falling behind the company's competition. However, firms can continue their business by selling new products, so they need to promote actively regardless of boom or bust periods (Nagal and Holden, 2002).

Firms are required to employ economic value-added analysis and strategic value assessment such as customer preferences, the rate of change of underlying technology, and competitive position in the marketplace (Fine et al., 2002). Most multinational firms are targeting bottom-of-the-pyramid market segments to acquire higher market share in the mass market, and these firms are endeavoring to develop a sustainable value chain by building local capacity through the "4As," comprising awareness, acceptance, adaptability, and affordability. Firms invest in educating local market players and alliance partners, developing infrastructure, and providing basic community services. Large firms also create shared value opportunities by improving products and reorganizing market segments, redefining productivity in the value chain, and enabling local cluster development. Large and emerging firms also aim at co-creation of products and business models to upgrade shareholder value and enhance the value-creation process. An emerging company like AXA Group, in the financial and insurance business, has dramatically redesigned both upper- and lower-end value chain architecture by reinventing the concept of customer value. Companies should focus not only on operational efficiencies, but also modify their activities in the value chain to reach low-income consumers or small suppliers (Anderson and Billou, 2007). The creation and governing value chains in firms are critical to successful implementation of strategy for achieving effective backward and forward linkages. Firms should stay in the marketplace, constantly innovating new products and processes, and understand the changing behavior of markets to develop long-term customer-centric strategies and efficient value chain models (Esko et al., 2013).

Consumer values toward new and differentiated products

The customer value concept is utilized to evaluate product differentiation and to determine the competitive structure of new products. An analytical approach to the new product-market structure based on customer value may be fitted well within the microeconomic framework. The measure of customer value as product efficiency may be viewed from the customer's perspective toward a ratio of outputs (e.g., perceived use value, resale value, reliability, safety, comfort) that customers obtain from a product relative to inputs (price, running costs) that customers have to deliver in exchange. The efficiency value derived can be understood as the return on the customer's investment. Products offering a maximum customer value relative to all other alternatives in the market are characterized as efficient. Different efficient products may create value in different ways using different strategies (output–input combinations). Each efficient product can be viewed as a benchmark for a distinct sub-market. Jointly, these products form the efficient frontier, which serves as a reference function for inefficient products (Bauer et al., 2004). Thus, customer value of new products is defined as a relative concept. Market partitioning is achieved endogenously by clustering products in one segment that are benchmarked by peers. This ensures that only products with a similar output–input structure are partitioned into the same sub-market. As a result, a sub-market consists of highly substitutable products. The individual values of the customer may be estimated as base values, and changes in such values are affected by the corresponding measures of specific value drivers. The base value ties to the most important of all complements, which may be determined as customers' needs. Estimating value drivers for a new product can be tricky because there is no direct historical data. However, we can assume that the impact from changes in price or availability of complements is similar to what other markets have experienced.

It has been observed that there is an increasing number of customer goods and services offered in recent years, which suggests that product-line extensions have become a favored strategy of product managers. A larger assortment, it is often argued, keeps customers loyal and allows firms to charge higher prices. There also exists a disagreement about the extent to which a longer product line translates into higher profits by keeping the customer value higher. Academics, consultants and business people speculated that marketing in the new century would be very different from the time when much of the pioneering work on customer loyalty was undertaken. Yet there exists the scope for improving applied concepts as there have been many changes over conventional ideologies. A study using market-level data for the yogurt category, developed an econometric model derived from a game-theoretic perspective, explicitly considers firms' use of product-line length as a competitive tool (Dragnska and Jain, 2005). On the demand side, the study analytically establishes the link between customer choice and length of the product line, and includes a measure of line length in the utility function to investigate customer preference for variety using a brand-level discrete-choice model. The study reveals that the supply side is characterized by price and line length competition between oligopolistic firms.

Companies need to ascertain a continuous organizational learning process with respect to the value-creation chain and measure performance of new products introduced into the market. In growing competitive markets large and reputed firms are developing strategies to move into the provision of innovative combinations of products and services as "high-value integrated solutions" tailored to each customer's needs than simply "moving downstream" into services. Such firms are developing innovative combinations of service capabilities such as operations, business consultancy, and finance required to provide complete solutions to each customer's needs in order to augment customer value toward innovative or new products. It has been argued that the provision of integrated solutions is attracting firms traditionally based in manufacturing and services to occupy a new base in the value stream centered on "systems integration," using internal or external sources of product designing, supply, and customer-focused promotion (Davies, 2004). Besides the organizational perspectives of enhancing customer value, functional variables like pricing play a significant role in developing customer perceptions toward the new products.

Value and pricing models have been developed for many different products, services, and assets. Some of these are extensions and refinements of conventional value-driven pricing theories. Also there have been some models that are developed and calibrated to address specific issues such as a model for household assets demand. The key marketing variables such as price, brand name, and product attributes affect customers' judgment processes and derive inference on quality dimensions leading to customer satisfaction. The experimental study conducted indicates that customers use price and brand name differently to judge the quality dimensions and measure the degree of satisfaction (Brucks et al., 2000). The value of corporate brand endorsement across different products and product lines, and at lower levels of the brand hierarchy, also needs to be assessed as a customer value driver. Use of corporate brand endorsement either as a name identifier or logo identifies the product with the company, and provides reassurance for the customer (Rajagopal and Sanchez, 2004). A perspective from resource-advantage theory is used to formulate expectations on the degree to which the use of information on customer value, competition, and costs contribute to the success of a price decision. It is argued that the success of these practices is contingent on the relative customer value the firm has created, and the degree to which this position of relative value is sustainable in the competitive marketplace. These expectations are empirically tested on pricing decisions with respect to the introduction of new industrial capital goods (Hunt and Morgan, 1995).

Conventional wisdom advocates building customer value through relationship marketing approaches for the benefit of generating long-term value and loyalty among consumers. Most importantly, consumers are expected to raise their spending and association with the products and services of the company with increasing levels of satisfaction (Reichheld and Sasser, 1990). Hence relationship marketing with a customer value orientation thrives on the concept that increases the length of the customer–company relationship, which contributes in optimizing profit for the company. Improving customer value through faster response times for new products is a significant way to gain competitive advantage. In the globalization process many approaches to new product development emerge, which exhibit an internal focus and view the new product development process as terminating with product launch. However, it is the process output that really counts, such as customer availability.

Enhancing customer value toward product differentiation needs to be appraised continuously by managers, and appropriate changes should be proposed in a timely manner, which will help in improving market effectiveness, services efficiency, and dealer performance. It is commonly perceived by marketing managers that market-oriented campaigns are expensive, but actually they can lower operating costs and increase market share, yielding high sales. It is more profitable for a retailing firm to establish long-term customer relationships than to adopt a short-term transaction-oriented approach. The customer-centric strategies in a firm should go beyond customer relationships and cater to cross-functional integration of processes, people, operations, and marketing capabilities that are enabled through information, technology, and applications (Payne and Frow, 2005).

Implementation of effective customer-centric strategies by retailing firms results in developing a TIC effect among consumers. The TIC effect comprises the three cognitive factors of trust, involvement, and commitment that drive consumer behavior in a given marketplace. In a retail environment, trust may be understood as a concept that is often related to a customer's willingness to rely upon the retailing firm's services quality and customer relations. This concept represents quality in the sense that it helps to reduce uncertainty in complex consumer–retailer relationships (Bruhn, 2003). Consumers' involvement with the retailing firm, store brand, and promotions develops loyalty in the long run. When consumers feel satisfaction in their association with the retail brand, their sense of commitment and involvement is enhanced. Higher levels of involvement lead to greater levels of consumer loyalty and a lower need for scarce marketing resources. Hence, involvement does play a significant moderating role, and in most cases the relationships with retailing firms and their store brands are stronger for consumers with higher involvement (Baker et al., 2009). Commitment as a concept is closely associated with the customer relationship strategy where two parties lean toward loyalty and show stability to each other. A common opinion is that customer commitment only relates to a seller or a relationship with a seller. It is also observed that a high commitment level might be seen as an important emotional barrier in switching behavior (Hulten, 2007). Customer relationships with retailers are dependent upon specific cultural contexts in which buyers and sellers interact, and the type of relationship developed over the period determines the strength of the commitment (Dash et al., 2009).

Improving customer value through faster response times for new products is a significant way to gain competitive advantage. In the globalization process many approaches to new product development emerge, which exhibit an internal focus and view the new product development process as terminating with product launch. However, it is the process output that really counts, such as customer availability. Many firms with shortening product life cycles try to penetrate into the market as quickly as possible. It is observed that the commercial success of a new product is significantly associated with a more ambitious and speedier launch into overseas markets as the process of innovation is only complete when potential customers on a world scale are introduced effectively to the new product (Oakley, 1996).

Product choice among consumers will be difficult when products have marginal differentiation in reference to attributes, price, and use value as compared to competing products available in the market. Hence, many manufacturing and retailing firms provide default options to consumers in order to facilitate their buying process. Well-designed defaults benefit both company and consumer, simplifying the buying decision process of consumers, enhancing their levels of satisfaction, reducing risk in purchases, and driving profitable purchases. On the other hand, misconceived options to choose products can leave money on the table, fuel consumer backlash, put customers at risk, and trigger lawsuits that may cost companies dearly (Golstein et al., 2008). As competition among companies manufacturing consumer goods and number of routes to market is increasing, customers today are faced with an overwhelming array of choices. Thus, companies should stop creating new brands and product extensions to alleviate customer frustration and consolidate their product and service functions by following a "4R" approach, comprising replace, repackage, reposition, and replenish. In the race of acquiring and retaining strategies tested by companies, customers are rapidly becoming smarter than the companies that pretend to serve them (Locke, 2000).

Companies engaged in manufacturing and marketing of consumer and industrial goods seek competitive distinction through product features – some visually or measurably identifiable, some cosmetically implied, and some rhetorically claimed by reference to real or suggested hidden attributes that promise results or values different from those of competitors' products. The offered product is differentiated, though the generic product is identical. The desired position for a product may be determined using the following procedure:

- Analyze product attributes that are salient to customers.
- Examine the distribution of these attributes among different market segments.
- Determine the optimal position for the product in regard to each attribute, taking into consideration the positions occupied by existing brands.
- Choose an overall position for the product (based on the overall match between product attributes and their distribution in the population and the positions of existing brands).

In the growing competitive markets large and reputed firms are developing strategies to move into the provision of innovative combinations of products and services as "high-value integrated solutions" tailored to each customer's needs rather than simply "moving downstream" into services. Such firms are developing innovative combinations of service capabilities such as operations, business consultancy, and finance required to provide complete solutions to each customer's needs in order to augment customer value (Rajagopal, 2007). Manufacturers' high-technology product sales increase the economic satisfaction of the customer with the distributor as it reveals competitive advantage in making the buying decision. A strong market-oriented strategy by the firm alleviates the possibility of using coercive influence strategies by competitors and offers advantage to customers over competitive market forces (Chung et al., 2007). High-technology products sales is an organization-wide concept that helps explain sustained competitive advantage. Since many manufacturing firms have linked their marketing strategies with services delivery attributes, the concept of high-technology products sales is expanding as a system in global corporate settings.

Universal Electronics Inc. (UEI) manufactures and markets a universal remote control that is packed with infrared codes that allow it to operate virtually any remote-capable device. The product replaces remotes for several consumer electronics items, including CD and DVD players, satellite receivers, surround sound systems, tuners, and TVs. Universal Electronics sells and licenses its products and technologies worldwide to consumer electronics and computer manufacturers, as well as to cable and satellite companies such as Direct-TV. The One-for-All branded remotes are sold by retailers worldwide. UEI designs, develops, and delivers innovative solutions that enable consumers to control entertainment devices, digital media, and home systems. The company's broad portfolio of patented technologies and database of infrared control software has been adopted by many Fortune 500 companies in the consumer electronics, subscription broadcast, and computing industries. UEI expanded its operations to Hong Kong, Singapore, Taiwan, and South Korea to address the region's rapid growth. The company operates a customer-friendly philosophy across its client organizations as well as marketplaces worldwide. It manages its inventory by carrying additional safety stock to meet just-in-time supplies as well as to maintain high customer service levels with existing and newly acquired customers. UEI is committed to settle service warranty claims directly through customer service department or contracted third-party warranty repair facilities. The services transparency policies of the company are well regarded by consumers as it builds confidence in the quality products and services of the company. UEI provides estimated product warranty expenses, which are included in the cost of sales, as the company sells the related products. Warranty expense is a forecast primarily based on historical claims experience; however, actual claim costs may differ from the amounts provided. The culture at UEI is one of dedication and a pursuit of customer satisfaction. UEI associates are committed to do what it takes to get the job done right for customers throughout the globe.[1]

---

[1] Corporate website of Universal Electronics Inc., http://www.uei.com.

The process of high-technology products sales contributes to continuous learning and knowledge accumulation by an organization that continuously collects information about customers and competitors and uses it to create superior customer value and competitive advantage (Slater and Narver, 1995). In order to cope with increasing competition, high-tech firms need to continuously launch new products. However, adoption of new products may require substantive cognitive efforts from consumers. Therefore, firms should be able to monitor and influence their consumers' knowledge base. A consumer learning roadmap is a relevant instrument, and indeed a successful concept for high-tech marketing. The fact that this process has so far been used only marginally means that the most prominent high-technology marketers are likely, little by little, to dominate their market (Hanninen and Sandberg, 2006).

A cognitive attributes of innovativeness among consumers enhances the actual adoption of new products whereas sensory innovativeness and perceived social and physical risks enhance consumers' propensity to acquire novel information about high-technology products. Financial risk, on the other hand, has a negative impact on the propensity to acquire novel information about new products. Time, performance, psychological, and network externalities risks show no significant relationship with the tendency to acquire novel information about high-technology products (Hirunyawipada and Paswan, 2006). In order to drive the adoption of high-technology products and augment consumer value toward differentiated and improved products in the market, companies may encourage service-cantered sales by designing and offering a service-mix. It is perceived by core customers as of superior quality, while high-technology products sales strategy could be catalytic for retailers and distributors in driving profit and building competitive advantage in the market (Chang et al., 1999).

Customers' needs and perceptions tend to change frequently, and it is imperative to routinely evaluate the competitive status of the firm by offering quality services to enhance customer satisfaction and the market efficiency of the firm. As a result, improved customer services, quality of products, sales and post-sales services influence the effectiveness of the sales of high-technology products and reflect the corporate culture among consumer segments. The orientation of the retailing strategy is positively related with market effectiveness and creation of a customer culture in the integrated sales and services in an organization (Heiko et al., 2008). Retailing firms build their most profitable strategies through services differentiation and competitive advantages, offering customers something new they value that other retail outlets do not have. Self-service retail stores differentiate at every point of customer services and relationship from the moment customers express store loyalty. Large self-service retail stores open up their promotion strategies to stimulate shopping behavior of customers and uncover new opportunities for them to gain long-term benefits with the retail stores and remain loyal (McGrath and MacMillan, 1997). The strategy of point of sales promotions has helped large self-service retail stores to slash costs on advertising and publicity, increase volume of sales, and sharpen their focus on core competencies. Hence retailers use point of sales promotions to build shopping arousal, gain satisfaction, and build loyalty to the stores (Deshpande et al., 1986).

Co-creating differentiation

After the globalization effect experienced by companies in the recent past, the markets have changed in many ways as companies bring differentiation in products and services continuously to consumers. The switch from a shared house phone to a personal phone has had a significant impact on product appearance as well as product use. People do not use their personal phone only for calling, but also for taking pictures, making movies, playing games, listening to music, and as an agenda. This has changed consumer attitudes towards phones. What once was a rather functional product has become a product that expresses one's personality. Therefore, customers require their phone to be modern, easy to use, and of good quality. In the meantime, they do not want the phone to be expensive, as they would like to buy a new one periodically. The change in needs reflects in shifting customer demands and increasing product complexity, requiring a far-reaching integration of the different knowledge domains of the actors from different disciplines during collaborative differentiation or the new product development process with consumers (Garcia and Calantone, 2002). During this process knowledge management should focus on knowledge integration instead of on knowledge transfer. The effectiveness of knowledge integration also requires a mutual understanding of the actor's contributions. This is in line with research on design communication, which finds that the quality of the co-differentiation project is dependent on the process of creating a shared understanding (Dong, 2005). In developing collaborative product designs, managers should consider the following perspectives:

- Be an involved consumer of your own and competitor's goods and services:
  - transfer of knowledge;
  - document experiences to retain personal knowledge;
  - relativity of needs in reference to average consumers;
  - obtaining information through mutual cooperation.
- Critically observe and live with consumers:
  - critical observation rather than casual viewing;
  - investing time;
  - realistic and precise conclusions.
- Talk to consumers and get information on their needs:
  - structured, in-depth, one-on-one, situational interviews;
  - engineer trade-offs during product development;
  - technical design information;
  - exploring tacit and product-related needs of consumers.

Co-differentiation and the change management process are considered to be a socio-organizational process. In advancing collaborative new product development there are many players who are involved in the process. A player, who may be a consumer or retailer, executes three main activities during this social process. The first activity is the construction of the task that an actor needs to perform. This allows the actor to understand that the task is a part of a system and that others perform different and complementary tasks in the system. Thus, a co-differentiation player engages himself in the interactive ambience of knowledge management and diffusion (Weick and Roberts, 1993). The pivotal role of creativity in organizations has been widely recognized by the academic community. Creativity is associated with that part of the innovation process that is labeled as idea generation. The ideation process for new product development can be stimulated through metaphors, pictures, and experience. It is rooted in the philosophy of rationalism and empiricism, implying "the truth is out there" approaches. It is observed that defining cognitive idea generation is based on personal experiences and beliefs driven by individual and social information. However, these forms of cognitive-based idea generation process are individualistic and not amenable to team contexts (Bhatt, 2000) Managers engaged in documenting new product ideas from users should communicate to them on the following lines:

- use consumer language;
- keep ideas simple, focused, and organized;

- maintain clarity – from the consumer's point of view;
- do not overpromise or oversell;
- focus on major consumer benefits;
- differentiate the brand from the competition;
- keep all concepts that will be tested in the same format;
- use experienced professionals to prepare the concepts;
- address the right target audience;
- understand the level of errors in information acquisition;
- include diagnostic questions.

A product development manager should actively observe the activities of his team during their regular meetings by taking notes about the most important issues concerning communication on the design content. During regular face-to-face meeting with the separate actors, which are now mostly about planning and monitoring issues and design problems or changes, the project leader could use the notes as input for discussing collaborative aspects with the actors. This form of storytelling will provide the project leader with knowledge about the collaborative aspects of the design process. A project leader should also learn to distill the barriers and enablers from these conversations (Maaike et al., 2010).

Customer involvement in developing differentiated or new products has been widely used in American and Japanese manufacturing firms. Quality Function Deployment (QFD) is a popular tool for bringing the voice of the customer into the product development process from conceptual design through to manufacturing. The process of QFD begins with a matrix that links customer desires to product engineering requirements, along with competitive benchmarking information, and further matrices can be used to ultimately link this to the design of the manufacturing system. Unlike other methods originally developed in the USA and transferred to Japan, the QFD methodology was born out of Total Quality Control (TQC) activities in Japan during the 1960s and has been transferred to companies in the US. It has been observed that companies in the US showed a higher degree of usage, management support, cross-functional involvement, use of QFD-driven data sources, and perceived benefits from using QFD. American companies are more suitable for using newly collected customer data sources such as focus groups and methods for analyzing customer requirements. Japanese companies have been found using existing product services data such as implications of a guarantee, warranty and a broader set of matrices. The use of analytical techniques in conjunction with QFD including simulation, design of experiments, regression, mathematical target setting, and an analytic hierarchy process are also considered as supporting tools for analyzing customer data (Cristiano et al., 2000). Similarly recent studies have described how "lean" Japanese car assemblers assigned the design and development of whole modules to a group of first-tier suppliers, who in turn utilized a team of second-tier suppliers for the detailed development and engineering. Customer-involved product development strategies were also found to be common with firms in different industries, including Apple, Benetton, Corning, McDonald's, Nike, Nintendo, Sun, and Toyota. The customer firm, often a large original equipment manufacturer, perceives that its power may be cascaded throughout its supply base. At the basic level, cascading is a way for a customer to delegate responsibility to its suppliers. In practice, it has been contended that cascading more often takes the form of a more imposing style of leadership (Lamming et al., 2000).

Companies engaged in introducing the differentiated products for larger benefits and consumer outreach should develop arousal-led sales with affordable on-trend communications and endorsements to attract consumers. Lack of engaged emotions among consumers may cause dissatisfaction and prompt a decision to reject the differentiated product and trigger switch behavior. Such retail conditions may drive negative emotions in terms of merchandise choice, visual merchandising, store environment, sales personnel attitude, pricing policies, and promotional activities among consumers. On a tactical level, managers need to consider the optimum spread of consumers on a matrix of product attractiveness and sales. It needs careful attention and application of managerial judgment and experience to measure the customer-value driven performance of retail stores considering the innovative leisure sales approaches, store layouts, location issues of retail stores, shopping behavior, and loyalty parameters of the consumers. Managers driving differentiation in a company need to consider promoting the shopping arousal with the advent of one-on-one marketing, media-targeted direct mail or Internet marketing, and explore the opportunities to develop relationships with consumers.

Driving quick marketing results within shorter differentiated product lifecycles is pushing companies to introduce new products more frequently. Though differentiated products can offer tremendous value, the subsequent product improvements and their transitions in the marketplace pose enormous challenges to managers. A common problem faced by many companies in the process of developing new products has been the lack of a formal process to guide managerial decisions. Drawing from research at Intel and examples from General Motors and Cisco Systems, a process to facilitate decision-making during new product transitions may be illustrated. The proposed process analyzes the risks impacting a transition, identifies a set of factors across departments tracking those risks, monitors the evolution of these factors over time, and develops playbook mapping scenarios of risks and responses. This process helps level expectations across the organization, reduces the chance and impact of unanticipated outcomes, and helps synchronize responses among different departments. It assists managers in designing and implementing appropriate policies to ramp up sales for new products and ramp down sales for existing products, balancing the supply and the demand for both so that combined sales can grow smoothly (Erhun et al., 2007). A marketer has to make more crucial decisions at the growth stage of the product. The major strategies are decided on at this stage to provide adequate support to the product in the market in reference to:

- Rationalizing the product line and width.
- Innovative promotional approaches.
- Identifying new market segments.
- Evolving a comprehensive distribution policy.
- Changing the strategy of product awareness, advertising to the product preference, and launching advertising campaigns accordingly.

It is essential to rationalize the product portfolio with differentiation strategies in the company and develop strategies to promote only those categories of product that had gained considerable response from consumers. Such product categories need to be promoted through innovative approaches giving more emphasis on product preference-based advertisements and advertising campaigns. However, the possibilities of exploring new market segments and comprehensive coverage of distribution also need to be worked out in tune with competitors. As there will not be encouraging growth in profit through product marketing in the short run, there exists enormous scope for developing business relationships and renovating product attributes. The most important need for product differentiations is to sustain the brand image and rebuild this through product and institutional advertising.

One of the challenges for the marketing manager of a firm is to incorporate the preferences of the customer into the design of new products and services in order to maximize customer value. An augmented and sustainable customer value builds loyalty toward the product and the brand. Systematically explored concepts in the field of customer value and a market-driven approach toward new products would be beneficial for a company to derive a long-term profit optimization strategy. Hence, a comprehensive framework for estimating both the value of a customer and profit optimization needs to be developed. On a tactical level, managers need to consider the optimum spread of customers on a matrix of product attractiveness and market coverage. This needs careful attention, and the application of managerial judgment and experience, to measure the value-driven performance of the firm's products. It is necessary for the managers to understand that customer value is context-dependent and that there exists a whole value network to measure, not just a value chain. Appropriate promotional strategies considering the economic and relational variables discussed in the study may be developed by managers upon measuring the intensity of leisure shopping and the scope of expanding the tenure of leisure shopping in view of optimizing customer values and the profit of the firm.

6
Darwinism in the Marketplace

Customers have proven to be a precious source of new solutions in various product categories and, by becoming directly involved in the innovation process, they can help companies better anticipate market changes. Darwinism in business is a concept derived from the Darwinian ideology of biological evolution. Many successful global companies have set the example of their evolution in the market over a long period by sustaining in various conflicting situations. This chapter discusses the survival of the fittest and struggle for existence axioms of Darwinism in reference to companies operating in varied market taxonomies. The chapter especially refers to notions of struggle for existence being used to justify various business policies, which make no distinction between those companies that are able to support themselves and those unable to cordon their growth in business against competition. This chapter addresses the competition matrix with two-dimensional focuses in reference to the shifts in marketing-mix elements, and the causes and effects of firms on consumer values in general. The discussions are woven around market complexities emerging out of the diffusion and adoption of technology.

Evolution and growth in business

The evolution of markets over the centuries has been a perennial phenomenon congruent with shifts in social, economic, and technological knowledge in society. The evolution of business and growth has promoted economic behavior to explore markets. Sociologically the evolution of markets was based on the understanding that individuals are embedded in various cognitive structures involving business activities. Shifts in market processes in society are induced by fundamental beliefs and shared assumptions, and resemble elements of social culture in defining norms of markets, expected behavior, and thought.

144

Such business evolution paradigms are resistant to minor discrepancies between their fundamental models and contradicting (potentially empirical) evidence. Thus, discrepancies in market behavior are considered as socio-economic abnormalities, paradoxes or puzzles in a given place and time (Hedaa and Ritter, 2005).

Historical documentation reveals that market evolution is a long process that enables some causal attribution. Historical analysis can sometimes enable identification of the reasons for important transitions by highlighting key events that triggered change and their patterns. Marketing patterns in society are commonly believed to have evolved through five distinct phases of growth. These phases can be categorized as the simple trade era, the production era, the sales era, the marketing department era, and the marketing company era. At the end of the eighteenth century most of the developed countries gradually escaped the Malthusian trap of stagnant living standards as technological progress accelerated along with population growth (Goldthorpe, 2000). Consequently the industrial revolution adapted to technological progress and began to keep pace with the population. Such growth in industrial products and services for consumption and business needs created new markets, and by the middle of the nineteenth century a global transformation in product and financial markets was observed. Such phenomenal change in the global marketplace resulted in economic dynamism in both developed and developing economies. Accordingly many countries entered the market fray and started to produce a larger variety of products, making them more substitutable, raising the price elasticity of demand, and strengthening competition. Such market development had driven higher competition to modern growth, and competitive firms aimed at larger territorial expansion at lower markups with prolonged breakeven. As firms become larger, they find it easier to cover the fixed costs of innovation and technology diffusion and adaptation. As the size of the market is large, with significant competitive driving force, market innovation grows endogenously. This, in turn, pushes the market to grow exponentially, providing additional incentives to mount competition. The market economy thus graduates in the global marketplace to the era of competition and contests, determining the Darwinian fitness theories of struggle for existence and survival of the fittest.

In growing market competition small firms always face major threats from large companies as the latter possess more resources (physical, financial, human, and technological). Hence most smaller firms develop a cocooning attitude and confine themselves to a niche as they could not continue their struggle for existence in the marketplace. Figure 1.1 illustrates the chaos in the market and muddle among firms struggling to establish their business in a given marketplace. It may be observed that large firms will enter new market niches created by small firms through technological innovation and ingest the market share of the small firms. In view of Darwinian theory it may be argued that market conditions and company-specific characteristics explain the entry timing and underlying goals of large firms, and that such entry might be a continuous process for large firms in different marketplaces. The dominating behavior of large firms is more likely to be backed by innovations in the industry in response to competing firms. Small firms are affected by the entry of firms that are similar in size and resources. When a highly similar company enters the new market, it raises the probability that the company enters beyond levels based solely on the attractiveness of the market (Debruyne and Reibstein, 2005). Hence, small firms play both aggressive and defensive strategies to stay in the marketplace despite competitive attacks by new entrants. On the other hand, a consortium of small firms manufacturing identical products also poses a major threat to large firms in sustaining the competitive marketplace. For example, more than 20 companies have joined the Taiwan Blu-ray Disc (BD) Consortium, a special interest group, under the Taiwan Information Storage Association, formed by Taiwan-based companies involved in the BD market in 2010. The consortium includes makers of Blu-ray optical disc drives (such as Lite-On IT), optical discs (such as CMC Magnetics and Ritek), integrated circuit design and components, which hope to join forces to negotiate better licensing terms for producing BD-related products (Hwang, 2010). This consortium may cause a major threat to international BD manufacturers such as Sony to compete in the global marketplace against the consortium firms in reference to price and supply of BD products.

Business consortia are alliances of individual business enterprises specifically of small and medium size. Businesses involved in these sorts of consortia are often in the same broad field or industry, though they are rarely in direct competition with one another. Instead, members usually offer products or services that are complementary to those available through other consortium members. Unlike associations and other similar organizations, which engage in efforts to shape legislation and present a unified industry front, business consortia ally themselves for basic business functions, such as marketing. These alliances are not commonplace, but some analysts indicate that in the future, increasing numbers of small business owners may investigate consortia as a way of sharing common costs, increasing purchasing power, and competing with larger companies. Business consortia usually come into being for specific reasons such as competitive threats from a common enemy (whether another business or an unwelcome economic trend), changes in competitive structures, or deregulation. Consortia of small and medium companies helps in developing collective bargaining and purchasing power as well as marketing efforts that can provide the member firms with increased recognition and stature in the community. Further, joint marketing and advertising efforts save members money because they can pool their resources for better rates. and they also save member businesses time because they do not have to undertake as much work themselves (Doz and Hamel, 1998).

Darwinian fitness in market evolution argues that when consumer demand increases, more varieties of products and services penetrate in the market, driving more demand. Such market thrust in positioning products and services increases the price elasticity of demand. Some management studies exploit this feature and show in a one-period model how the higher elasticity of demand, due to a larger population or more liberalized trade, facilitates innovation (Desmet and Parente, 2010). As trade liberalization continued in the global marketplace, transforming the regional markets, multidimensional growth appeared to be a strong catalytic thrust in the economy of developing countries. Multidimensional growth, in which a corporate firm manages relatively freestanding business units, was the most successful design of marketing organizations of the twentieth century. However, some firms have evolved organizational designs to sustain market competition. These firms are organized around multiple dimensions such as regions, products, and services, and hold different strategies accountable for performance on these dimensions. The multidimensional growth of marketing organizations is best understood as the next step in the evolution from a resource-centric business model to a customer-centric knowledge-sharing model. It is a way of managing competitive markets that is particularly well adapted to stimulating the market leadership necessary to create economic value in complex markets (Strikwerda and Stoelhorst, 2009).

The continuum of market evolution across regions, products, and services drove the rapid diffusion of new products in the marketplace. Quicker time to market and shorter product lifecycles are pushing companies to introduce new products more frequently in the global marketplace. While new products intend to offer high value, product introductions and transitions pose enormous challenges to managers.

Drawing from the best practices of General Motors and Cisco Systems, it may be argued that these companies identify operational risk factors across departments and keep tracking them. These companies monitor the evolution of these factors over time, and develop strategies by mapping scenarios of risks and responses in the market. This process of market evolution by nurturing the demand for new products helps firm's expectations in the marketplace, lowers the chance and impact of unanticipated outcomes, and helps synchronize responses among different consumer segments (Erhun et al., 2007). The factors discussed below contribute to the evolution of markets:

- Long-run changes in growth, demographics, consumption trends, changes in substitutes and complementary products, and improvements in the attributes of the products.
- Changes in buyer segments.
- Improvement in consumer knowledge.
- Adapability to change among consumers.
- Reduction of uncertainty.
- Shifts in the consumer experience.
- Changes in the scale of business operations.
- Product and market innovations.
- Structural change in adjacent industries.
- Government policy change.
- Liberalization of entry and exit barriers.

The evolution of markets over a period has been driven by both strategic and tactical growth. The strategic evolution of the market is attributed to long-range planning, while tactical growth appears to be myopic and causes disequilibrium in the marketplace. At some point in the process of market evolution, every emerging market can be considered a growth point, with sales considered as a major measure of growth over other functions of marketing. This might be a wrong notion, because selling focuses on the needs of the seller, whereas marketing concentrates on the needs of the buyer. For markets to ensure continued evolution, they must define their industries broadly to take advantage of growth opportunities. They must ascertain and act on their customers' needs and desires, not bank on the presumed longevity of their products. A market must learn to think of itself not as producing goods or services but as doing the things that will make people want to do business with it, which determines the extent of growth of markets in a given time and territory (Levitt, 1960).

The global scenario is changing very fast with the emergence of new markets, including the new business opportunities developed in the European Community, enhanced by the reunification of Germany, and the thriving economies of the Pacific Rim countries during the 1990s. The prospective business growth areas in the current decade are China, Latin America and the emerging market-based economies in Eastern Europe. Additionally, the growing momentum towards privatization and liberal policies shows further promising markets in developing countries. Companies planning on territorial expansion have used a three-pronged attack in their strategy to penetrate emerging markets: offensive, defensive, and efficiency initiatives. Offensive initiatives were intended to gain market share where the company had not traditionally been a leader, and thus bring in new revenue streams. Defensive initiatives attempted to preempt competitors' move into markets where the company had traditionally dominated. Efficiency initiatives delivered cost savings to the bank from customer self-service or from straight-through processing that squeezed costs out of back office processes.

Asian markets are very sensitive to most of the top brands of Western companies. The markets in Asian countries, including Japan, shoulder one third of the luxury goods and fashion business, and by 2005 this region made up to half of the global business in luxury goods. However, there remains an absence of well-functioning product markets in transition economies as a sufficient condition under which a "big bang" reduces output initially, while a Chinese-style reform increases output. A "big bang" in business is caused by the massive consumer impact of breakthrough technologies that shifts market demand and attracts higher competition in the market. Governments introducing a big bang dismantle central planning or centralized organization of production, permitting monopolistic and vertically interdependent enterprises to pursue their own monopoly profits by restricting output and inter-firm trade with overseas markets. The Chinese style of reform, by maintaining central planning but allowing enterprises to produce for emerging product markets after they have fulfilled their output quotas under planning, gives enterprises incentives to expand output beyond planned targets (Li, 1999).

Understanding market competition

Increasing competition in the global marketplace has induced large companies with high market share and brand equity to undertake spatial expansion in their market operations. In this process large companies tend to acquire smaller firms or get them merged with larger organizations on win–win negotiations. Although such a process has been established in the global marketplace as an effective strategy for the growth of business for larger companies, it has been considered as a survival mechanism for smaller and weak business companies in the market. In the context of global competition this approach may be considered as a process of cannibalization. At the lower end of the market, value-added resellers (VAR) also catalyze the cannibalization in the global market. Remanufactured products do not always cannibalize new product sales. To minimize cannibalization and create additional profits, firms need to understand how consumers' value remanufactured products. This is not a static decision and should be re-evaluated over the entire product lifecycle. While firms exhibit responsibility to maximize profits for the firm, this is not necessarily equivalent to maximizing new product sales. A portfolio that includes remanufactured products can enable firms to reach additional market segments and help block competition from new low-end products or third-party remanufacturers (Atsu et al., 2010).

The role of brand prices contributes toward product cannibalization in the market. Price elasticity of competing firms poses a major threat in the market and induces cannibalization. It has been observed that new entrants cannibalize the market share of a large company's brand by the growth in sales of low-cost brands (Meredith and Maki, 2001). Hence, there has been a growth in the literature studying the effects of cannibalization, since an assessment of the expected cannibalization effect of a new product can help in deciding on suitable times for new product introduction and promotions. Successful companies encounter unique competitive challenges to grow in the competitive market. However, there are several product strategy initiatives that are relevant to all organizations seeking to develop market-driven strategies. Key initiatives include leveraging the business design, recognizing the growth mandate, developing market vision, achieving a capabilities and value match, exploring strategic relationships, building strong brands, brand leveraging, and recognizing the advantages of proactive cannibalization (Cravens et al., 2000).

Cannibalization in the global marketplace is very common in the liberal entry policies adopted by many countries in response to globalization. The expansion of product lines and continuous innovations drive cannibalization not only for competing products but also within the product line of a company. Companies often design product lines by segmenting their markets on quality attributes that exhibit a "more is better" or "value for money" property for all consumers. Since products within a product line that have marginal differentiation serve as close substitutes and as consumers self-select the products they want to purchase, competition among the products within the product line is increased. Multiproduct firms need to meticulously address the cannibalization problem in designing their product lines and avoid product overlaps. It has been observed that if lower-quality products are attractive, consumers with a concern for "value for money" may find it beneficial to buy lower-quality products rather than the higher-quality products targeted to them. Accordingly, lower-quality products can potentially cannibalize higher-quality products. The cannibalization problem forces the firm to provide only the highest-valuation segment with its preferred quality while other segments receive lower qualities than anticipated. The firm may not serve some of the lowest-valuation segments when the cannibalization problem is very severe. However, not much is known about how and when the cannibalization problem affects product line design in an oligopoly. Also, consumers may differ not only in their quality valuations but also in their taste preferences (Desai, 2001).

Under some conditions, the cannibalization problem does not affect the firm's price and quality choices, and each firm provides each segment with that segment's preferred quality. Each firm finds it optimal to serve both segments. In case consumer preferences of the high-valuation segments are sufficiently weak, more intense competition in the high-valuation segment is expected to reduce that segment's incentives to buy the product meant for the low-valuation segment. This mitigates the cannibalization problem and makes it more likely for the low-valuation segment to receive its preferred quality. Similarly, when firms are less differentiated in the low-valuation segment, stronger competition between the firms makes the cannibalization problem worse, and the low-valuation segment may not get its preferred quality (Desai, 2001).

Cannibalization has also become a critical phenomenon in selling products and services of identical nature in the competitive consumer segment. Consider a seller who faces two customer segments with differing valuations of quality of a durable product where demand is stationary and known, the technology exists to release two products simultaneously, and the seller can commit in advance to subsequent prices and qualities. Should the seller introduce two differentiated products simultaneously? In the simultaneous strategy, the lower quality would cannibalize demand for the higher quality. To reduce cannibalization, the seller could lower the quality of the low-end model and reduce the price of the high-end. Alternatively, he could increase the quality of the low-end model, but delay its release (Moorthy and Png, 1992).

Large firms in the global marketplace strive to reach the lowest consumer segments by generating the social impact and financial viability that provide optimal value for money to consumers. Thus popular firms demonstrate higher brand equity in various tiers of the market in a given region and assume the challenging role of meeting the twin goals of commercial profitability and social development of the firm. Firms with larger market share and higher equity implicitly signal lower perceived risk and higher acceptance by the marketplace. Such firms also tend to have larger resources, higher brand equity, buying incentives, and increased loyalty, and undertake higher advertising levels in bottom-line markets (Anderson, 1979).

Competing firms show higher concerns on quality, cost, and management factors in order to succeed against others in the marketplace. Competing firms try to attract consumers by various means to polarize business and earn confidence in the marketplace. It is necessary for successful business firms to look for a place of business that provides them better location advantage and attracts consumers for their goods and services. Business cordoning or securing trade boundaries are essential decisions for competitive firms in building competitive strategies to attack rivals in the marketplace.

Managing low-end market segments

In growing global competition multinational companies are exploring remote markets to position their global brands. This strategy has leveraged market access of global brands to the regional level. Such accessibility to markets is further reinforced by reducing trade barriers through far-reaching business communication strategies, product and market development programs, and consumer relations. Markets for implementing brand strategies can be divided into the three levels of premium markets, regular markets, and low-end markets located in rural habitats in a region. Consumer behavior toward large firms in premium and regular markets is generally driven by push factors, including brand equity, brand personality, and brand endorsements, while brand strength is determined by consumer pull factors such as price advantage, social status, and perceived use value in the low-end market segments (Rajagopal, 2009).

The Darwinian principle of struggle for existence for firms at the bottom-of-the-pyramid market segments argues that moving beyond decades of mutual distrust and animosity, competitors keep learning to cooperate with each other for mutual gains. Realizing that their interests are converging firms are working together to create innovative business models that are helping to grow new markets in bottom-of-the-pyramid market segments. Firms from Brazil, Russia, India, and China are also eager to enter the global marketplace. Yet multinational companies typically pitch their products to the tiny segments of affluent buyers in the emerging markets, and thus miss out on much larger markets further down the socioeconomic pyramid (Prahalad and Lieberthal, 2003). The low-end philosophy of business further argues that by stimulating commerce and development at the bottom of the economic pyramid, multinationals could radically improve the lives of billions of people and help create a more stable, less dangerous world. Achieving this goal does not require MNCs to spearhead global social-development initiatives for charitable purposes but to rationally establish business by also positioning global brands in the low-end markets (Prahalad and Hammond, 2002).

It may be cited in this context that in the 1970s, the early marketing activities of Hindustan Unilever Limited (HUL) in India tended to focus upon the urban middle class and elite. Meanwhile, an Indian entrepreneur produced and marketed a detergent, *Nirma*, targeting the bottom of the consumer segments sector, and the brand became the second largest volume seller in the country by 1977 (Sabharwal et al., 2004). In the skin care market, besides competition from leading global players, HUL has also been losing share to South-based player, Cavincare Ltd. In the foods business, Tata Tea in packet tea, Nestlé in coffee and culinary products, Gujarat Cooperative Milk Marketing Federation with its Amul brand in ice creams, and Godrej Pillsbury in staple foods are HUL's main competitors. Profitable growth is the revised focus of HUL in contrast to a strategy of expansion through acquisition, woven around rationalization. A focus on 30 power brands, which are major contributors to profitability, seeking new avenues of expanding distribution reach, and improving profitability of the foods businesses, which is in the investment phase, are the target areas in low-end market segments. The marketing strategies for slow-moving consumer goods of multi-brand firms are being strengthened by partnerships through the technological expertise in rural or suburban retailing (Rajagopal, 2006).

Low-end marketing strategies are contemplated as stimulating commerce, which implies that multinationals could radically improve the lives of billions of people and help create a more stable, less dangerous world. Achieving this goal does not require a multinational company to spearhead global social-development initiatives for charitable purposes. The philosophy of managing bottom-line markets gave a clear indication to the multinational companies that reluctance to invest is easy to understand, but it is, by and large, based on outdated assumptions of the developing world. Although individual incomes may be low, the aggregate buying power of poor communities is actually quite large, representing a substantial market in many countries for what some might consider luxury goods like satellite television and phone services. Because these markets are in the earliest stages of economic development, revenue growth for multinationals entering them can be extremely rapid.

The debate on low-end markets throws up various perspectives concerning global firms, which confront their own preconceptions, particularly about the value of high-volume and low-margin businesses for companies to master the challenges or reap the rewards of these developing markets. Thus global firms need to start thinking about their marketplace as all six billion people on the planet. Global firms could augment revenue through poverty alleviation as the poor deserve world-class products and services. The lifestyles of the poor are different than their income levels might suggest, as can be seen from the way poor people allocate their income to consumption (Prahalad, 2002).

Global companies are targeting their brands in low-end market segments comprising large consumer communities with small per capita purchases. These companies are developing low-end market strategies based on personal brand relationships with local institutions, retailers or distributors of global brands in the region. Low-end market segments have been identified as potential outlets for global brands when the semi-urban and rural markets are modernized. Globalization has segregated consumer behavior in rural and semi-urban marketplaces and noted the influence of urban marketplaces (Cruickshank, 2009).

Intensive competition from global firms not only decreases the market share of small and medium enterprises that are grown locally but also induces price wars, reducing profit margins and limiting market growth of firms. This situation motivates companies to consider positioning their brands in unexplored markets and targeting these segments with products in small packs at lower price points (Dubey and Patel, 2004). The low-end market segment, which constitutes a large number of small consumers, has become the principal target of most of the consumer brands emerging from multinational firms. The brands penetrating the low-end of the market should provide consistency and agility at the same time. Consistency is required if the brand is to build awareness and credibility, while agility in the brand builds perceived value among consumers. Agility is required if the brand is to remain relevant in a free marketplace (Blumenthal, 2002).

Globalization trends in the market have increased competition on one hand and behavioral complexities of consumers on the other. The traditional marketing and branding strategies of multinational firms are gradually refined in reference to changing business dimensions to gain competitive advantage. It is observed that in current times marketing-mix strategies considerably influence branding strategies in different types of markets. Marketing-mix has now stretched beyond product, place, price, and promotion dimensions to packaging, pace (competitive dynamics), people (sales front liners), performance of previous brands, psychodynamics (consumer pull), posture (brand and corporate reputation), and proliferation (brand extension and market expansion).

Previous research has established that there is a close relationship between a firm's attributes and its corporate image concerning the emotional values of consumers. This relationship in turn influences the consumer's responses toward building brand loyalty in the lower layer of markets in a region. The quality connection between personality traits and corporate image depends to a large extent on the perceived attractiveness of the brand. However, the role of attractiveness in the relationship varies across individual brand personality dimensions (Hayes et al., 2006).

Firms penetrating the bottom-of-the-pyramid market segment largely affirm the value to consumers in reference to the strategies pertaining to product, price, place, promotion, packaging, and psychodynamics. When a firm in the low-end market segment is supported by these strategies, it develops a consumer pull effect and becomes more tensile. Such firms face consumer sluggishness in the beginning but become strong over time with increasing consumer satisfaction in the brand. On the other hand, global firms are found to be initially stronger in perceptional values of consumers, which become sluggish overtime as new brands penetrate in the low-end market. Thus, consumer brands in the premium markets prioritize agility. The relationship between the brand and consumer personalities has three dimensions – strong, vacillating, and weak. The strong dimension of the relationship leads to loyalty development while the weak links form a discrete relationship. The vacillating dimension cultivates the risk of brand switching owing to uncertainty of consumer decision to be associated with the brand or otherwise.

Firms in low-end market segments are largely identified in the context of packaging. A study revealed that rural residents in India found that packaging is more helpful in buying, that better packaging contains a better product, and that they are more influenced by the ease of storing a package than their urban counterparts. Easy to carry size of package, gross weight, simplicity, transparency, and similarity of packaging have also emerged as critical brand identity factors among consumers of low-end market segments in urban areas (Sherawet and Kundu, 2007). Low-end brand strategy demands intensive advertisements, sales schemes, and an aggressive sales force. Low-end brands should feature strong point of purchase displays, sales promotion schemes, and consumer response analysis at retail outlets. Brand equity and price premium on consumer products in low-end market segments delineate the role of uniqueness, together with the awareness, qualities, associations, and loyalty as the principal dimensions of a brand. Relevant brand associations like origin, health, organizational associations, and social image along with the quality attributes such as taste, odor, consistency/texture, appearance, function, packaging, and ingredients are the major variables that influence consumer behavior toward brands in low-end market segments.

Managing brand differentiation

A firm may choose to develop a brand as a reference at the first stage of the brand architecture process as competitive pressures kindle differentiation of their goods from those of other producers. The brands should be architected in the consumer space, working with the consumer and achieve differentiation primarily through changes in physical product attributes and augmented consumer perceptions of its use value. Consumers' extended memory networks help consumers to use brand names based on their image of the brand, though many consumers primarily value brands for their utilitarian qualities. Utilitarian values may be instrumental in making buying decisions because they enable consumers to reach higher levels of satisfaction derived from owning or using the object.

In the following stage marketers may labor to shape their brand's personality. The personality idea responds to the tendency in contemporary society to value personal relationships. It also refers to the idea that relationships are important in social life. In terms of Maslow's hierarchy of needs, it tries to lift products to higher levels of need satisfaction, including belongingness, love, and esteem. Brand personalities are created in different ways and with different tools. An example may be cited of the Escudo anti-bacterial soap, a Latin American brand of Procter & Gamble, which has been established by creating the personality of the caring mother; the firm has injected emotion into the consumer's learning and valuing process. The brand, through such personality appeal, pulls it closer to the consumer through an emotional bonding of caring for the child. In the previous two stages, there was a distinction between the consumer and the brand. Incorporation of personal characteristics into the brand makes it more appealing to consumers who are more likely to affiliate with brands possessing desirable personalities. While crafting the brand personality a firm may try to keep the balance between the personalities of the consumer and the brand when they begin to merge and the value of the brand becomes self-expression. Cultural and ethnic values also influence the products and brands and establish their categorical preferences among consumer segments. The companies may attempt to classify the users on the basis of brands, for example, the affluent drive a Rolls-Royce and the less affluent drive a Ford. However, in a cross-cultural market environment, confusion may result in buying behavior of consumers as goods may not be valued for the same reasons in other cultures. So, the values communicated by products and brands must be consistent within the group and the culture.

Subsequent to the association of an appealing personality to the brand, the firm may develop the brand as an icon to hold as a top of the mind perception. At this stage of brand architecture, the brand may be conceived by the consumer, endorsed by their self-reference criteria, such that the firm may be confident of the brand being "owned by customers." An example may be cited of Marlboro cigarettes where the rugged cowboy representing a man standing against the odds is a symbol or a brand icon enveloped with a set of values. Similarly, Nike shoes and sports apparel have primary associations with Michael Jordan's athletic prowess and secondary associations with the Chicago Bulls. Hence, the more associations a brand has, the greater becomes its network to stimulate brand recall. The management of such brands with multiple associations strengthens the iconic stature of the company.

In the fourth stage the brand may be described as a synonym for the firm, and it is a complex stage to run thorough wherein brand equals the company as all stakeholders may also perceive the brand (as a constituent of the firm) in the same fashion. The firm must have integrated communications throughout all of its operations. However, communication may not be unidirectional as it flows from the consumer to the firm as well as from the firm to the consumer so that a dialogue is established between the two. The delivery of Ford cars seeking collaborative customization in the process in which customers are involved in designing the interior of the cars, may be an appropriate example where customers identify the brand as a company. Such interaction strengthens the relationship that consumers feel with the firm. A brand is said to have positive (or negative) customer-based brand equity when consumers react more (or less) favorably to marketing-mix activity for the brand, as compared to when the same marketing activity is attributed to a hypothetical or unnamed version of the product or service. Consumer response to marketing activity for competitive brands or an alternatively named version of the product or service can also be useful benchmarks (i.e., for determining the uniqueness of brand associations and the opportunity cost of brand extensions, respectively).

Few firms reach stage five of the brand architecture, which is distinguished by an alignment of firm with ethical, social, and political causes. Before moving into this stage, firms have to consider both the risks and their credibility of brand as company. New brands can enter the market at any stage of development as long as other brands have laid the groundwork of consumer understanding to support the understanding of the new brand. The brand image at the end of the evolutionary process is similar to Kapferer's conceptual model of the brand. He indicates that brands display a physique, personality, culture, relationship, reflection, and the consumer's self-image. It is necessary for the managers of a firm to know that no brand can incorporate all of these facets without having traveled through the six stages (Kapferer, 2000).

Product markets continue to change rapidly. As markets evolve, firms need to consider how to modify their brand architecture and look for opportunities to reduce the number of brands and improve efficiency as well as to harmonize brand strategy across product lines and country markets. Focus on a limited number of strategic brands in international markets enables the firm to consolidate and strengthen its position and enhance brand power. Effective management of international brand architecture in the light of changing market conditions and the firm's market expansion is, however, crucial to maintaining its position and strengthening key strategic brands in international markets.

The brand architecture should incorporate the entire firm's existing brands, whether developed internally or acquired. It should provide a framework for consolidation in order to reduce the number of brands and strengthen the role of individual brands. Brands that are acquired need to be merged into the existing structure, especially where these brands occupy similar market positions to those of existing brands. Equally, when the same or similar products are sold under different brand names or have different positioning in each market, ways to harmonize these should be examined. Another important element of brand architecture is its consistency relative to the number and diversity of products and product lines within the company. A balance needs to be struck between the extent to which brand names serve to differentiate product lines, or alternatively, establish a common identity across different products. Establishment of strong and distinctive brand images for different product lines helps to establish their separate identities and diversify the risk of negative associations (for example, between food and chemicals). Conversely, use of a common brand name consolidates effort and can produce synergies (Rajagopal and Rajagopal, 2007).

The value of corporate brand endorsement across different products and product lines, and at lower levels of the brand hierarchy also needs to be assessed. Use of corporate brand endorsement either as a name identifier or logo identifies the product with the company, and provides reassurance for the customer. In international markets, corporate brand endorsement acts as an integrative force unifying different brand identities across national boundaries. At the same time, corporate endorsement of a highly diverse range of product lines can result in a dilution of image. Equally, negative effects or associations can harm and have long-lasting effects across multiple product lines. Thus, both aspects need to be weighed in determining the role of corporate brand endorsement in brand architecture.

It may be stated that the brand endorsement with a strong and associated name would be helpful in market penetration for new brands and extended brands. The presence of the co-drivers would also provide an added impact on the endorsed brands where competition is intensive. Independent brands may be able to make a high impact in a niche market by differentiation over closely competing brands. It is of critical importance for companies to understand the increasingly complex variety of factors underlying and influencing the linkages between brands. Manufacturing companies may have to exercise several options on brand sponsorship.

Differentiation and the chaos matrix

Increasing market competition has become an essential phenomenon in globalization, which does not always have a pattern. Competition in regional markets often grows randomly by the free entry and exits of firms of all categories while competition among large firms operates in a streamline with reference to a particular product or service category. However, in both market situations competition generates chaos, and companies try to implement various strategies to overcome chaotic market conditions.

One of the common practices followed by most companies to create a distinct space in market chaos is to carry out a well-defined differentiation in products and services that provides unique posture to the companies. Amidst the competitive fray, most companies drive enormous intellectual and financial resources into creating differentiated products or services for acquiring consumers and creating a defection in the competitor's consumers. However, in many situations, differentiation may not be a profitable strategy. Companies drive consumers to learn about their preferences from advertising and pick up the right differentiation for gaining competitive advantage. As many consumers do not see advertising for all relevant alternatives, a significant fraction of them make decisions with limited information about the available alternatives. The value of creating differentiated products is ambiguous when awareness of products and their characteristics is the key determinant of consumer behavior (Soberman, 2003).

Market chaos and differentiation have a complex juncture, where competing companies are always risk averse in achieving their desired success. However, profitable strategies built on differentiation often deliver customers the tangibles they value, which competitors do not have. Thus, most companies concentrate on continuous differentiation of their products or services to create unique selling propositions and wider outreach of consumer segments despite the variable outcomes across markets and strategies. The differentiation matrix needs to be understood by companies in reference to communication and advertisement, price, quality and perceived value, technology, and environment. In fact, companies can differentiate at every point where consumers' preferences are guided by needs, value for money, and peer response. Most companies open up their thinking in tune with consumers' experience to uncover opportunities to position their differentiated products in the markets through ways that keep competitors inaccessible (MacMillan and McGrath, 1997).

Companies in complex competitive market conditions differentiate any product or tangible deliveries with intangible values to augment customer satisfaction. The differentiated product includes generic products, competitive differentiation to add value to products, and affordable price to drive customer purchase intentions. Purchase intentions are driven by variables such as delivery, terms, support efforts, and new ideas, and the sale of generic products depends on how well the customer's wider expectations are met by the differentiated products and services. Most companies believe that successful differentiation with a wider outreach is made possible by penetrating lower-income consumer segments in emerging markets through slashing price and adding value to the product features. Besides, companies appeal to potential customers by demonstrating that differentiations introduced by the companies act as competitive agents to enhance the value and lifestyle of consumers. Offering product differentiations with culturally appropriate positioning helps companies to succeed in lower-income consumer segments in emerging markets (Flores et al., 2003). Figure 6.1 shows how companies can develop strategies in reference to advertising, pricing, quality, technology, and environment to drive small differentiations in products and services for larger benefits with wider outreach.

Figure 6.1 illustrates four different matrices in relation to marketing elements and differentiation. Section A exhibits the relationship of advertising and communication, and differentiation in reference to the high and low limits in the competitive markets. This section indicates that effective advertising and communication strategies with a high order of differentiation would lead to wider outreach of products and drive positive peer response and purchase intentions among consumers. Contrary to this situation, if companies experience weak advertising and communication effects with low level of product differentiation, it would lead to failure, low satisfaction, and drive the product to decline soon in its lifecycle.

The functionality of differentiation in reference to variability in price is illustrated in section B, which shows that companies positioning products with high differentiation and high price could target consumers in the premium segment and acquire high profit, though the lifecycle of the differentiated products might be shorter than the mass market segment. However, the low-price/low-differentiation strategy would not allow companies to be competitive in the marketplace. Companies with such strategies narrow down their business into niches, which causes low psychodynamics among consumers of the products and services offered. The above market conditions generally appear in the decline stage of the product life cycle.

Quality and perceived consumer value play an important role in determining the sustainability and marketability of differentiation in products and services offered by a company in the competitive market, as explained in section C of Figure 6.1. High quality and perceived

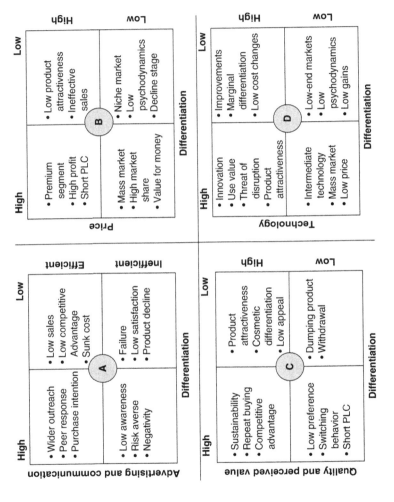

Figure 6.1 Differentiation and market chaos matrix

value with high product differentiation enables companies to achieve sustainability in marketing and will deliver competitive advantage to consumers over other products and services. Also high-quality product differentiation carrying high perceived value of consumers drives repeat buying behavior among consumers, which strengthens the sustainability and competitiveness of the products in the market.

Contrary to these marketing conditions companies have to sell products at cost price or lower and tend to withdraw them from the market. Section D reveals that innovation, appropriate use value, and product attractiveness are built when companies launch highly differentiated products using high technology. However, companies also face the threat of disruptive innovations below the market as the products become successful.

Disruptive innovation may be a product or a service designed for a new set of customers by leading them to defect them from the existing stream of buying. Generally, disruptive innovations are technologically straightforward and convincing to consumers, and generate value for money. Some disruptive innovations offer more for less to customers through a different package of attributes that will have higher significance to the consumers in the bottom-of-the-pyramid market segment than to those of the mainstream market. Clayton (2003) argues that disruptive innovations can damage successful brands and the well-managed products of reputed companies that are responsive to their customers and have invested resources in conducting excellent research and development to support innovation. These companies tend to bypass markets that are most susceptible to disruptive innovations as there appears the risk of low profit and low scope of business growth. Thus disruptive technology provides products and services with focus on the customer and drives a strategically counterproductive impact on existing products in a market. However, in a positive sense disruptive innovation may be considered as the constructive integration of attributes to existing technology. Disruptive innovations generate radical insights that could help in improving the economic benefits to consumers and provide better opportunities for the firms to grow in the mass market.

Most managers presume that the purpose of developing and implementing an effective marketing strategy is to drive optimal profit and gain sustainability in the competitive marketplace. Thus, embracing chaos seems the opposite of discipline and planning in marketing theory. However, in practice uncertainty often delivers opportunities amidst the threats in the market. Companies that ignore this fact and follow rigid strategies blind themselves to unexpected complexities and miss potential opportunities. In order to gain a competitive edge in market chaos, companies need to learn how to adapt quickly in changing circumstances. A study of US, Japanese, and European companies shows that large companies can be more rapid in technological innovation than small companies but conventional products might be capable of giving a tough battle for the large companies to carry out regional expansion of business. However, effective management of innovation is surprisingly similar in both, where only the scale of operations differs (Quinn, 1985). Small companies pursue their technological goals slowly by keeping costs low and protecting them over uncertainties and setbacks, but demonstrate the potential for adapting to market needs and delivering differentiated products for larger benefits. Innovative large companies face the unruly realities of the innovative process when competing companies turn to aggressive marketing strategies and local markets are engaged in hatching disruptive innovations.

Technology has created an attractive product market and consumers are continuously motivated to consider a new option with better value for money. Technology innovation has made emerging business firms into creative think-tanks. The twenty-first century is largely driven by the development of technology, and business enterprises are becoming dependent on technology not only to offer new products but also to drive consumers to more convenience-bound behavior. Technological growth in society affects people (including consumers), products, operations, materials, manufacturing, and the marketing process, and the state of consumer preferences. Before employing any new technology firms need to assess its social, economic, and legal perspectives.

New technologies drive customer value and increase market competitiveness. As an advancement in technology emerges, existing businesses are threatened. Firms in the marketplace strive to make a seamless transition to the new technology to lead the competition. Such responses of competitors cede most of the established market to the adaptation of new, dominant technology and develop strategic alternatives to head-on competition. Competing firms develop two types of bold strategies encompassing retrenchment to a niche of the traditional market, where the old technology has an advantage over the new one in addressing customer needs, and relocation to a new market, with superior offerings and low risk (Adner and Snow, 2010). Increasing globalization and competitiveness in the retail environment is thrusting retail firms to reach high levels of consistent experimentation of new technology in store management, product information, and customer services. Technology management can be used to help retailers test new ideas and implement the most successful ones. However, human behavior is particularly important in the retail setting, where projects are generally focused on testing new concepts, increasing collaboration, and implementing new technologies (Thomas et al., 2008).

In the scenario of growing competition, retailer firms can also establish how a customer relationship management and monitoring system ensures the buying decision-making process through the use of joint project teams and facilitating technology. Development and innovative applications of e-commerce transactions as well as the integration of available technology can provide an organization with a unique opportunity to remain competitive within today's global business environment. Although technology plays an important role in gaining competitive advantage for organizations worldwide, information technology professionals, consumers, and e-retailers ensure proper security measures to overcome any harmful impact of the misuse of these same technologies (Medlin and Romaniello, 2008).

The technology impact on the various functions in retailing has been increasing. As the number of channels for a retailer rises, managing the dynamics of customer behavior in the rapidly emerging multichannel environment becomes complex. Building and retaining a long-term association with customers requires that relationship management applications should be able to accommodate the various channels. Multichannel customers are the most valuable customers, and hence multichannel integration would improve customer loyalty and retention (Ganesh, 2004). Besides self-service retail stores and grocery stores, the technology has enormously supported the buying process of consumers for capital goods like automobiles. The purchase of a car is a highly involved process when compared with other retail experiences. Despite the range of purchase channels available and the increased level of accessible information, the majority of customers still choose to buy a car through a traditional dealer network. However, since the end of twentieth century the computer-assisted buying process has been well received by customers (Reed et al., 2004).

The most evident reason to drive companies to go global is the market potential in developing countries that act as major players in the world market. Companies such as Nintendo, Disney and the Japanese motorcycle industries have been greatly benefitted from exploiting the markets of developing countries and reassuring their growth in the world market to harness the promising market potential. The emerging scope of spatial diversification has also been one of the drivers for enhancing global business by utilizing the additional production capacity of economies of scale and low-cost outsourcing. The saturation of demand for the products and services of a company in a domestic market may also be an effective driver to globalization wherein the company looks for building value for its brand across boundaries. A product that is near to the end of its lifecycle in the domestic market begins to generate growth abroad. Sometimes the cross-cultural attributes of overseas markets become the source of new product ideation. Such backward sourcing of technology insights may also be considered as one of the potential drivers for globalization of business and for exploring the strategic alliances with prominent regional or multinational brands.

7
Business Growth and Local Effects

The main goal of consumer-centric changes and user-oriented improvements in products, services, and marketing strategies of competing firms in the marketplace is to manage large differences with small, cost-effective changes. Yet firms often fail to exploit market and production discrepancies, focusing instead on the tensions between standardization and localization of technology. It is argued in this chapter that such situations arise largely as firms fail in maintaining economies of scale, which escalates the cost of production and price. Accordingly, many companies are thrown out of market competition. This chapter analyzes business drivers, the complexities grid, total innovation and risk factors, and factors affecting innovation and technology adaptation in reference to economies of scale and market structure. New product development and managing consumer markets are addressed in this chapter. It is argued that strategic choice for firms requires prioritization toward popular technologies, and the innovation framework can help the firms to become consumer-centric. While it is possible to work on economies of scale, companies must usually focus on building competitive advantage to grow sustainable.

Differentiation drivers

Product differentiation has become one of the prerequisites for companies to stay competitive in growing global and local marketplaces. Most companies are engaged in meticulously designing and positioning their product differentiations as a continuous strategy and invest enormous resources, including financial, intellectual, and technological, to keep abreast of market demand. Five major drivers that actively catalyze the product differentiation process consist of market, competitive, cost, technology, and advertising and communication drivers. In introducing product differentiations, large firms often face tough challenges from local firms to match ethnic values and consumer orientation. Local enterprises that operate in niches compete with large firms as their markets are firmly based in local culture. Some local firms move from their ethnic strengths and develop understanding of global production and consumption dynamics in due course, becoming capable of challenging the innovation and technology of large companies. Large firms can offer product differentiations in products and services by ways of standardization, price competitiveness, convenience, and sustainability in the market as against the products available locally. However, large companies need to develop an ethnic innovative perspective and a local business vision, guard against disruptive and counterfeiting products in local markets, develop partnerships and alliances at the destination market, and drive a supportive consumer ambience (Ger, 1999). Broadly there are five factors that influence innovation differentiation of companies to gain competitive advantages in the marketplace, as exhibited in Figure 7.1.

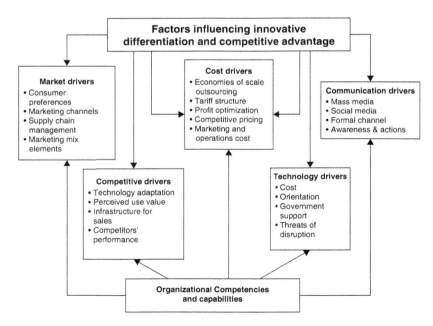

Figure 7.1   Drivers of competitive differentiation

All five factors shown in the figure are discussed in detail in the following sections. It is very important that organizations craft competencies and capabilities in market, competitive, cost, technology, and communication drivers in order to derive competitive advantage and gain sustainable growth in the marketplace.

The market drivers of product differentiation and new products development comprise the needs of common customers, global customers, global channels, and transferable marketing. Customers' needs become a compelling factor for multinational companies when customers of different countries have the same needs in a product category. The freeing of trade and relatively unrestricted travel have created homogeneous groups of customers across the world in reference to specific industries. However, some markets that typically deal with the culture-bound behavior and resistance of consumers toward adoption of differentiated products seek companies to offer customized products to consumers within niches. Global channels, distribution, and logistics companies offer seamless transport, storage, and delivery services. Companies can expand internationally provided the channel infrastructure meets the distribution needs of the company. Hence their integrated networks thrive to bring new products and technologies close to the global distributors, and retail stores like supermarkets and departmental stores in order to generate a systems effect. Transferability in technology marketing is applied in congruence with marketing ideas on brand names, packaging, advertising and other components of marketing-mix in different countries. Nike's campaign anchoring the basketball star Michael Jordan pulled up the brand, which was associated with technology-led new products in many countries. This is how the good ideas of multinationals obtain leverage for new-technology and innovative products in global markets.

The competitive drivers of product differentiation support companies in matching their technology development and marketing strategies in accordance with consumer preferences. The existence of global competitors indicates whether a new technology or products are ready for international business operations. Firms need to develop market infrastructure for the new technologies and products to be able to explore the scope of expansion. Competitive efforts put pressure on companies to globalize their marketing activities and derive optimum performance of their new products by interpreting competitor signals appropriately.

The cost drivers of technology and new products are largely based on economies of scale that involve cost of production functions in large and complex industries, along with cost of outsourcing, diffusion and adaptation of technology, tariffs and taxes, and costs associated with basic and advanced marketing functions. The macroeconomic factors of neighboring countries also govern the cost drivers. When a new automobile plant is set up, it aims at designing, manufacturing or assembling, and delivering a particular model by penetrating neighboring markets to gain the advantages of economies of scale. High-market share multi-domestic companies derive gains from spreading their production activities across multiple product lines or diversified business lines to achieve their economies of scale advantage. Developing new technologies, products, manufacturing, and marketing activities of Procter & Gamble, Unilever, and Colgate-Palmolive may illustrate this global attribute that is explained by the cost drivers. The other cost drivers include global sourcing advantages, low global communications, and automation processes. The location of strategic resources to production plants, cost differences across the countries, and transport costs are also some important considerations of cost drivers.

The lowering of trade barriers made globalization of markets and production a theoretical possibility, and technological change has made it a tangible reality. The technology drivers play a significant role in global business. Global expansion of multinational companies has been highly stimulated by technological advancements in the designing, manufacturing, and marketing of consumer and industrial products. Services have also been improved by many technological breakthroughs. The Internet revolution has triggered e-commerce as an open access channel that acts as a strong driving force for global business in its consumer and industry segments. Improved transport and communication now makes it possible to be in continuous contact with producers anywhere in the world. This makes it easier for companies to split production of a single good over any distance. Storage and preservation techniques have revolutionized the food industry, for example, so that the idea of seasonal vegetables is no longer relevant today as anything can be exported all year round from anywhere. Technological upgrading, in the form of introduction of new machinery and improvement of technological capabilities, provides a firm with the means to be successful in competition. In the process of introducing better technologies, new lower-cost methods become available, which allow the firm to increase labor productivity, that is, the efficiency with which it converts resources into value. Firms adopt these newer methods of production if they are more profitable than the older ones. The ability of a firm to take advantage of technical progress is also enhanced if the firm improves its entrepreneurial and technological capabilities through two competitive strategies, namely, learning and adaptation, and innovation. The latter is a process of searching for, finding, developing, imitating, adapting, and adopting new products, new processes, and new organizational arrangements. Because rivals do not stand still, the firm's capacity to develop these capabilities, as well as its ability to compete depends on the firm's maintaining a steady pace of innovation (Asian Development Bank, 2003). Containerization has revolutionized the transportation business, significantly lowering the costs of shipping goods over long distances. Before the advent of containerization, moving goods from one mode of transport to another was very labor-intensive, lengthy, and costly. It could take days to unload a ship and reload goods onto trucks and trains. The efficiency gains associated with containerization have caused transportation costs to plummet, making it much more economical to ship goods around the world, thereby helping to drive the globalization of markets and production. The government drivers for globalization include diplomatic trade relations, custom unions, or common markets. These government drivers add favorable trade policies, foreign investment regulations, bilateral or regional trade treaties and common market regulations.

Communication is another important driver of innovation and differentiation. Mass media channels are the most rapid and efficient means of communicating to a large number of potential adopters, but interpersonal communication is more effective in persuading potential adopters to accept a new idea. Direct communication among users of the same socioeconomic segment and educational level increases the potential of acceptance even more. Although scholarly writings and curriculum resources provide an abundance of information about the effectiveness and benefits of media literacy training, a majority of potential adopters will be more influenced by conversations with their peers.

The most evident reason to drive companies into going global is the market potential in developing countries that act as major players in the world market. Companies such as Nintendo, Disney and the Japanese motorcycle industries have been greatly benefitted from exploiting the markets of developing countries and assuring their growth in the world market to harness its potential. The emerging scope of spatial diversification has also been one of the drivers for enhancement of global business, utilizing additional production capacity with economies of scale and low-cost outsourcing. The saturation of demand for the products and services of a company in a domestic market may also be an effective driver to globalization wherein the company looks for building value for its brand across boundaries. A product that is near the end of its lifecycle in the domestic market may begin to generate growth abroad. Sometimes the cross-culture attributes of overseas markets become the source of new product ideation. Such backward sourcing of technology insights may also be considered as one of the potential drivers for globalization of business and to explore strategic alliances with prominent regional or multinational brands thereof.

Information and communication technologies, optical technologies, production technologies, materials technologies, biotechnologies, nanotechnologies, microsystems technologies and innovative services are considered to be the drivers of innovations and differentiation – above all in areas of application such as automotive engineering, medical technology, mechanical engineering, and logistics. Developments in these key technologies provide solutions for the challenges of our time. The dynamic differentiation and product innovations have created high product attractiveness. Increased involvement of consumers and market players in new product development has led to co-creation strategies and the demand for intelligent products and services. Flexible differentiation architectures and application frameworks tie new products, technologies, and users together. Rapidly changing consumer markets in many industries have called for strategies to expedite support services for technologies and product development. However, an unplanned or ad hoc technology in the market makes the managerial tasks of forecasting, marketing and its user values indistinct and erratic. Fast-cycle decision-making for the induction of new technology and products should be based on rethinking of the decision-making model, where managerial intuition replaces extensive analysis as the main driver of decisions (Prewitt, 1998).

The development and marketing of new or improved technology-led products with competitive performance is currently receiving more attention in business-to-consumers and business-to-business industries. A more innovative strategy to push technology products in the market has proven to be successful for industries operating in mature markets. It is also important to be cost-competitive to develop and launch new technologies, which depends on an efficient production process. The drivers that move the technology as well as new products toward success also include measuring performance for the management of technology. It is recognized that success at project level does not necessarily means success at company level (Lager and Horte, 2002).

The performance of a business organization can be viewed from many perspectives. However, performance does not necessarily endorse growth of business in a competitive marketplace. The financial performance of a firm may unveil a different scenario of growth as compared to the performance of various brands within a product category in the overall product-mix. Achieving good organizational performance requires more than the will of a single person; indeed, it requires the united commitment of an organization's members. This commitment must also move beyond mere talk and encompass concrete action (Adler, 2010). The top management of the firm needs to evolve the true definition of performance and its relevance in the competitive market environment. Performance expectations, which are fundamentally a manager's expectations in envisaging the competitive stand of the firm in a marketplace, have a big impact on decision-making in firms (Stone, 1994), particularly in relation to investment decisions. Strategists may contribute toward improving the performance of the firm by linking expectations to the capability and competence of managers and employees, and providing the necessary support to improve the capability and competency in first instance.

Successful consumer led-products in the competitive marketplace always try to gain a distinct place among competing firms and focus on acquiring new customers and retaining existing ones. Repeat buying behavior of customers is largely determined by the values acquired on the product. Attributes, awareness, trial, availability, and repeat (AATAR) factors influence customers toward making subsequent buying decisions in reference to the marketing strategies of the firm. The perception on repeat buying is affected by the level of satisfaction derived from the buying experience of customers (Rajagopal, 2008). Among growing competition in retailing consumer products, innovative point of sales promotions offered by supermarkets are aimed at boosting sales and augmenting store brand value. Purchase acceleration and product trial are found to be the two most influential variables of retail point of sales promotions. Analysis of five essential qualities of customer value judgment in terms of *interest, subjectivity, exclusivity, thoughtfulness, and internality* needs to be carried out in order to make the firm customer-centric and its strategies reaching the bottom of the sales pyramid (Dobson, 2007). Dynamic complexity in business may arise in oligopolistic market systems with high risk in investment, brand development, and generative customer loyalty. It may be observed that the switching behavior of consumers occurs when distribution of a company is weak in the market. In many cases companies are not able to carry out controlled experiments on implementing business strategies for cost-related and ethical reasons. Hence, dynamic complexity not only slows the learning loop but also reduces the learning gained on each cycle.

Developing the right business strategies in the right market situation is a growing challenge among systems thinkers and business strategists. Delays in developing appropriate strategy can create instability in market dynamic systems and add negative feedback loops, which reduces the sustainability of the company in the competitive marketplace.

The complexity grid

Market competition and growth of innovation and technology have always featured the unpredictable, the surprising, and the unexpected in the global marketplace. However, the increasing deployment of information technology in firms has developed hyper-connectivity on one hand and complexity in business management on the other. Market competition and growth of technology are now intertwined and interdependent as market need has become the principal driver of innovation and technology. New products are embryonic to the consumer need and market demand, and are grown largely on predicting outcomes. There are too many continuously changing interactive elements in play that create complexities in managing the marketing of technology-led innovative products in different market segments. Managers looking to handle these difficulties need to adopt strategic rather than tactical approaches for sustainable results, and to overcome conventional wisdom by using models that simulate the behavior of the market players, including consumers, in order to make technology-led new products sustainable. They should also make sure that their strategies are future-oriented and can manage market risk. Firms introducing new products rapidly in the marketplace should minimize the need to rely on predictions and work with user-oriented product design and applications. They can list the complexity factors in a system and build resistant production systems to minimize the consequences of failure in the business system, develop strategic alliances to share the unforeseen risks in the innovation and technologies-led products, and enhance organizational capabilities and competencies (Sargut and McGrath, 2011).

Administrative complexities play a significant role in explaining new technology drive. Process simplification, zero defect products, cost and profit, and overall governance of new products development have many obstacles to be either eliminated or managed within the organizational system. Most managers are not involved in setting up business thinking about managing probable odds and complexities during the innovation process, and tend to withdraw their role if complexity occurs. Such behavior is also significantly affected by the perception of administrative complexity (van Stel and Stunnenberg, 2006). Firms that are engaged in rapid development of new products find there is a gap between diffusion and adoption. It is expensive for companies to manage excess inventory of obsolete products unless they can be improved and reverted to active demand. Expensive downtime for production line changeovers, and merchandise languishing on retailers' shelves or in their showrooms also cause serious concerns to firms engaged in developing new products. For service companies, though, complexity is much harder to spot and root out, largely due to the ease with which new products can be created and marketed (Gottfredson and Schwedel, 2008). The complexities that companies face in competitive differentiation in markets are exhibited in Figure 7.2.

Figure 7.2 illustrates four possible complexity areas that companies can meet while introducing differentiations in products and strategies in the competitive marketplace. These complexity areas are observed by companies toward internal and external fit. The complexities in the internal fit consist of possible problems a company may face while developing and implementing strategic and tactical approaches

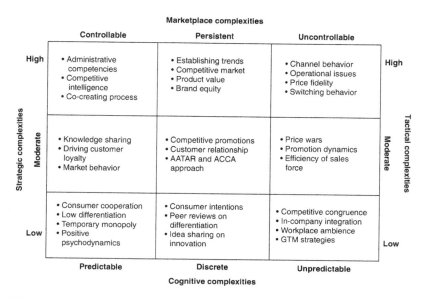

Figure 7.2   Complexities in competitive differentiation: A multifactor grid

in introducing differentiations. Besides administrative complexities, most companies are unable to build strong competitive intelligence for collecting market information and sharing knowledge within the company. Such internal difficulties would render the companies less competitive in the market in driving the co-creation of differentiated products, seeking consumer cooperation, and understanding market behavior. Every company expects to enjoy temporary monopoly on the differentiation of products and services for a while until disruptive or competitive products appear in the marketplace. The complexities in implementing tactical differentiation might arise in the short term but cause long-term effects for companies to manage their business in the competitive marketplace. Tactical complexities are often observed when companies enter into price wars, competitive promotions, and go-to-market (GTM) strategies involving the sales force and consumers in selling and buying of differentiated products. Another complexity in the market might be observed by companies when competitive congruence grows in the marketplace. This situation may occur when competitors follow identical strategies for introducing their innovative differentiations in products and services to grid consumer decisions.

External fit consists of marketplace and consumer complexities that are highly uncontrollable and unpredictable. The inconsistent behavior of distribution channels and operational difficulties are considered to be highly uncontrollable marketplace factors that trigger complexity in managing the competitive differentiations of companies. The response of consumers toward the strategies of firms on creating awareness, illustrating attributes, assuring availability, demonstrating trials, and creating repeat buying behavior (AATAR) of competitively differentiated products are often also intercepted by competitors. Such situations in the marketplace could cause complexities in positioning products in the market. Price fidelity is another major concern for most companies to uphold marketing in the mass and bottom-of-the-pyramid consumer segments. It has been observed as common practice among retailing firms to appoint mystery shoppers who collect information on pricing from rival companies to help break the price fidelity of consumers with competing companies. These mystery shoppers are often paid employees of retail companies or of local business intelligence organizations. Aggressive or deceptive advertisement and communication strategies for launching and marketing differentiated products create marketplace complexities as such strategies might affect awareness, comprehension, conviction (purchase intention), and action (buying) among consumers in reference to a competitor's call and peer review.

One of the major complexities that arise during the process of product differentiation is deciding about the mass production and commercialization of the differentiated products to optimize both revenues and market share. Most firms begin with a low scale and find it difficult to get into economies of scale if the new product becomes attractive in the markets. The fact is, companies have strong incentives to be overly innovative in new product development but making competitive decisions in view of the anticipated consumers' and competitors' behavior often rolls back corporate decisions in the market. However, continual launches of new products and line extensions adds complexity throughout the market operations of a company and as the costs of managing that complexity multiply, profits tends to shrink. To maximize profit potential, a company needs to identify its innovation pivot, the point at which an additional offering either increases or pulls back the profit of the company to enable the right decision on differentiation. The usual solutions to complexity remain unsolved because companies often treat the problem on the market platform rather than at its source where consumer value, product-line requirements, and latent demand in the market exists (Gottfredson and Aspinall, 2005).

Large organizations are complex by nature and face new business challenges such as globalization, innovative technologies, and regulations. Market uncertainties and competitive threats add layer upon layer of complexity to the corporate structure and management. The technology marketing grid has several factors that pose conflicts and challenges to innovation and technology development firms during different levels of the process. The complexity grid comprises twelve commonly observed points of conflicts, and has independent effects for each point as well as in matrix form. The conflict points in the grid comprise ideation, resources management, process management, capabilities and competencies, technology marketing, growth and next-generation innovation and technology issues, involvement, organizational policies, operational efficiency, competitive decisions, business environment, and organizational culture, all of which nurture the innovation and technology development projects in the firm.

In the complexity grid the ideation process and the extent of involvement of employees, consumers, and market players stage cognitive and organizational conflicts and challenges while management of resources and organizational policies raises various challenging issues during different phases of innovation and technology development. Similarly, the process and operational efficiency commonly drive various issues of concern in reference to capabilities and competencies and work culture of the organization. Firms face many conflicts during the innovation process on marketing of technology-led products and the existing business environment. Moving the innovation and technology to the next generation is not an easy step as firms often get snared in unwise competitive decisions in an effort to push their innovation and technology-led products in the marketplace.

Large firms have been the driving force behind the market economies of developed countries. Traditional theories suggest that new products that are not consistent with existing demand retard economic growth, hence classical theories propose that serving products to existing market demand is safer than creating demand in the market to position the products. However, global competition and changing consumer behavior in experimenting with new products have raised new theoretical concepts on the relationship of launching new products with market demand. Large firms are engaged in continuously developing new products and could benefit, in contrast to small firms, from economies of scale and scope. Many economists believed that the presence of more large firms would lead to more economic growth and that the share of small firms eventually would disappear or decline to only a small fraction. Globalization has induced extensive cross-culture working ambience and driven most firms to multidimensional manufacturing and marketing operations to sustain in the competition marketplace. Hence, most firms have become increasingly complex and ungovernable, causing decline in performance, unclear accountability, and opaque decision-making processes that raise questions on the sustainability of the firm. To avoid frustration and inefficiency, executives need to systematically address the causes of complexity using a simplicity-minded strategy in their companies by streamlining the structure, pruning non-responding products before introducing new products to create space, building disciplined processes, and improving managerial behavior (Ashkenas, 2007).

Firms operating in niche environments have tried to secure themselves against risks by focusing on potential threats outside the organization, such as competitors, shifts in the strategic landscape, natural disasters, or geopolitical events. They are generally less skillful at detecting internal vulnerabilities that creep into organizations through various interrelated systems. Indeed, as firms increase the complexity of their systems they often tend to draw insufficient attention to the introduction of new products and strategies and manage growing system flaws. The possibility of random failure rises as the number of combinations of factors that can go wrong increases, while the opportunity for competitors to counter strategies also goes up. Firms should meticulously assess the risks in technology marketing and stay aware of market information to guard against market uncertainties and make appropriate decisions. It is also necessary for technology marketing firms to identify vulnerabilities in the marketplace and fix them before competitors or disruptive innovation products attack the new technology products (Bonabeau, 2007).

Business leaders have expressed the view that previous assumptions and business models developed to cater to regional oligopolistic market requirements are inadequate to help managers in understanding the strategic needs of global markets. Management practices that are guided by complexity science will lead to a highly human-oriented approach to business that not only brings greater purpose and fulfillment to people's lives but also steers organizations to greater financial success (Hoe, 2001). In today's increasingly competitive global marketplace, companies create value and ensure survival based on their ability to manage the complex web of suppliers and customers comprising their value chain. At the heart of this process is the accurate, timely, and complete disclosure of information between value chain partners to enable the types of coordinated action mandated by exchange partners (Hausman et al., 2005).

Differentiation failures and risk factors

Product innovation and new differentiation projects often fail for various organizational and market-related factors. It has been observed that when companies undertake a large, complex, systems project, the realistic expectations are either very high or intrinsic, and this can lead projects to fail. In particular, manufacturing process reengineering and differentiation improvement projects have an even higher failure rate because of their expanded scope. Differentiation or innovation projects are built using a multilayer strategy spread across various factors constituting backward and forward linkages. New product development using differentiation reengineering is an integrated process, and fragmentation of the process at any stage may cause damage to its end value and market response.

The sustainability of new products and associated technologies depends largely on organizational support towards employees' creative production and marketing ideas, and innovative solutions to consumer needs. Business organizations should improve their human resources performance to increase their employees' initiatives toward innovation and differentiation change, and drive involvement in the innovation projects. Often innovation and differentiation projects are unsuccessful due to the lack of organizational support to employees. It has been observed that supportive behavior from top management significantly increases the involvement of employees in new production, differentiation, and business initiatives. In most firms with sustainable development policies, operations managers are found less supportive when managing new products or differentiation issues as compared to managing other business issues due to perceived risk factors (Ramus, 2001).

Most organizations back off from providing adequate resources support to the ancillary units associated with innovation and differentiation development projects. Commonly, support units have been regarded as discretionary expense centers in most companies, and are often underplayed. But it is a serious mistake to view them this way as they are aligned to the business projects of the organization. Differentiation support units may be encouraged to involve intensively with the innovation and differentiation development projects through strategy maps and balanced scorecards that could help support units to become value-creating organizations. However, firms should understand that support unit alignment is a continuous process toward establishing better production processes, working relationships, and managing technological requirements. Organizations need to consider the following requirements for carrying out innovation and differentiation projects successfully:

- The necessity of top management support throughout the process of new product and differentiation development.
- Following a rigorous and complete process design.
- Effective technical leadership to drive the project through the predetermined process.

Each of the above factors is a driver for success in any innovation and differentiation project. Besides the above core considerations in managing differentiation projects, companies also need to measure the extent of work diversity, fix accountability among the project members, support flexible process arrangements, provide leadership education, and offer quality role models to encourage carrying out differentiation and innovation.

Project failure in the innovation and differentiation area is an expensive issue, and troubled projects in organizations pursuing innovation are not uncommon. These projects need strong commitment of employees, and organizations should continue to pour in more resources. Employees in most companies escalate commitment to a failing course of action in technologically sophisticated projects with a strong information differentiation component. Such situations have to be judged in terms of benefit–cost ratio of the project. Through de-escalation, managers may successfully turn around or sensibly abandon troubled projects. Organizations should manage troubled projects by carefully appraising the problem, re-examining of the prior course of action, search for an alternative course of action, and implement an exit strategy (Keil and Montealegre, 2000).

Managers often do not understand the design of a differentiation process or innovation engineering system. Innovation and differentiation projects should be subjected to a regular audit process to review the performance of the project in each stage. A project may be discontinued simply because of lack of coordination among various teams in performing the designated tasks satisfactorily. In such cases, a technical audit can validate the actions of the development team and provide management with the information required to continue supporting the project. In any innovational differentiation project, there are four interdependent factors, namely, cost, quality, speed of project activities, and risk.

Project failures sometimes generate new organizational insights to develop better ways to carry out innovation and differentiation projects. Hence, failures in projects should not be viewed always in negative terms, as they also exhibit a positive side of the effect by providing improved opportunities. A certain amount of failure can help managers keep the project revival options open and explore points of weakness in the process. Managers can create the conditions to attract resources and attention to revive failing innovation and differentiation projects and develop radical intuitions and skills. The key to reaping these benefits is to foster radical intelligence against failure throughout the project process in an organization. Organizations should assess the potential success and failure factors prior to initiating an innovation and differentiation project, and document initial assumptions, test conditions, and convert them into working knowledge. However, managers should attempt to limit the number of uncertainties in new projects, and build organizational tolerance in achieving results (McGrath, 2011).

Large differentiation and new product development projects can fail because they are laid over multiyear time frames. Government agencies typically execute large-scale programs in multiyear cycles, which increases the complexity of programs and leads to higher failure rates. Long time frame cycles often drive duplication of tasks within the project process as the team seeks to build all project components with each stage being managed by different team leaders, causing a process jam at any point of time. The problem worsens when teams try to prevent failure by diligently using conventional wisdom to resolve complex issues despite non-compliance to deadlines and customer dissatisfaction. Organizations express more concern on the failure or delay of innovation and differentiation projects as the pace of technological change continues to accelerate and they cater to the market with new products, differentiation, and demand. Unpredicted alterations in the product lifecycles and differentiation shifts make the existing project activities more complex and augment program risk and probabilities of failure. Often multilayers and time-overrun projects fail in the market despite being successful in completing the project. They end up delivering functionality on outdated differentiation that often does not meet true business needs. Most innovation and differentiation products fail for the following very common but overlooked reasons by organizations:

- Differentiation projects with broad scope and multilayer processes spread over a long time frame often face setbacks. It is necessary for firms managing large differentiation projects to limit the requirements and process cycle. In order to prevent further delays and damage in the differentiation development process, managers prioritize project requirements and decide to derive timelines, resources, and business needs. Innovation and differentiation products also suffer as firms fail to accommodate the preferences of stakeholders. Developing products that do not match consumer demand increase complexity exponentially, resulting in significant delays and cost overruns. Besides, weak governance and new requirements in the mid-development process add to the complexity, causing further delay.
- Delays and suspensions of new product development projects occur due to complex budgeting and funding processes within the organization. Large-scale innovation and differentiation development projects suffer from protracted funding cycles, budget uncertainties, and administrative challenges. Funding approval is largely considered by the large business organizations in advance, and such financial proposals are often articulated to set the project budgets in advance. In this process requirement of funds are considered as the priority in the differentiation lifecycle. Consequently, by the time firms complete the innovation projects and launch their new products and

differentiation in market, they have become obsolete, causing failure of the project.

- Most differentiation-led new product development projects end in closure due to inadequate financial resources. When project managers develop long-term budgets the financial appropriations are often inaccurate due to shifts in organizational and market requirements. Another budgetary complication may be the availability of finance as funds are typically appropriated for a given fiscal year, and project teams have limited ability to move portions of current-year funding to the next year or to reallocate money among activities spread over a wider time span in the same portfolio. It is difficult to move funds across the periods even when changes in the differentiation landscape or in business needs require a reallocation.

- Every innovation and differentiation project in a company has a broad set of stakeholders, including agency leaders, business-process owners, and functional departments like information differentiation, acquisitions, finance, security, general administration, and legal operations. Large companies face the intimidating task of integrating the interests of multiple stakeholders. Though the general intent behind this multiple stakeholder focus is to ensure that companies operate for the benefit of society as a whole, weak governance and oversight of many interrelated factors in carrying forward innovation and differentiation-related projects often causes failures.

- Such difficulties in managing innovative products arise because stakeholders are not fully aligned on the desired outcomes. Projects also suffer as accountabilities in managing various tasks are not determined and decision-making is centralized. Most firms do not consider analyzing their stakeholder inputs significantly and integrate the results into the innovation and differentiation development process (Crittenden and Crittenden, 2012).

- Differentiation projects are also decommissioned while incorporating various insights emerging from consulting on the operational issues. Project leaders sometimes receive conflicting direction from multiple players involved in the project while stakeholders sometimes make decisions outside the project that may have a material impact on carrying out the innovation and differentiation projects.

The consequences of failure lead over time to the multiple layers of costs of materials, capital, and know-how management. These costs may be classified as sunk costs as they cannot be recovered for a process that has failed. The overhead costs of failed innovation and differentiation projects include technical components (e.g., backup systems, "safety" features of equipment) and human components, comprising cost of training and knowledge diffusion. Reviving a sick project demands changes in a variety of organizational, institutional, and regulatory defenses consisting of policies and procedures, certification, work rules, and training of employees. Organizations deciding to revive or re-initiate differentiation projects need to provide a series of defenses to prevent further failures in the process.

Differentiation management and organizational culture

Working with competitive innovation and differentiation projects drives many changes in an organization in terms of work-culture and on-market behavior of the products in particular and the company in general. Often in carrying out new products and technology projects there comes resistance among the employees in the organization as well as market players once the product or technology is ready to launch. Thus, an organization carrying out innovation and technology projects should simultaneously develop strategies for managing the organizational change. Organizational change is a structured approach for ensuring that changes are smoothly and successfully carried on within the internal system to achieve strategic benefits for the long term. Dynamic innovation and technology changes develop a non-sustainable work ambience in the organization and often induce rapid transformation. Globalization and the constant innovation of technology result in a constantly evolving business environment. Social media has revolutionized business organizations to continuously think of developing new products and technology, which causes an increasing need for change, and therefore change management in business organizations has become an essential discipline. The growth in technology also has a secondary effect of increasing the availability and therefore the accountability of knowledge. With the business environment experiencing so much change, organizations must then learn to become comfortable with change as well. Therefore, the ability to manage and adapt to organizational change is essential in the workplace today. There are various factors affecting the change management process in an organization.

The rapid growth of technology and continuous penetration of new products in competitive markets has pushed unforeseen organizational changes in a company motivated by external market behavior rather than internal conflicts and changes. Organizations that adapt quickly to changes in organizational culture and move to market with new products and technologies create a competitive advantage, while companies that refuse to change are left behind. Organizational change directly affects all departments, and the entire company must learn how to handle changes to the organization. Regardless of the many types of organizational change, the critical aspect is a company's ability to win the confidence of employees and market players on the change. Organizational change management should begin with a systematic diagnosis of the current objectives of the company in order to determine both the need for change and the capability to change. Change management process may include creative thinking and developing effective communications, group dynamics, and integrating teams to manage training for employees and market players. Firms should use performance metrics such as financial results, operational efficiency, leadership commitment, communication effectiveness, and the perceived need for change to design appropriate strategies.

Most organizations implement large-scale organizational change initiatives according to predetermined time frames with limited resources. However, anticipated performance is often discouraging as internal resistance among employees and market players may run counter to the set change management initiatives. A combined assessment of work-culture and organizational structure can help firms in identifying barriers to change in the organization and marketplace, and develop change initiatives accordingly (Johnson-Cramer et al., 2007). The change management process comprises a sequence of steps for a management team or project leader to follow in an organization. It is vital for the change management team and executives to build change leadership. Individual change management activities should be put through the scheduled change process. Simultaneously the project team members should develop training requirements based on the skills, knowledge, and behaviors necessary to implement the change. Resistance from employees and managers is very common for any new initiatives in an organization toward innovation and technology, and continued resistance may threaten a project. The change management team needs to identify, understand, and manage resistance throughout the organization.

The effectiveness of change management efforts is largely determined by various organizational factors, comprising a company's structure, work processes, reward systems, and business policies orchestrated over time to support market sustenance. Change management is also affected by the strategic intent, identity, existing capabilities and competencies of an organization. In a competitive marketplace that is continuously changing, an organization's design must support the idea that implementation of the change management strategies is a continuous process. Most traditional organizations tend to resist change. However, emerging companies are built to change and invest in continuous thinking on modifying basic organizational design assumptions with a focus on managing talent, delineating effective job descriptions, redefining the relationship between company and worker, and restructuring reward systems from a subjective pay system for objective assessment of remunerations based on performance. Companies intending to apply a change management process in their organization should work on redesigning the organization to maximize its interactivity surface among employees by breaking a hierarchical system into peer reviews and talent-mapping paradigms. It is also important for change management-oriented companies to open information sharing and analysis and decision processes for the frontline requirements in the market. Change management in an organization is largely successful when the leaders cooperate in replacing hierarchical command-and-control with a democratic team leadership approach to drive confidence among employees. Successful change in a growing organization requires not only sound strategic and financial decisions, but also effective bi-directional communication from both top-down and bottom-up directions.

Product design strategy

The product and business strategies of a foreign firm should be developed in reference to the macroeconomic conditions of the host country. The definition of product objectives should emerge from the business definitions developed in accordance with the macroeconomic requirements of the host country. Foreign firms need to analyze whether the success of their product or product line can be replicated in a new market destination abroad and explore the factors that may lead the product approach to success in the host country. In other words, a decision must be made about which is the more appropriate of the two product design strategies of standardization or customization. *Standardization* refers to offering a common product on a national, regional, or worldwide basis, while *customization* signifies adapting a product, making appropriate changes in it, to match local perspectives.

Customization of the product may be chosen over standardization in order to cater to the unique situation in each country. Yet, there are potential gains to consider in product standardization. International

marketers must examine all the criteria in order to decide the extent
to which products should vary from country to country (Aaker and
Joachimsthaler, 1999). If there are no new needs to be catered for to
make the product offering ready for any market, resulting in a significant cost saving, the firm may decide to standardize its products.
Product standardization may be a risky proposition in the long run, as
consumer behavior is flexible and tends to change over time. However,
some multinational companies have succeeded in standardizing products for offering in many countries. General Electric Company's deba-
cles in the small-appliances field in Germany and Polaroid's difficulties
with the Swinger camera in France are classic examples of failed product
standardization. At the same time, Volkswagen's success worldwide with
Beetle supports standardization.

Excessive concern with local customization can be troublesome,
too. Holland's Philips Company learned the hard lesson that it cannot
afford to customize television sets for each European market separately.
International markets are not always homogeneous, and markets in
different countries for a given product are at different stages of development at the same time. This phenomenon may be explained through
the product lifecycle concept wherein products go through several lifecycle stages over a period of time, and in each stage different marketing
strategies are appropriate. There are four stages, usually identified as
introduction, growth, maturity, and decline, even for products distributed in markets overseas. In a developing market environment, firms
should develop their product policies in accordance with the requirements of the local markets. If customer needs tend to be basic and the
alternatives for customers in the home market are found to be weak, it
would be appropriate for a firm to offer standardized products from the
existing product line. Under such circumstances, a firm may decide to
offer a narrow range of choices in product selection at a local market
level. This would help in confirming the choice of cost-effective and
high-profitability product offerings in developing markets. However,
product adaptation to match local conditions involves consideration
of many cost factors, and it is necessary for a foreign firm to undertake
cost–benefit analysis prior to making firm decisions on product policy.
These costs may relate to research and development, physical altera-
tion of the product's design, style, features or changes in packaging,
co-branding, performance guarantee, and the like. In contrast with
standardization no research and development is required in the process
of customization, since manufacturing technology and quality control
procedures have been established, and performance has been tested and

improved. Hence, standardization brings certain cost savings. Among various cost factors, direct and indirect, it would be difficult for a firm to quantify the opportunity cost. If a product is customized, presumably it will have greater appeal to the mass market in the host country. A cost–benefit analysis would help in determining the cost to customize and realizing a benefit. The results of cost–benefit analysis on product customization should be compared with the same analysis applied to standardization. The net difference indicates the relative desirability of the two strategies.

A review of research on product development indicates that analytical attributes technique plays a vital role in product design for both business-to-consumers and business-to-business companies. The analytical attributes approach is defined as the transformation of a market opportunity into a product available for sale. This technique of new product design also encompasses the functional fields of marketing, operations management, and engineering design. The value of this breadth is in conveying the shape of the entire research landscape. The analytical attributes technique looks inside the "black box" of product development at the fundamental decisions that are made by intention or default. In doing so, managers can adopt the perspective of product development as a deliberate business process involving hundreds of decisions, many of which can be usefully supported by knowledge and tools (Kishnan and Ulrich, 2001). The analytical attributes approach capitalizes on the concept that any feature change in a product must involve one or more current attributes.

Although the role of attributes in new products development is not well understood, research suggests that personality plays a critical role in the effective performance of attributes. Product attributes should be especially important for new product development that typically includes highly coordinated activities among multidisciplinary members. There are two specific types of new product development processes, namely, incremental innovation and radical innovation (Reilly et al., 2002). The analytical attributes approach can be used in designing new products in the following ways:

- dimensional analysis uses features;
- checklists use all attributes;
- trade-off analysis also uses determinant attributes.

Materials selection has emerged as a major issue for product design engineers. The available set of materials, rapidly growing both in type and number, has vastly expanded the number of possibilities meriting serious consideration for many engineering applications. Today, engineers are forced to look for systematic techniques for managing and analyzing engineering data on the growing array of materials. While advances in materials science continue to expand the horizons of material performance, the material developer finds it increasingly difficult to establish what constitutes a desirable material. By its nature, the designer's process of material selection happens outside the ken of the suppliers of the alternative materials. Because suppliers are frequently isolated from this process, they receive little insight into the rationale for the success or failure of their offerings. The lack of this information not only limits their ability to identify and rectify the limitations of their current offerings, but it also makes it very difficult to ascertain what success new offerings will have. Product design engineers should make the following analysis of attributes in designing new products:

- cost–benefit analysis;
- unique sales proposition (USP);
- use analysis;
- hierarchical design;
- functions analysis;
- weaknesses;
- attribute extension;
- relative brand profile;
- systems analysis.

Inventory constraints, costs of lost production, safety and environmental objectives, strategies of maintenance adopted, and logistics aspects of spare parts are some of the criteria to be taken into account, and spare parts classification is thus defined with respect to multiple attributes. In virtue of the large number of potential operational characteristics to be considered, the decision diagram is integrated with a set of analytic hierarchy process models used to solve the various multi-attribute decision sub-problems at the different levels/nodes of the decision tree. An inventory policy matrix can be defined to link the different classes of spare parts with the possible inventory management policies so as to identify the "best" control strategy for the spare stocks (Braglia et al., 2004).

Most firms build their marketing strategies around the concept of the product lifecycle. However, by positioning their products in non-conventional ways, companies can extend the span of product lifecycle in reference to how customers perceive them. In doing so, managers can shift products lodged in the maturity phase back and propel new products forward into the growth phase. Some non-conventional positioning strategies firms can use to shift consumers' thinking include reverse positioning, breakaway positioning, and furtive positioning. The reverse positioning strategy holds products in a particular stage of the lifecycle for a longer period while adding new ones. Breakaway positioning associates the product with a radically different category, as, for example, Trendy, a brand of Swatch Company, associated its watches in the category of fashion accessory. A furtive positioning strategy offers consumers, who are not confident in the products of the company, a new offering by concealing the product's true nature. A company can use these techniques to go on the offensive and transform a category by demolishing its traditional boundaries (Moon, 2005). Detailed knowledge on how innovation, market performance, and competition serve as a basis for a firm making decisions is important for companies to gain and determine the lifecycle of a product. Managers should consider consumer preferences and product knowledge as the significant drivers in the course of changing market conditions (Werker, 2003).

It has been observed that increasing global competition and heterogeneous market segments, together with shorter product lifecycles, are forcing many companies to simultaneously compete in the three marketing domains of products, processes, and value chains. Uncertainty in decision-making across these domains makes competitive strategies of companies highly complex in the marketplace. Companies should develop consistency in the product attributes comprising commonality, product service platforms, product designs and values, and product modularity. This framework can be used to focus product design and product architecture dimensions, which are critical for a given operational strategy. In order to assess advantages and limitations of operational strategies in conjunction with the given product architectures, firms need to develop dynamic capabilities such as planning effective product and operation strategy combinations (Fixson, 2005). Firms should understand that the process lifecycle is distinct from the product lifecycle in terms of facilitating the strategic decisions of a firm in positioning new products in the innovation and technology sectors in the competitive marketplace. A company may seek competitive advantage in the market, but should understand the implications of each move (Hayes and Wheelright, 1979).

The success of new products is a major concern of companies as it determines their standing in the marketplace. Strategies that can provide innovative combinations of products and services as "high-value integrated solutions" tailored to each consumer's needs instead of simply "moving downstream" into services are being developed by large and reputable firms in order to sustain in increasingly competitive markets (Davies, 2004). Innovative combinations of service capabilities such as operations, business consultancy, and finance are required to provide complete solutions to every consumer's needs in order to augment consumer value perceived in innovative or new products. The time gap between changes in customer preferences and product mix affects the introduction of a new product and its lifecycle in a given market environment. Consumer product manufacturing and marketing firms observe seasonality within markets, and are exposed to demand volatility for certain elements of the complex product mix. Market responsive manufacturing strategy entails adaptive and flexible production and supply capability in conjunction with real-time market interaction through profit optimization.

Among growing market competition many companies are introducing new products with short product lifecycles and quick market penetration attributes. While new products offer tremendous value, product introductions and their transitions to market pose enormous challenges to managers. The new product development process should analyze the risks impacting a transition and identify factors across departments in the business organization tracking those risks, monitor the evolution of these factors over time, and map scenarios of risks and responses. This process helps managers to understand the expectations of firms, lessens the chance and impact of unanticipated outcomes, and synchronizes responses among different departments. It assists managers in designing and implementing appropriate policies to enhance the sales for new products and ramp down sales for existing products, balancing supply and demand for both so that combined sales can grow smoothly (Erhun et al., 2007).

The key factors fostering growth in packaged food markets are convenience, functionality, and indulgence, with packaging becoming an integral constituent of processed food products that contributes to consumer value and market demand. Recent trends in the marketing of functional foods suggest that multiple-benefit products are becoming more common, and frequent introduction of new processed food products in the market is being encouraged. Companies stimulate consumer preferences for new product introductions based on some specific nutritional attributes, for example, tomato juice with soy positioned on its organic and nutritional attributes. While naturally occurring nutrients are preferred over fortification, health benefits and the use of natural ingredients are positively valued. However, such preferences and valuations are influenced by an individual's education, income, and food purchase behavior (Teratanavat and Hooker (2006).

There are many marketing concepts, including market orientation, marketing competencies and resources, and competitive marketing strategies, that explain success among small agro-food companies in international markets. Some research studies indicate that the influential impact of adopting a market orientation, developing competencies in advantage-generating consumer food products, channel and relationship management areas, leveraging strategically relevant managerial, production and brand resources, and deploying appropriate competitive marketing strategies significantly affect the process of new product introductions and variability in their cyclicality (Ibeh et al., 2006). Consumer-oriented innovation is an increasingly important source of new product development and competitive advantage in reference to the speed with which product innovations are introduced to the market (Davenport et al., 2003). In many cases, aesthetic properties are as important as technical functions. When one considers the subjective part of the requirements, the feelings, impressions, sensations or preferences of consumers must be quantified and modeled in advance. This is a major challenge in new consumer products design.

An international firm should develop country-specific product lines for achieving success in overseas markets. To achieve this viability, the composition of the product line needs to be periodically reviewed and changed. Such environmental changes as customer preferences, competitors' tactics, host country legal requirements, and a firm's own perspectives, including its objectives, cost structure, and spillover of demand from one product to another, can all render a product line inadequate. Thus, it may become necessary to add new products or eliminate existing products from the product line to customize the product line specifically to each country. Alternatively, certain specific products may be for a particular foreign country, either locally abroad or in the home country. The extension of domestic products to foreign markets follows the logic of the concept of market demand in consumer segments. Such product extension into the market of a host country is generally adopted through a process wherein the products are developed first for the home market, which may prove successful and lead to some export orders. As the exports grow, the firm may consider setting up a warehouse, a sales branch, or a service center in the foreign locale. Ultimately, the firm finds it more economical to assemble or manufacture the product in the country selected for entry. Firms operating in the overseas market may also choose to add new products to the line in order to serve an unfulfilled customer need in a particular market overseas or to optimize the existing marketing capacity of the firm in a given market. For example, a dairy firm selling different categories of liquid milk and milk products overseas in developing countries may discover a dire need for cattle feed and veterinary products for the dairy farmers to augment the procurement of liquid milk. Hence the firm may add such items to its product line. Alternatively, the same company may establish a good distribution network to serve semi-urban and rural milk producers, though such products may not be directly related to the firm's business.

The firm's decision to add a product to the line is influenced by its compatibility with reference to marketing, finances, and environment. *Marketing competitiveness* involves the match between the new addition and the current and potential marketing compatibilities of the parent company and its foreign subsidiary in matters such as product, price, promotion, and distribution. The firm needs to analyze the risks pertaining to financial operations and opportunities related to the addition of any new product line. The common criteria in determining the *financial compatibility* of the proposed addition may be profitability and cash flow implications. Besides, to ensure that the newly added product line would not encounter any legal and political problems, it is necessary for the firm to analyze the factors of *environmental compatibility*, which include concern for the customer, competitive action, and legal or political problems. The inclusion of a product in the line should not pose any problem for either existing or potential customers.

8
Sustainable Marketing

Consumer marketing focuses on integrating sustainability principles into both marketing theory and the practical decision-making of marketing managers. This chapter examines how the complexities of sustainability issues can be integrated into marketing decisions through a systematic step-by-step approach. The steps involve an analysis of socio-environmental priorities to complement conventional consumer research; an integration of social, ethical, and environmental values into marketing strategy development; a new consumer-oriented sustainability marketing-mix to replace outmoded and producer-oriented strategies; and finally an analysis of how marketing can go beyond responding to social change to contribute to a transformation to a more sustainable society. This chapter explores answers to the fundamental problems of disruptive innovation and technologies to which most companies succumb. Accordingly, this chapter addresses theoretical perspectives associated with sustainable marketing concepts in the global marketplace, delineates the key elements and discusses the market chaos-producing factors in pursuing tactical market growth against sustainable market development.

Sustainability in business can be developed by companies by inculcating a responsive organization culture to contribute to society and the environment, and driving expected returns to the business from every investment of the company. Sustainability programs must be subjected to alternative business performance models. Companies could develop sustainability in their business by assessing its strengths, choosing the right market segments, building productive partnerships, and convening other sources of strength. As the principal stakeholders of the company, consumers offer insights that can stimulate ideas to develop socially acceptable and sustainable business strategies. These contribute directly to internationally recognized sustainable development goals, social entrepreneurship, and also to encourage business firms in performing corporate social responsibility (Seelos and Mair, 2005). The major factors that have contributed to the emergence of the entrepreneurial economy include:

- The rapid evolution of knowledge- and technology-promoted high-tech entrepreneurial start-ups.
- Demographic trends accelerating the proliferation of newly developing ventures.
- The venture capital market becoming an effective funding mechanism.
- Industries in developing countries beginning to learn how to manage entrepreneurship.

The context-specific practices of knowledge management followed in financial organizations influence organizational design and its effectiveness. There is a possible mediating role of knowledge management in the relationship between organizational culture, structure, strategy, and organizational effectiveness. An appropriate convergence of these factors has made financial institutions stronger and sustainable during recent economic recessions. It is observed that knowledge management fully mediates the impact of organizational culture on organizational effectiveness, and partially mediates the impact of organizational structure and strategy on organizational effectiveness (Zheng et al., 2010).

Sustainable business development has emerged as an influential concept for firms to develop contextual policies, and it is increasingly felt within various sectors of industries that fundamental transformation is needed from conventional enterprise management patterns to the best business practices led by innovation and technology. Entrepreneurship is increasingly being recognized in the above context as a significant channel for bringing organizational and managerial transformation to the sustainable growth of enterprises. Many high-profile thinkers advocate entrepreneurship leading toward the transformation of products and processes as a solution for growing socioeconomic concerns across the regions in the world. Entrepreneurs have long been recognized as an instrument for exploiting emerging market opportunities. There is need to map the business prospects that lie beyond the pull of existing markets (Hall et al., 2010).

Companies also run as family businesses. Firms desiring continuously generative returns on investment and increasing margin of profit cannot rely on either strategy or entrepreneurship alone, but instead they must successfully engage in strategic entrepreneurship. However, profitable niches evolve, shift, and disappear rapidly in the competitive market economy. Thus, some firms focus solely on entrepreneurial strategy, which might become an effective tool to sustain market competition in the long run. Without an effective strategy to create competitive advantage in pursuing these entrepreneurial opportunities, a firm will soon experience imitation by competitors whose offerings will erode its profits. Strategic entrepreneurship begins with an appropriate mindset among executives and decisions that are then made within this mindset shape the firm-level actions on exploring and exploiting opportunities. The balance of exploration and exploitation results in the key outcome of continuous innovation. One of the most pertinent challenges involved in pursuing strategic entrepreneurship is developing an appropriate mindset within the firm that can balance short- and long-term entrepreneurial objectives. A mindset refers to the cognitive frameworks through which new and existing knowledge is interpreted and used to inform decisions such as those regarding strategy and entrepreneurship (Webb et al., 2010).

Many competitors develop their own products and services system, and marketing culture to protect their brands from market competition. Pharmaceutical companies, for instance, derive competitive advantage while their products are sold under exclusive patents, which provides them lead time in developing sustainable competitive advantage and recovering the cost of research and development incurred by the firm. Despite several protections activated by pharmaceutical firms, competing firms often develop similar products and patent similar formulae, which can lead to competitive threats in short run and maintain industry equilibrium in the long run (Narver et al., 2004). For instance, upon the introduction of Viagra in the market by Pfizer and positioning it as an arousal-triggering medication, there has been an abundance of consumer response to it. The success of the product attracted the attention of many large pharmaceutical firms and prompted them to seek a similar product in the market and duly patent it. Over a period Eli Lilly came out with a product with a similar effect bearing the brand name Cialis, and positioned it as a medication for erectile dysfunction, though it is broadly categorized as an arousal stimulant. All firms operating in the competitive marketplace are driven by Darwinian principles following a lifecycle pattern.

Most companies explore ways to transform the various organizational practices used to enhance business sustainability. Current management expectations and practices are affected by growing societal and economic understanding about sustainability (Hopkins, 2009), through such factors as:

- Increasing productivity at sustainably designed workplaces.
- Developing sustainability-related business choices.
- Building a company's sustainability profile for driving the organization's overall management quality.
- Improving innovation results and linking them with sustainability-related outcomes.
- Developing sustainability efforts within an organization to drive productive collaboration.
- Inculcating transparency and trustworthiness among stakeholders to ensure competitive success.

Companies in emerging economies are largely known as environmental laggards but are being pushed on addressing environmental as well as consumer values. These companies observe that in markets where resource depletion is common, innovation and conservation of energy in products would be the value-added differentiation to gain competitive advantage. For example, LED television screens and computer screens have emerged as value-added differentiations in existing product lines besides offering value for money for consumers. Some enterprises pursue sustainability out of pragmatism while some others do so out of idealism, but all companies will generate sustainable growth rates and profit margins as long as they stay consumer-centric and deliver desired values. Large companies intend to achieve sustainable goals by taking a holistic view and investing in technology-led operating methods that could lead to lower costs and higher yields in business. Companies that have a longstanding reputation in the market also follow bootstrapping by making small adjustments that generate big savings and drive sustainable butterfly effects in the global marketplace. Companies that are successful in developing butterfly effects through small change models buy advanced technologies over the period and extend their sustainability efforts to the operations of their subsidiaries, customers, and suppliers. Collectively, such companies demonstrate that no trade-off is needed between sustainability and financial performance, and advocate strategies leading to sustainability as a powerful path to reinvention to standout in market competition (Haanaes et al., 2013).

Sustainable business growth and decision factors

Result oriented performance control and market volatility are positively related to performance and growth of the firms in the competitive marketplace. The effect of market-oriented strategies on business performance is stronger in firms that encourage outcome-based control measures. Firms that provide information on the background of crash-competitive strategies to employees through internal communications will help in managing a market crisis and ad hoc situations by minimizing the risk. It has been observed that managers who simultaneously exhibit commitment and effort will drive higher levels of performance in business firms. Overall performance in an international context has emerged over the period of globalization to show the significance of managerial competence to sustain competitive advantage. Most managers possess the sense of responsibility and power to grow their companies that vests in them, but growth is a hard task in an increasingly competitive market environment, where investment capital is difficult to come by and firms are reluctant to take risks. Managers also know that process improvement and innovation are the principal channels to business growth. But often firms cannot seem to get innovation right. In the situation of fast-growing market competition, more than ever managers need to guide their decision-making around innovation to help move their companies in the right direction to stimulate growth.

In customer-centric companies, marketing decisions are held singularly accountable for the performance and results of the company, as realizing not only goals but also driving value among competing external stakeholders. Hence, growth-related business decisions are responsible for linking the inside to the outside in considering the following tasks:

- Defining meaningful strategy inside: Such a notion emphasizes that the consumer is the kingpin in business growth, and the company should design and implement competitive strategies by putting the consumer at the core of the process. The company may also lean toward setting up win–win partnerships with other market players such as retailers and suppliers.
- Deciding core strategy: After a thorough analysis of market strengths, current competitive position and structural conditions, business strategies may be developed to grow from its core and also to focus more on low-income consumers and developing markets. Such insights would help in streamlining the strategy focus as to where to compete and where not to compete.
- Balancing present and future strategies: A firm may define realistic growth targets and use a flexible budgeting process with complementary short-term, mid-term, and long-term goals.

Asian markets have shown dynamic growth in international markets by shifting their business strategies and reorienting decision-making processes toward integrating discrete stages into sustainable long-term marketing strategies. Considering the growth in Asian markets, it is important for the managers of global organizations to understand what drives the success of Japanese and South Korean business groups such as *keiretsus* and *chaebols*.

Keiretsu refers to the framework of relationships among Japanese companies organized around a common bank for their mutual benefit after World War II. The *keiretsu* structures cooperated with and received strong support from the Japanese government. In the late 1980s, *keiretsus* contributed 17 percent of the total sales and 18 percent of the total net profits of all Japanese businesses. The *keiretsu* structure helped the companies affiliated to a keiretsu to maintain business relationships with their partners. These long-term relationships between different companies helped each of them to share resources and increase their competitiveness, especially in the export market, which provided the revenues that helped the Japanese economy to grow during the post-World War II period. There are two types of *keiretsu* – vertical and horizontal. Vertical *keiretsu* illustrate the organization and relationships within a company (for example, all factors of production of a certain product are connected), while a horizontal *keiretsu* shows relationships between entities and industries, normally centered on a bank and trading company.

Chaebol is a form of business conglomerate in South Korea. These are powerful global multinationals that own numerous international enterprises, such as Samsung, Hyundai and LG. *Chaebol* were able to grow because of two factors: foreign financial resources and government-backed policies. Access to foreign technology was also critical to the growth of the *chaebol* through the 1980s. These organizations are often compared with Japan's *keiretsu* business groupings. While the *chaebol* are similar to *zaibatsu*, there are major differences between *chaebol* and *keiretsu*:

- *Chaebol* are still largely controlled by their founding families, while *keiretsu* are controlled by groups of professional managers.
- *Chaebol* are centralized in ownership, while *keiretsu* are more decentralized.
- *Chaebol* often formed subsidiaries to produce components for exports, while large Japanese corporations often employed outside contractors.

The purpose of this discussion is twofold – to analyze, compare, and contrast the ownership, structure, government influence, financing, and culture of these two types of business groups, and to analyze how each has dealt with the recent financial crisis in Asia by making dynamic decisions. From this analysis emerge important lessons for strategic international management and decision-making oriented to business growth. *Chaebols* and *keiretsus* both emphasize the idea of harmony, but they have different interpretations of this concept and enact it differently. Both groups have altered their structures in response to the new global financial environment: the *chaebols* have taken the opportunity to solidify and expand their core business units and become more vertically integrated, whereas the *keiretsus* have succeeded only in the limited disposal of some non-performing units (Tu et al., 2002).

DuPont traditionally has grown by diversifying its business and implementing growth-oriented business strategies. The business growth of the company has been proportional to the amount of raw materials and energy used as well as the resulting waste and emissions from operations. Over the years, though, DuPont became aware that cost-effective supplies of non-renewable resources would be scarce and that ecosystems in future might not absorb the waste and emissions of production and consumption. The company believed strongly that the challenge of sustainable growth creativity and scientific knowledge needed to be used effectively, so that strong returns for shareholders would emerge and drive the growth in its businesses, meeting the human needs of societies and reducing the environmental risks on operations and products. In fact, a focus on sustainability helped the company identify new products, markets, partnerships, and intellectual property, and ultimately lead to substantial business growth. Focusing on integrated science, knowledge intensity, and productivity improvement, the strategy was accompanied by a new method to measure progress quantitatively. Du Pont delivers lessons that sustainable growth should be viewed not as a program for stepped-up environmental performance but as a comprehensive way of doing business, and as the one that delivers tremendous economic value and opens up new opportunities. Emerging companies might find that they can generate substantial business value through sustainability while both enhancing the quality of life around the world and protecting the environment (Holliday, 2001). Figure 8.1 exhibits the organizational and environmental factors affecting sustainable decision-making competencies and capabilities in a company.

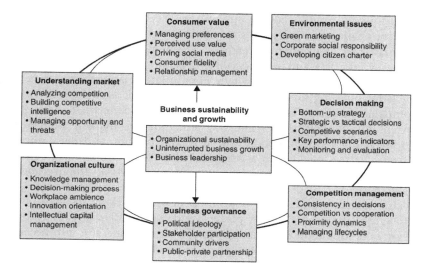

Figure 8.1 Factors influencing sustainable business growth

Sustainability in business and growth depend on various organizational, managerial, environmental, value-centric, and governance-related factors, as illustrated in Figure 8.1. Sustainability in business grows in organizations that have strong business leadership and are based on a cohesive organizational culture. Effective management of knowledge by ways of generating and sharing information, collective decision-making, maintaining an innovation orientation, and utilizing intellectual capital in the right ways will help in developing sustainable organizational culture, which contributes to the overall sustainability of the business of a company. Companies should also understand the market environment appropriately by analyzing the competition, building competitive intelligence, and managing opportunities and threats to sustain in the competitive marketplace. Competitive intelligence is collecting and analyzing the available market information for guiding decisions of the company to remain market-oriented. Competitive intelligence and market-oriented strategies consider the manager's role in creating an environment that generates, disseminates, and responds to live marketplace situations.

In the global business environment today, companies need to develop competencies to stay on both market-oriented and customer-centric platforms to be sustainable amidst growing competition. Consumers play a pivotal role in adding strength to the company against competitive challenges. Companies may deliver enhanced consumer value by managing consumer preferences, augmenting the perceived use value of products and services, driving their opinion through social media, and serving them through appropriate relationship management for building loyalty to the organization. It is also necessary for companies to attend to social and environmental concerns to grow in an environmentally sustainable way alongside the market. Strategies on green marketing, corporate social responsibilities, and developing citizen charters could help a company to serve environmental issues effectively. Organizational sustainability also depends on the decision-making philosophy of companies. Companies that are not autocratic in decision-making and follow bottom-up decision-making strategies by involving employees, market players, and stakeholders possess better chances of long-term sustainability in the marketplace. It is also necessary for companies to establish their rationale in marketing strategic and tactical decisions to drive business growth and competitive advantages. Consistency in decision-making will help companies to manage competitive challenges efficiently. One of the new global business management philosophies demonstrates that in order to be sustainable in global competition companies should lean more toward arranging cooperation with new entrants on various business functions rather than perceiving them as competitors and launching competitive strategies. In order to play safe in market competition, companies should adapt to proximity dynamics, which would guide them to expand business from one market to another by evaluating the potential of the market to influence neighboring markets. The business governance of companies conducted around the prevailing political ideology, stakeholder values, and community drivers would provide opportunities for growing sustainable in the marketplace.

Consumers are the kingpin of business and just by managing the competition without customer-centricity businesses could not succeed. Customer-centric strategies have therefore become synonymous with proactive business strategy and are regarded as a strong business driver for sustainable growth in the competitive marketplace. As innovations and technologies grow continuously, consumers experience a dynamic shift in marketing – from a previous focus on products and companies to a spotlight on consumers. Sociocultural platforms disseminate efficiently the products and services differentiations derived by the growth of technology and provide consumers a much stronger voice in both the business-to-business (B2B) and business-to-consumer (B2C) sectors.

Customer-centricity fits into an organization as part of a knowledge management system toward understanding the customer and as part of the development of strategic competence in a learning organization in building a customer-centric culture. It also incorporates the sustainability of companies as a foundation for corporate strategy development and implementing of customer services strategies (Deshpande, 2014).

In order to sustain itself in the growing competition of globalization, a company needs to reinvent continuously, leaning out of the flattening end of one business performance curve to the rising slope of another. There are some companies that make the leap successfully at an appropriate time because they lag in the reinvention process. Once its current business begins to stall and revenue growth drops significantly, a company has a narrow chance of ever fully recovering. High performers manage their businesses not just along the growth curve of their revenues but also along three much shorter, though equally important, S-curves tracking the basis of competition in their industry, renewing their capabilities, and nurturing a ready supply of talent. Hence, by planting the seeds for new businesses before revenues from existing ones begin to stall, these companies enjoy sustained high performance (Nunes and Breene, 2011).

Globalization and increasing competitiveness in the services industry have driven the service delivery firms to thrust innovativeness in marketing operations to gain sustainable competitive advantage in the marketplace. Service innovation involves innovating intangible products for a more radical service-logic perspective that challenges the conventional attribute-based view of services delivery designs. This has led the firms towards service innovation as a way to deliver high-value services at competitive prices to their target clients. In the context of proliferating innovations among services in the competitive marketplace, the focus of services delivery and measures of effectiveness has shifted toward co-creation of innovative services with customers that generates higher customer satisfaction and loyalty towards the services firms and their brands. Today, firms compete on the basis of services, not on the basis of physical products. Innovative partnering, co-creation, effective resource utilization efforts have improved shareholder value, capability for service innovation and in-turn firm performance. Firms carrying innovative business architecture reap substantial benefits by providing new solutions to the customer interface, new distribution methods and improved application of technology in the service process, new forms of operation with the supply chain or new ways to organize and manage services. To differentiate businesses from competitors, firms look for the competitive advantage in terms of technology, knowledge and networks. Firms should combine their resources and skills into core competencies distinctively well against their competitors (Verma and Rajagopal, 2013).

Holland's Philips Company learned the hard lesson that it cannot afford to customize television sets for each European market separately. This internationally popular Dutch company offers its electrical products according to regional standardization based on power supply categories (in North and Latin America the power distribution for the domestic use is 110 volts, while in England it is 120 volts and in India in ranges further to 220 volts). However, a greater extent of standardization may be more feasible in the case of industrial goods rather than consumer goods. Among consumer goods, non-durables require greater customization than durables, because such consumer goods appeal to tastes, habits, and customs pertaining to host countries. Retail markets are not always homogeneous, and markets in different countries for a given product can be at different stages of development at the same time. This phenomenon may be explained through the product lifecycle concept wherein products go through several lifecycle stages over a period of time, and in each stage different marketing strategies are appropriate. There are four stages, usually identified as introduction, growth, maturity, and decline even for the products distributed in markets overseas.

In developing market environments, firms should arrive at product policies in accordance with the requirements of the local markets. If customer needs tend to be of a basic variety and the alternatives for the customers in the home market are found to be weak, it would be appropriate for a firm to offer standardized products from its existing product line. Under such circumstances, a firm may decide to offer a narrow range of choice in product selection at a local market level. This would help in confirming cost-effective and high-profitability product offerings in developing markets. General Motors uses this strategy. The company has developed a special automobile for use in rural areas in Southeast Asian countries such as the Philippines, where roads are rough and wearying. The chassis can be constructed from steel bars that come in a kit and require only simple tools for assembly. The engine and transmission are then mounted on the frame together with two seats and a canopy. The vehicle comes from global brand leaders in automobiles, and is cheap, runs high off the ground, and is easy to repair. Such a product policy is developed specifically for the requirements of the region keeping in view customer preferences in terms of use value, affordability, and convenience (Badarcco Jr, 1988).

In the retail food sector it has been observed that entry-based advantages for new products are due to the relationship between market demand and consumer perceptions. Perceptual measures of overall preferences and attribute-level beliefs contribute to the success of new products. However, early entrants are perceived by customers to be significantly superior to later entrants (Denstadli et al., 2005). The success of new products is a major concern of companies as this determines their standing in the marketplace. Strategies that can provide innovative combinations of products and services as "high-value integrated solutions" tailored to each consumer's needs, instead of simply "moving downstream" into services are being developed by large and reputable firms in order to sustain in increasingly competitive markets (Davies, 2004). There are many marketing concepts, including market orientation, marketing competencies and resources, and competitive marketing strategies that explain the success of small agro-food companies in international markets. Some research studies indicate that the influential impact of adopting a market orientation, developing competencies in advantage-generating consumer food products, channel and relationship management areas, leveraging strategically relevant managerial, production and brand resources, and deploying appropriate competitive marketing strategies significantly affect the process of new product introductions and variability in their cyclicality (Ibeh et al., 2006). Consumer-oriented innovation is an increasingly important source of new product development and competitive advantage in reference to the speed with which product innovations are introduced to the market.

Competition and corporate sustainability

The customer value concept is utilized to assess product performance and to determine the competitive structure of new products. The analytical approach to new product-market structuring based on customer value may be fitted well within the microeconomic framework. The measure of customer value as product efficiency may be viewed from the customer's perspective toward a ratio of outputs (e.g., perceived use value, resale value, reliability, safety, comfort) that customers obtain from a product relative to inputs (price, running costs) that customers have to deliver in exchange. The efficiency value derived can be understood as the return on the customer's investment. Products offering a maximum customer value relative to all other alternatives in the market are characterized as efficient. Differently efficient products may create value in different ways using different strategies (output–input combinations). Each efficient product can be viewed as a benchmark for a distinct sub-market. Jointly, these products form the efficient frontier, which serves as a reference function for inefficient products (Bauer et al., 2004). Thus, customer value of new products is defined as a relative concept. Market partitioning is achieved endogenously by clustering products in one segment that are benchmarked by peers. This ensures that only products with a similar output–input structure are partitioned into the same sub-market. As a result, a sub-market consists of highly substitutable products. The individual values of the customer may be estimated as base values, and changes in such values are affected by corresponding measures of the specific value drivers. The base value ties to the most important of all complements, which may be determined as customers' need. Estimating value drivers for a new product can be tricky because there is no direct historical data. However, we can assume that the impact from changes in price or availability of complements will be similar to what other markets have experienced.

Knowledge-based competition has magnified the importance of learning alliances as a fast and effective mechanism of capability development. The parameters of success and effective knowledge transfer are used interchangeably to indicate a relatively high level of achievement of intended as well as the unintended benefits to a firm (Daghfous, 2004). However, Kohn argues that cooperation is more effective when the size of the organization is smaller and the degree of interdependence is higher among its units. He strongly phrases his idea on cooperation as a rider over the negativity of competition. In his view competition works just as any other extrinsic motivator does (Kohn, 1986). The movement of public services into direct competition with their private enterprise counterparts is a common feature of public sector policy throughout the developed world. The publicly funded provision of school education has not been exempt from this trend. The creation of a competitive climate is placing public school leaders and teachers under pressure to improve performance in an environment where parents-as-consumers choose the schools to which they send their children (Dempster et al., 2001). However, we may disagree with the fact of involving increasing competitive efforts for augmenting the extent of achievements, and argue that, far from making us more productive, a structure that pits us against one another tends to inhibit our performance. Children simply do not learn better when education is transformed into competitive struggle. Many teachers conclude that competition holds attention better even though they have never worked with cooperative alternatives (Kohn, 1986).

Relationships between competition, athletic skill, and social relationships among children have received considerable attention from social psychologists and have also sparked lively public debate. Most studies of these relationships have concentrated on sports programs involving upper elementary or older boys. Competitive environments heightened the tendency for athletic skill to function as a generalized status element in peer networks. After-school sports programs contributed to the reproduction of athletic skill as a basis of peer status, even for young children (Landers-Potts and Grant, 1997). A passive argument has also emerged on pushing children to competition, though at times the arguments seem to be pro competition. It has also been observed that forcing children to compete is something defended precisely on these following grounds (Kohn, 1986):

- Early experience with competition will lead to more effective competition in later life; competition works just as any other extrinsic motivator does.
- The distinction between trying to do well and trying to beat others is not the only explanation we can come up with competition failure.
- Competition precludes the more effective use of resources that cooperation allows.
- The dynamics of cooperative effort make this arrangement far more efficient, while competitors hardly are predisposed to like and trust each other enough to benefit from it.

Some studies have shown that cooperation is a better tool for growth and achievement as compared to competition. While analyzing the behavioral attributes of children it has been observed that combining cooperation with other behaviors has been a successful strategy in competing for resources. Children quickly learn to cooperate, although viewing times varied significantly between them, suggesting that they were competing against each other even while cooperating. The inequitable outcomes appear to be due to individual differences in the ability to combine helping others with more competitive behaviors (Charlsworth, 1996). It has been evident from the Kohn debate for and against competition that when we compete, we do so out of the primary concern of our own welfare. Working together as a group would not be a strategy for maximizing individual gain but a logical consequence of thinking in terms of what benefits all of us. Sometimes such a tradeoff will occur, but it will not be seen as catastrophic. More to the point, this question will not occur to someone whose worldview is different from our own.

The contemporary concepts of economic advancement are largely based on the concepts of collaboration, cooperation, and competition for developed countries that include the entire range of governmental functions, including sectoral policy reform, economic integration, privatization, public sector enhancement, labor market competitiveness, investment climate enhancement, e-government, soft infrastructures for developing a knowledge economy, macroeconomic management, and effective long-range planning. The weight of the public sector constitutes a serious impediment to more rapid growth for many countries. Importantly, the large expenditure burden it requires does not always translate into an efficient and equitable distribution of services. Such performance is reflected by public sector efficiency and governance in promoting the economic advancement of a country (Rajagopal and Rajagopal, 2007). Competition is a pivot of economic development that allows cooperation to take the lead in some aspects of development. The inadequate functioning of some product markets and lack of competition has undermined the dynamism of the economy, in particular productivity growth. While discussing economic environment Kohn seems to be pro-competition and states that despite the enormous discrepancy between perfect competition and the actual state of our economic system, competition is still the stated ideal. Businesspeople and public officials use the term as an honorific, discussing ways in which they can make their companies and countries *more competitive*, never pausing to ask whether a competitive system really is the best possible arrangement.

The need for economic as well as market competition has been endorsed by many applied studies conducted to evidence the driving factors in economic growth. Market competition is essential for any economy to be efficient. In order to develop competition in a transition economy, it is conventionally thought that privatization should take place first. This wisdom has been challenged by the Chinese reform experience of the last two decades, which modified the incentive structure of state enterprises and created markets and market competition in the absence of large-scale privatization. China's experience, however, raises the question of whether its chosen type of reform is sufficient to promote competition in a market dominated by public firms (Liu et al., 2001). It has been observed in Kohn's readings that he delineates competition as a driver of growth but at the same time argues that it is not a healthy psychological attribute to nurture growth of either an individual or an organization. Kohn argues that the distinction between trying to do well and trying to beat others is not the only explanation we can come up with for the failure of competition. Competition also precludes the more effective use of resources that cooperation allows. The dynamics of cooperative effort make this arrangement far more efficient, while competitors are not predisposed to like and trust each other enough to benefit from it (Kohn, 1986).

However, contemporary economists favor competition as an important tool for economic growth. They discuss whether standard procedures and widely accepted insights of competition policy remain valid when one deals with potentially anti-competitive conduct in innovative industries. The question of appropriateness arises because competition in these industries displays features that are radically different from those encountered in traditional sectors of the economy. Competition is for the market rather than in the market, and the dynamic aspects of competition matter more in knowledge-based industries (Encaoua and Hollander, 2002). In reference to international economic development, competitiveness among nations in exploiting resources has certainly proved to be a major attribute. It is also been noticed that global competitiveness is the key element to survive in business, and this is a task that the business sector along with governments have to confront.

Competition may be characterized as striving together to win the race, not to destroy other competitors from the point of view of the supporters of globalization. The local market competition is targeted toward customers, and competitors strive to win over the customer, temporarily or permanently. However, in the business-to-business process, competition may turn more tactical and strategic in order to outperform rival firms. In this way competition can be seen as regulated struggle. Competitive roles can be radically altered with technological advances or with the right marketing decisions. In growing competitive markets, large and reputed firms are developing strategies to move into the provision of innovative combinations of products and services as "high-value integrated solutions" tailored to each customer's needs than simply "moving downstream" into services. Such firms are developing innovative combinations of service capabilities such as operations, business consultancy, and finance required to provide complete solutions to each customer's needs in order to augment customer value toward innovative or new products. It has been argued that the provision of integrated solutions is attracting firms traditionally based in manufacturing and services to occupy a new base in the value stream centered on systems integration using internal or external sources of product designing, supply and customer-focused promotion. However, competition varies strongly with the values associated with the brand, industry attractiveness, knowledge management, and ethical issues of the organization (Rajagopal and Sanchez, 2005).

The contemporary ideology on competition emphasizes the competitive environment, which contributes to various dimensions of rivalries. It has been observed that a low-end competitor confronting a company by offering much lower prices for a seemingly similar product has been the common fear of each industry leader managing his business among competitors. The vast majority of such low-end companies fall into one of the four broad categories of strippers, predators, reformers, or transformers (Potter, 2004). Global companies often try to promote competition among their salespeople by offering incentives to the best performer, and marketing planners develop strategies to defeat their competitors as a way of ensuring their company's success. Hence it may be stated that in corporate business management practices competition is largely accepted as a desirable and effective way to improve performance (Armstrong, 1988). Certainly one would expect competition to be more effective under some circumstances.

Hence, it is surprising to learn how difficult it was to find empirical evidence about situations in which competition proved superior, especially when one may look at the range of evidence examined by Kohn. However, he emphasizes that competition leads to produce a less positive regard for people of different ethnic backgrounds. Many organizations feel that in growing competition establishing strategic alliances would better check a competitor's penetration than an own brand or a technology-driven company. They recognize that alliances and relationships with other companies of repute are fundamental to outwit, outmaneuver, and outperform competitors by methods of better branding, better service, and tagging global brands for assuring the quality of goods and services. Alliances and relationships thus transform the concept of the competitor.

A competing firm intends to push its aggregate sales in short run by leveraging the marketing-mix components, particularly those related to price and promotion to obtain short-run market advantages. However, such efforts may lead to higher risk and uncertainty to for sustainability, with competitive strategies in a given market causing variability in the market share of the firm. It is necessary for managers to look into the chain of cause and effect while adapting competitive marketing strategies as sometimes this process may induce irreversible results. Alternatively, if a firm chooses to develop its business through cooperation with existing firms in a given market, the firm may derive value-centered goals with a focus on strategic alliances. The alliance firms would have the advantage to share risk, uncertainty, and profit in a given market over a specified time. The managers of a firm may opt for leaning to cooperation as a safe and mutual growth driver to go international or expand their business in the domestic market with a long-run business equilibrium. However, the proper choice of strategy is situation- and firm-specific, and a more effective approach for managers may be to act on the particular circumstances in which they find themselves (Krubasik, 1988).

There has been much work done to determine whether competition is better than cooperation, and some research has compared competition with doing the best for oneself. The studies emerge from diverse fields, but primarily from education, sports, the performing arts, and psychology. However, the results have been consistent, clear-cut, and surprising: competition typically results in less creativity, poorer performance, and reduced satisfaction. It has long been a debatable issue to weigh the role of competition and cooperation in social and economic development, and at times the arguments favoring each tool seem to be appropriate. Certainly one would expect competition to be more effective under some circumstances. Kohn has described varied and interesting research outcomes to support his arguments on cooperation socially, anthropologically, and economically. Competition has been identified by some researchers as an aggressive tool to achieve market power while cooperation is determined as a management instrument for defensive positioning against competition. Though both forms of organizational tools lead to growth and development, cooperation is considered to be more balanced and welfare-oriented (Rajagopal and Rajagopal, 2007). Hence there has been major emphasis on cooperation in international trade among nations who have joined the stream of globalization. Collaboration across the supply chain has become a crucial element in the creation of business value in such a complex manufacturing environment. The collaborative planning, forecasting, and replenishment (CPFR) process is a powerful tool to enhance cooperation between partners from upstream to the vendor/suppliers and downstream to the customer.

In fact both competition and cooperation are used to build organizational and customer value in varied business situations. The optimal portfolio demand for products in competition varies strongly with the values associated with the brand, industry attractiveness, knowledge management, and ethical issues of the organization. The extent of business values determines the relative risk aversion in terms of functional and logistical efficiency between the organization and supplier, while a switching attitude may influence customers if organizational values are not strong and sustainable in the given competitive environment (Rajagopal and Sanchez, 2005). The success of a firm largely emerges from the three different management practices that refer to the use of information on customer value, competition, and costs respectively. It is argued in a study that the success of these practices is contingent on relative product advantage and competitive intensity, which reveals that there are no general "best" or "bad" practices, but that a contingency approach is appropriate. This may be competition, collaboration, and strategic cooperation (Ingenbleek et al., 2003).

Some arguments are contradictory, with expressions such as that competition will lower achievement markedly for individuals who seriously affect the performance of the whole group (class, corporation, society). One way that a competitive culture deals with those who find competition unpleasant is to accuse them of being afraid of losing. It has been argued that across many fields the assumption that competition promotes excellence has become increasingly doubtful. Such competitive pressures ultimately benefit no one, least of all the public. Working against, rather than with, colleagues tends to be more destructive than productive. This corroborates the bulk of evidence on the topic – evidence that requires us to reconsider our assumptions about the usefulness of competition. However, it remains true that competition is an essential constituent of development, as has been evidenced by large number of research studies in reference to animal and human behavior, and social, national and international growth. The more competition there is the more likely are firms to be efficient and prices to be low. Economists have identified several different sorts of competition. Perfect competition is the most competitive market imaginable in which everybody is a price taker.

Sustainable global business strategies

There are many new hybrid business cultures emerging internationally. Of these, regional types are re-emerging through international partnering under the aegis of globalization. The evolution of trade partnerships with companies of other countries is a phenomenon that often reflects deep structural changes in the whole economic system of a country. It usually takes long to unfold since comparative advantages in international business partnering have long-term gains. Globalization has increased access to markets as remote markets have been reduced following political and economic changes world-wide. Structural reforms in developing countries have broadly focused in five major areas comprising international trade, financial markets, labor markets, and the generation and use of public resources. Consequently financial development has improved, especially the depth of financial intermediation, private sector participation in banking, and the size and activity of stockmarkets.

The challenges for firms are growing in managing business in future. The first challenge is to keep pace with the rapid growth and greater involvement of firms in global business activities. Social media has emerged as one of the new and powerful platforms for the firms to stay abreast of consumer dynamics in the global marketplace. In particular, the tremendous growth in interactive marketing activities has necessarily engaged new entrants in global business-to-business activities, to which much greater attention should be paid. The second major challenge for firms is in business process transition, which demands managing supply chain systems through greater coordination of entire distribution channels, alliances, and relational exchanges. Most companies are relying on social network platforms for faster exchange of communication on one hand and implementing sophisticated technology of market communication through radio frequency identification platforms on the other. Finally, another challenge fostering a major change in how firms conduct business and compete is the transition to electronic forms of exchange, particularly with respect to information access, storage, and retrieval (Samiee, 2008).

Market access has also been improved by the growing trade blocs at the regional level. Such accessibility to markets is further reinforced by reducing trade barriers through far-reaching business communication strategies, product and market development programs, and customer relations. This situation has given a boost in determining market opportunities as the narrowing of trade barriers has helped in deregulating certain sectors of trade, such as financial services. However, there may be some exceptions to this common pattern. The global marketplace, equipped with the application of global communications, has become the focus of the global business arena that keeps world markets open and involved in fair competitive practices.

A route to market is a distinct process followed by customers in buying a selected product or service through a market channel. Globalization and growing urban retailing practices have introduced multi-channel retailing in the recent past. It is observed that multiple channel retail strategies enhance the portfolio of service outputs provided to the customer, thus enhancing customer satisfaction and ultimately customer–retailer dyadic loyalty (Wallace et al., 2004). There are diverse communication strategies used by retailing firms to attract shoppers, which include closed circuit television in shopping malls, public television commercials, advertisements in print media, and direct marketing. It is observed that urban shoppers showed confidence and a fashion-conscious shopping orientation, and catalog and Internet shopping orientation, as key predictors of customer satisfaction level with an information search through multi-channels (Lee and Kim, 2008).

In emerging urban shopping centers multi-channel technology marketing provides a sustainable and attractive blend of new and existing retail formats for consumers. It has been observed in a research study that major components in channel choice among consumers include risk reduction, product value, and ease of shopping and experiential attributes (McGoldrick and Collins, 2007). As the use of technology is increasing in retail channels, consumer's preferences significantly vary between shopping in brick-and-mortar stores, or catalogues and e-retailers. The importance of retailers is to span multi-channel operations including brick-and-mortar stores, catalogues, and websites, which has created an opportunity for consumers to choose products from a variety of retailers and retail channels, lessening the probability that others have bought the same collection (Bickle et al., 2006). Retailers located in large shopping malls and busy street retailers are increasingly adopting multi-channel distribution strategies to defy the growth of online technology marketing and targeting potential shoppers through physical and electronic channels as multiple routes to encourage purchasing behavior (Nicolson et al., 2002). Consumers' rising power and retailer's enhanced ability to serve consumers through multi-channel store formats affect shopping perceptions. Needs of consumers are found to be increasingly manifested in a propensity to shop that prompts them to look for alternative channels of shopping in order to strike the best bargain across available routes to shopping. Globalization in the technology marketing sector has evolved an empowered consumer behavior in developed countries, which determines the choice of store format and quality of the business–consumer relationship (Vrontis and Thrassou, 2007).

Multi-channel technology marketing strategy caters to the wide shopping preferences of customers at various price options. This strategy generates more routes to shopping for customers in reference to products and price differentiation. In a multi-channel strategy, retailers offer superior products, typically accompanied by superior service outputs, to be sold at relatively higher prices for the premium market segment while a low-price strategy is followed for mass market retail locations

(Jindal et al., 2007). However, luxury goods are not commonly sold through the catalogue, e-bays or call centers, and differentiated products usually need relatively more intermediary support to be delivered satisfactorily to the end customer. Urban shoppers incur higher search costs when seeking a product across technology marketing channels and gathering information on prices as such shoppers are more guided by the value from money considerations in shopping. It is observed that price-sensitive customers always intend to strike a beneficial deal over the costs they incur during searching for such bargains through various channel options (Rajagopal, 2008).

Some studies have observed that there are striking changes in technology marketing practices with the increase of Internet usage among urban shoppers. The rise of non-store retailing in reference to direct marketing, catalogues, telephone, and the Internet coupled with consumers' increased willingness to buy via these alternative channels, imply that traditional retail stores either in shopping malls or on high streets do not seem to be necessarily a requirement in the present technology marketing environment (Crittenden and Wilson, 2002). Building and retaining a long-term association with customers requires that relationship management applications should be able to accommodate the various channels. Multi-channel customers are the most valuable customers and hence multi-channel integration would improve customer loyalty and retention. Effective customer relationship in multi-channel technology marketing has significant impact on the customer decision-making process and driving buyer behavior in a competitive marketplace (Ganesh, 2004). Thus, a meticulously designed multi-channel set-up enables consumers to examine goods in one channel, buy them in another channel, and finally pick them up at a third channel. Multi-channel technology marketing offers synergies as it results in the enhancement of customer portfolios, revenue augmentation, and growth in market share. Common attributes of a multi-channel retail strategy include highly integrated promotions, product consistency across channels, an integrated information system that shares customer, pricing, and inventory data across multiple channels, an appropriate order processing system that enables customers to purchase products on e-portals or through a catalog used for direct marketing, and lower search cost to buy products from available multi-channel technology marketing opportunities (Bermen and Thelen, 2004).

Multi-channel technology marketing is gaining importance amidst the globalization strategies of multinational firms as customer demands are growing for wider availability of buying options and greater convenience of purchase, including benefits at the point of purchase and post-purchase support. Previous empirical research studies have evidenced that technology marketing firms are adopting an increasingly broad variety of routes to market by ways of introducing a multi-channel technology marketing interface to facilitate urban shoppers. Firms following multi-channel technology marketing usually vary in their level of customer focus, or toward the magnitude of fulfilling customer needs and delivering customer satisfaction. This difference may be due to the attributes of the route to shopping through the channel and its associated services. A firm with strong customer-focus beliefs strives in catering to customer needs and delivering maximum satisfaction by ensuring a pleasant, positive, and value-adding purchase experience, which requires the commitment and support of channel managers in integration with the corporate philosophy of the technology marketing. Market research conducted by Sony Electronics Inc. showed that conventional electronics stores were not selling the products and services of the company successfully to women customers. It was observed that poor selling strategies of franchisee retail store not only lowered the revenue on sales but also developed poor customer relations causing some dissatisfaction among existing and potential customers. Consequently, Sony opened company-owned store outlets with the explicit objective of filling this gap and strengthening customer-focused philosophy of the company.

Markets today not only provide multiple goods and services to customers but also expose their behavior to cross-cultural differences and innovations. Specialization of the production process has also brought such cultural changes by business penetrations in the low production skills regions world-wide. Apparel from Asian countries such as Indonesia, South Korea and all types of consumer goods from China, electronics from Japan and perfumery from France are good examples to explain the specialization and cross-cultural sharing of consumer behavior. Conducting business is a creative enterprise, and doing it out of one's own country is more demanding. The industry structure varies dramatically across countries, and a global enterprise striving against odds requires strong adaptation behavior. In the international business a company needs to best prepare itself to achieve competitive advantage in the marketplace. International partnering in reference to production technology, co-branding, distribution and technology marketing may bring high success to the companies in the home country in increasing market share in the region as well as augmenting customer value for mutual benefit.

As the globalization has driven the market competition, companies are trying to earn their place in the market by outperforming competitors and staying omnipresent in the marketplace. In emerging urban shopping centers the multichannel retailing provides a sustainable and attractive blend of new and existing retail formats for consumers. Consumers enjoy liberally the choice of channels as competitive firms offer low risk, high product value, and ease of shopping. As the use of technology is increasing in retail channels, consumer's preferences significantly vary to shop among brick-and-mortar stores, catalogues, and e-retailers. The importance of retailers is spanning over multi-channel operations including brick-and-mortar stores, catalogues, and websites which has created an opportunity for consumers to choose products from a variety of retailers and retail channels lessening the probability that others have the same collection (Bickle et al., 2006).

As product innovations and new technologies are being frequently introduced into global markets, consumers would like to narrow down their choices and stay with their preferred products and technologies. However, few companies are able to exploit such consumer potential. Most managers churn out a greater variety of goods and services to tailor their finer market segments, but eventually consumers become confused with too many choices on innovations, products, and technologies. A technology company aiming to give customers what they want must use technology to provide individually customized goods and services, and elicit information from each customer about the value for money generated. The process of acquiring those skills will bind producer and consumer together in a learning relationship and collaboration to acquire potential consumers (Pine II et al., 1995).

In emerging innovation and technology product markets, producers and suppliers have to deal with customized demand, passive and active markets, interactions with any number of people, and interconnected relationships. This differs significantly from the marketing of fast-moving consumer products. Retaining loyal customers is important for firms upon investing resources on acquiring potential customers. In order to retain customers, firms should identify core customers and measure key satisfaction indicators. Large consumer goods companies engage market research organizations to rigorously analyze the reasons for consumer defections and find ways to customize their core market (Billington, 1995). Customer retention leads to higher profitability and to keeping loyal consumers, and technology marketing firms can apply adaptation and bonding strategies as two potentially useful approaches.

Most firms use e-mail newsletters and the reward-points card system as common strategies to acquire potential and retain existing consumers. Marketing is becoming more complex in the global marketplace, today with growing competition and increasing volume of new products and technology penetration. However, it is still possible to attract new customers and retain existing ones by employing new scientific technologies and research strategies in advertising and communication.

Marketing myopia

Every company grows in the competitive marketplace by virtue of the apparent superiority of its products and brand equity. However, most companies run tactical campaigns to gain competitive advantage in the short run and drive faster business growth. In the process companies usually emphasize selling to earn revenue as quickly as possible. However, selling-oriented companies largely compromise with long-term growth and sustainability because selling focuses on the needs of the company, whereas marketing concentrates on the needs of the buyer. Companies need to ensure continued growth and must define their goals broadly to take advantage of market opportunities. They must ascertain and deliver value to customers by managing their needs and desires for long-term sustainability. Companies must learn to develop strategic goals for sustainable business growth and market leadership (Levitt, 2004).

Sustainability in business is a long-term result for competing companies. However, most companies look for quick growth in business; thus they neglect market opportunities offering long-term growth. For example, investing in emerging markets to build sustainable long-term gains in the market is a credible strategy, but some companies do not carry the long-term advantage and sustainability arguments as far as this. They prepare for short-term results in the mistaken belief that such results are a trade-off for future profitability and drive the business through myopic objectives and tactical moves in the market. However, some management experts argue that myopic tactics for short-term advantage is a positive indicator that a company's strategy or practices may not measure up over the long run and establish temporary market leadership. Drawing on the examples of multinationals already competing in China, it may be observed that the success of companies in taking the competitive lead is more a factor of managerial capability, critical mass scale, and product portfolio than it is for length-of-stay, long-term strategies or myopic approaches. Conventionally it is presumed that companies with first mover advantages become market leaders. However, contemporary business practices suggest that to become market leader, companies need not be necessarily first movers but should be able to outperform competitors in the short run. For instance, Coca-Cola planned carefully for success and executed a series of smart short-term moves to make it happen. Companies that would like to gain high market share must attempt to make small changes in the marketing-mix and drive product differentiation for larger benefits. This strategy refers to the butterfly effect and may secure gains for the company from local and global scale. Thus, companies planning to enter the global marketplace and sustain in the long run should make the right moves in keeping a balance between long-term and myopic strategies. Turning myopic is not a mistake for companies aiming to be market leader or a market challenger as this would not seal a company's fate, but organizations need to broaden their rationale and use their new knowledge to build winning strategies. Companies that fail to adapt to the fast-paced market will never enjoy long-term success in the dynamic global marketplace (Yan, 1998).

Section III
Unveiling Future Effects

9
Social Psychology of Consumers

Random changes in the products and services of firms, competitive strategies of firms in the marketplace, and factors driving the cultural characteristics of consumers around the world are arguably the most critical issues in determining the success of modern business. This chapter provides an in-depth psychological analysis of social consumerism that draws from a wide range of theoretical and analytical approaches. Distant influences, such as advertising, consumption, materialism, and socioeconomic systems that affect the personal, social, and ecological well-being of consumers are categorically discussed in this chapter. Powerful forces on market changes driven by innovations, technology growth, communications, marketing and advertising, and psychographics are interacting to dissolve the boundaries across markets and cultures, and are accelerating the emergence of a homogeneous global consumer culture. This chapter addresses the concerns on effectiveness perspectives of linear and radical changes in the market in reference to cultural shifts, preparing customers for innovation and technology changes, changing psychographic paradigms, and demographic congregation that drive the market.

Sociocultural drivers

Culture consists of patterns, explicit and implicit of and for behavior, acquired and transmitted by symbols, constituting the distinctive achievement of human groups, including their embodiment in artifacts; the essential core of culture consists of traditional (historically derived and selected) ideas and especially their attached values; culture systems may, on one hand, be considered as products of action, on the other, as conditioning elements in future action (Heidrich, 2002). Culture has many complex dimensions to define in simple terms. It seems that each anthropologist has defined culture from his own perspective. However, certain anthropological thinkers had agreed-on fundamentals, as may be seen from the description by Hoebel (1969): "Culture is the integrated sum total of learned behavioral traits that are shared by members of a society." Culture may be described in reference to three basic concepts. Firstly, culture is a total pattern of behavior that is consistent and compatible in its components. It is not a collection of random behaviors, but behaviors that are related and integrated. Secondly, it is a learned behavior and not biologically transmitted. It depends on environment, not heredity. It can be called the man-made part of our environment. Finally, culture may be manifested in behavior that is shared by a group of people, a society. It can be considered as the distinctive way of life of a people. Accordingly a marketing manager of an international firm is supposed to be familiar with the reference groups, social class, consumption systems, family structure and decision-making, adoption and diffusion behavior, market segmentation, and consumer behavior in order to understand the cultural environment in the host country. In view of the varying definitions that exist on cultural concepts, the following broad areas of culture that are closely associated with international business may be addressed:

- technology and material culture;
- language;
- aesthetics;
- education;
- religion;
- perceptions and attitudes;
- Social Values and Life Style (VALS)
- social organization;
- political life.

Aesthetics may be described as the set of creative ideas embedded in culture concerning the sensory appeals of people to beauty, arts, and taste. Since actions or behavior can be said to have beauty beyond sensory appeal, aesthetics and ethics often overlap to the degree that this impression is embodied in a moral or ethical code. A value system, which is the prioritization of the values held by an individual or group in a society, forms the base of a moral code. Such dimensions are reflected in consumer behavior. In conservative societies in Asia, including Japan or India, any communication or art that exposes women is not socially accepted, despite the aesthetic standpoint of some critics.

In some cultures, relationships between moral and legal codes are often one and the same. Moral codes help drive personal conduct. Aesthetics include the art, drama, music, folk culture, and architecture prevalent in a society, and these aspects of a society convey its concept of beauty and modes of expression. In different societies colors have different significance, such that. in Western societies, wedding gowns are usually white, but in Asia, white symbolizes peace or sorrow. The aesthetic values of a society show in the design, styles, colors, expressions, symbols, movements, emotions, and postures valued and preferred in a particular culture. These attributes have an impact on the design and promotion of different products. In many situations the symbolic expressions of communication have greater appeal than the actual words, and people respond accordingly. Therefore, an international businessperson must understand nonverbal cultural differences to avoid communicating the wrong message.

Mary Kay Inc. operates on the Go-Give philosophy (Weston, 1999), namely, that all you send into the lives of others comes back into your own. All consultants and sales directors share experience and guidance with new team members until each reaches her potential. When illness or emergency keeps someone from a scheduled skincare class, it is not unusual to have some help from others. "In business for yourself but not alone," is a Mary Kay Ash philosophy that guides the independent sales force. Mary Kay skincare is taught, not sold. Rather than approach customers with "dollar signs in their eyes," consultants operate with the goal of helping women achieve a positive self-image and of leaving the customer feeling better about her. Mary Kay Ash said, "Ours is a business where selling results from a truly one-on-one personal relationship." According to Mary Kay, a career is not considered an end in itself, but a means to an end – to personal fulfillment, family comfort and harmony; to a balanced life; to self-expression. Hence the business philosophy of Mary Kay Inc. has been centered on the religion that reveals "God is first, family second and third is the career."

Consumer behavior is also significantly driven by human activity, and business, conducted under the guidelines of one of the major religions, will work better because the essence of business is trust, and religion teaches trust. Trust means an honest day's work for an honest day's pay, tough but fair dealing, and transparency without hidden agendas, and above all, trust means truth that is an outgrowth of religious sentiments in a society or an individual. The relationship between business and religion truly poses a self-challenge. There is a current sense that we must improve the fundamental actions of business in a global setting.

Besides, cultural aspects largely affect the products that people buy, the attributes they value, and the referrals that govern the buying decisions of consumers. It is observed that a person's perspectives or resources, problems, and opportunities are generated and conditioned by cultural values to a considerable extent. Culture creates the system of communication among consumers regarding acceptance and rejection of products and services, say in regard to food. Italian cultural influence in global markets plays an important role for the creation or expansion of markets for Italian products. One example is a collaboration project between the Italian and Japanese governments called the "Italian Year in Japan, 2001". Utilizing this kind of event, Italy succeeded in generating a sophisticated brand image in the Japanese market. An important part of this event is the generation of a network system through the Internet. Through this network, information about Italian technological products like automobiles and cultural products like paintings is distributed to members of the network (Yagi, 2003).

Consumer behavior is also influenced by the social status delivered by brands. A consumer may feel his self-esteem lies in buying an expensive foreign brand against similar brands available in the domestic market as it offers the social status of owning the brand. However, in conditions of globalization, store brands make sense in building consumer behavior more than manufacturer brands. Since the value of any imported goods from a Western country is perceived as much higher than that of domestic products in developing countries, the price of such products is often inflated in developing countries. It may happen that an Indian tourist buys an item of casual wear from Marks & Spencer during his trip to England, and later upon close examination finds that this item is labeled as "Made in India." In such circumstances the perceived value associated with the product as guided by cultural issues determines an acceptable price and not the actual value of the product. On the other hand, "Made in England" may be regarded by French consumers as promising more luxurious and more inventive products than "Made in the USA." Then, "Made in Germany" products may have greater perceived value for American than French consumers (Rajagopal, 2007b). Thus, channels of distribution largely function under the influence of local culture and may need to be adjusted to local sociocultural conditions.

Mary Kay Cosmetics uses door-to-door and other direct-selling methods in the US with great success. Americans appreciate the opportunity to make buying decisions in the privacy of their homes or workplaces. Such arrangements, however, did not work abroad. Mexican women, for example, considered calls by beauty consultants of Mary Kay Cosmetics as an intrusion on their privacy and safety, and the representatives felt uncomfortable as well. In another example, The Body Shop, Canada has developed fair trade relationships with local communities since the late 1980s. The company identifies this as community trade. These small communities, often in remote areas, do not usually have the chance to sell their products to global companies such as The Body Shop. The company buys accessories and natural ingredients such as cocoa beans, sesame oil and shea butter from them at a fair price. As a result, the community trade suppliers work together to meet their communities' goals and have more control over their futures.

In Thailand the Warner-Lambert Company used its US ad for Listerine, showing a boy and a girl being affectionate with each other. This type of appeal was ineffective since the boy–girl relationship shown was ultra-modern and hence ran counter to the cultural norms of Thailand's conservative society. A slight modification – two girls talking about Listerine – had a positive effect on sales. Localization of international advertising campaigns consists of adapting the company's communication to the specificities of the local environment of the hosting countries targeted by the campaign. The localization of communication should be aware of the sociocultural norms of the host country, which includes local particularities stemming from religion, customs, social and commercial habits, rules of conduct and ethical norms.

The one component of advertising that has grown over the past twenty years along with women's income and purchasing power is the percentage of advertisements objectifying men. A global brand may possess a stronghold in its home market, strength across other geographies, address similar needs worldwide, and show consistent positioning where consumers value the cultural issues and identify the corporate band within its purview. This statement can be discussed further, linking the product with universal human emotions and needs, being consistent over time and refreshing its appeal through cultural events like sports and using powerful symbols or icons. Marlboro has departed from its cowboy campaign to market its cigarettes in many countries and switched to a Formula-1 driver, which is thought to embody the same theme of the independent hero as cowboy, yet be more suitable in certain countries for a variety of cultural factors.

Ethnographic factors

Ethnography has often been portrayed as a lifestyle demonstration model analyzing people's homes to observe consumers' real-life situations. However, this description might not justify the role of ethnography in business and marketplace management. In the corporate world ethnography's increasingly important role has been observed in the twenty-first century in formulating business strategy. In the active social media-driven world ethnography focuses on what customers do and feel, and how they express themselves among peers, in the market, and with companies has become a powerful tool for gaining insights into the competitive market. Ethnographic behavior describes how consumers confront and overcome the hurdles they encounter in meeting their responsibilities and fulfilling their hopes in a globalized consumer culture (Cayala et al., 2014). Consistent with the idea that ethnography helps organizations deal more effectively with market complexities, the executives these authors interviewed often talked about ethnography as having helped them sort out puzzling data. While these discussions call into dispute the perception that ethnography is merely an exploratory technique, they also underline the point that ethnographic stories often provide an insight into consumer behavior that is hard to come by in other ways.

It has been observed that the largest share of commercials among the Hispanic population in the US tend to be of Spanish-language advertising programs. Since Spanish-dominant consumers tend to be relatively recent immigrants, Hispanic consumers strongly rely on advertising to guide their purchase decisions. These consumers tend to see Spanish-language advertising as information that they can use to make sense of the ample and confusing array of products they are faced with. Since few brands have decided to concentrate on the Spanish-language market, those that show an interest reap the rewards. But there is more than just advertising. Tradition from Latin American countries seems to contribute to brand preferences. After immigration to the US, many Hispanic consumers remain loyal to those brands they were accustomed to in their countries of origin. Colgate is a good example. Colgate is the traditional toothpaste par excellence in many Latin American countries. Colgate red or "*Colgate rojo*," aided by its Spanish-language advertising emphasis in the US, maintains and reinforces the tradition it established a long time ago (Rajagopal, 2007a).

Market integration allows consumers to buy goods from all over the world in their local shops and supermarkets. While local businesses must compete with these foreign goods on their home turf, they also have new opportunities to develop their export markets by selling in a multitude of other countries. Cultural goods and services are no exception to these new patterns of production, consumption, and trade. Cultural markets are increasingly going global, as may be observed by the trends in cultural goods trade in the post-1980 period across countries in different regions. As consumption of cultural goods and services spreads all over the world, production itself tends to concentrate. This results in an oligopolistic market with a highly asymmetric structure. The effects of this market profile are as yet unknown. While we are aware that a large share of the cultural products circulating in most countries are produced elsewhere, we know very little about the impact of this global cultural market on citizens, audiences, businesses, and governments.

The past few years have seen the emergence of a powerful interest in culture resulting from a combination of diverse phenomena such as globalization, regional integration processes, and cultures claiming their right to express themselves – all this in a context where cultural industries are progressively taking over traditional forms of creation and dissemination, and bringing about changes in cultural practices. The issue of "culture and trade" has now acquired prime strategic significance. Cultural goods and services convey and construct cultural values, produce and reproduce cultural identity, and contribute to social cohesion; at the same time they constitute a key free factor of production in the new knowledge economy. Culture is an essential dimension of business development. Business solutions should be tailored to locally relevant traditions and institutions, and these activities should make use of local expertise and knowledge. An international company entering the host country should ensure that people, their cultures, and society, and their organizations and institutions, are taken into account in formulating business goals and operational strategies. Such development coordination with local culture improves the lives of people, especially the poor, and builds social capital for a company to sustain itself long in the host country.

Culture contributes to core business development objectives by helping:

- Provide new opportunities for local communities to share skills and generate incomes from their own cultural knowledge.
- Catalyze local-level development through communities using their diverse social, cultural, and economic resources.
- Conserve and generate revenues from existing assets, that is, reviving city centers, conserving natural resources, and generating sustainable tourism revenues.

- Strengthen social capital by offering marginalized groups a basis to pursue activities that enhance their self-respect and efficacy, and to strengthen respect for diversity and social inclusion.
- Diversify strategies of human development and capacity-building for knowledge-based dynamic societies, e.g., through support to local publishing, library, and museum services.

Depending on the context, cultural industries may also be referred to as "creative industries," "sunrise industries," or "future-oriented industries" in economic jargon or "content industries" in technological jargon. The notion of cultural industries generally includes printing, publishing and multimedia, audio-visual, phonographic and cinemato-graphic productions, as well as crafts and design. For some countries, this concept also embraces architecture, visual and performing arts, sports, manufacturing of musical instruments, advertising, and cultural tourism. Cultural industries add value to contents and generate values for individuals and societies. They are knowledge- and labor-intensive, create employment and wealth, nurture creativity – the "raw material" they are made from –, and foster innovation in production and com-mercialization processes. At the same time, cultural industries are cen-tral in promoting and maintaining cultural diversity, and in ensuring democratic access to culture. This twofold nature – both cultural and economic – builds up a distinctive profile for cultural industries.

Social institutions play a significant role in nurturing the cultural her-itage, which is reflected in individual behavior. Such institutions include family, education, and political structures, while the media affects the ways in which people relate to one another, organize their activities to live in harmony with one another, teach acceptable behavior to suc-ceeding generations, and govern themselves. Status of gender in society, the family, social classes, group behavior, age groups, and how socie-ties define decency and civility are interpreted differently within every culture. Social institutions are a system of regulatory norms and rules of governing actions in pursuit of immediate ends in terms of their conformity with the ultimate common value system of a community. They constitute underlying norms and values making up the common value system of a society. Institutions are intimately related to and derived from the value attitudes common to members of a community. This establishes institutions as primarily moral phenomena, which leads to enforce individual decisions on all human needs including eco-nomic and business-related issues. The primary means for enforcement of norms is moral authority, whereby an individual obeys the norm because that individual believes that the norm is good for its own sake.

Social interactions establish the roles that people play in a society and their authority/responsibility patterns. These roles and patterns are supported by society's institutional framework, which includes, for example, education and marriage. Consider the traditional marriage of an Indian woman, which is customarily arranged by the parents. The social role assigned to women is to abide by the norms of their society and culture and yield to social pressures. Social roles are extensively established by culture. For example, a woman can be a wife, a mother, a community leader, and/or an employee. However, what role is preferred in different situations is culture-bound. Most Swiss women consider household work as their primary role, which leads to many of them resenting modern gadgets and machines. The recent social concerns on organic products has prompted a new thought process on green consumerism. It has been observed that women consumers are in the forefront of green purchasing and contribute a considerable share in consumption of green products. They do most of the shopping and although it appears attractive, they may naturally exhibit a maternal consideration for the health and welfare of the next generation. In conventional marketing, demographics are often a key determinant of intent to buy specific products. But in green marketing, what seem to determine willingness to purchase environmentally conscious products more than demographics or even levels of concern for a specific environmental issue is consumers' feelings of being able to act on these issues, or empowerment (Roberts, 1996).

It is necessary for a marketer to remember that self-referencing can be misleading while interpreting various cultural manifestations in different countries. A Self-reference Criterion (SRC) may be described as a process by which judgments on others are formed. It involves judging others' behavior against antecedents and experiences that are weighed on a preconceived platform of thinking. Before framing perceptions and conclusions, it would be wise to check with people who are familiar with the culture of the host country, and perhaps debate issues of concern on a knowledgeable base. However, the bottom line is that an international marketer should learn about a culture bypassing a blind trust on first impressions or preconceptions, and play down self-referencing in favor of more objective information. Cultural adaptation refers to the making of business decisions appropriate to the cultural traits of a society. In other words, decision-makers must ensure that native customs and conditions, and taboos, will offer no constraint to implementation of the marketing plan.

The high versus low context distinction and silent languages describing non-verbal communication elements provide useful concepts by which to think about various cultures. Hofstede's study of IBM employees around the globe conducted in 1980 was followed by his much more systematic assessment of cultures across countries. Although there have been significant cultural shifts since the study was done, cultures have changed less, and judging from recent events in Eastern Europe and Russia, ethnicity and cultural roots are stronger than ever. According to Hofstede's paradigm of cultural influences, countries can be classified along four basic cultural dimensions (Hofstede, 1993). The first dimension is individualism versus collectivism. In a collective society, the identity and worth of the individual is rooted in the social system, less in individual achievement. The second dimension is high versus low power distance, in which high power distance societies tend to be less egalitarian, while democratic countries exhibit low power distance. The third dimension is masculine versus feminine, which captures the degree to which a culture is dominated by assertive males rather than nurturing females and their corresponding values. The final dimension describes weak versus strong risk avoidance rates among various demographic segments in the culture.

General culture defines a set of acceptable and unacceptable behaviors within social norms. Individuals should learn to act according to these behavioral norms while managers need to learn how to do business. These are the processes of enculturation and socialization. They determine how individuals behave as consumers in the marketplace, how demanding they are, how they voice complaints, how managerial approaches are addressed to subordinates and peers, and so forth. In due course of time individuals become skilled in exhibiting acceptable behaviors and identifying unacceptable behaviors to be less risk averse. An American marketer will be good at briefly presenting his or her point of view, while a Japanese counterpart will be good at listening. But going beyond one's accustomed norms is hard to do. Acceptable behavior in a business firm is usually a reflection of acceptable behavior in society, especially if the company is large. In multinational companies employees cannot know each other personally and thus have to rely on more arms'-length relationships based on the general culture that may be stated as corporate culture. Regional business houses that are relatively smaller in size than multinational companies may be less orthodox, with an organizational culture that is cultivated, unique, and different from larger societies. Relationship-building is a prerequisite for an international firm to achieve success in business. The manager of an international firm should ask the local sales representative of his company how many new relationships were built and if the employee had participated in the local culture before evaluating his performance. The manager may then ask his local colleagues to give their impression of how well the expatriate is working out in their country.

An urban and ethnic marketing strategy requires an understanding of in-culture nuances and lifestyle of the marketing segment that a business is trying to reach. While urban marketing is employed to reach Hispanic, Latino, Asian American, and African American markets because of demographic clustering of these subcultures in metropolitan areas, it is also used to reach certain niche markets best found in urban environments. Urban and ethnic marketing strategies integrate consumer marketing solutions, including Internet and technology aspects, within the cultural environment of a host country. An international marketer should evaluate the psychographic and demographic profiles that indicate the target market of urban and ethnic groups. The firm may choose to provide marketing communications to the target segments close to their lifestyle.

Social psychology theories and butterfly effect management

One of the major challenges for innovation-led companies is to drive consumers to accept innovative or competitive-differentiation products and services. The differentiated products launched by companies move the social process while available in the marketplace. The social psychology of consumers is strongly influenced by the attributes of differentiated products, with specific reference to need for change, value for differentiation, extent of adaptability, perceived use value, and associated social values with the innovative products or competitive differentiation, as exhibited in Figure 9.1.

It may be observed from the figure that there are several factors that induce the socio-cognitive determinants toward consumers' decision-making on adapting product differentiations for competitive advantage. Attribution is one of the social psychology theories that explains how consumers attempt to understand the behavior of others by attributing feelings, beliefs, and intentions to them. Companies introducing new products thus focus on society to react to the differentiation and competitive advantages of new products to attract customers and roll out products. Consumers sometimes develop cognitive dissonance on own decisions but socio-cognitive motivation prompts them to adapt to the new products that exhibit competitive differentiation. As peer reviews on innovative products are disseminated in society, consumers can be

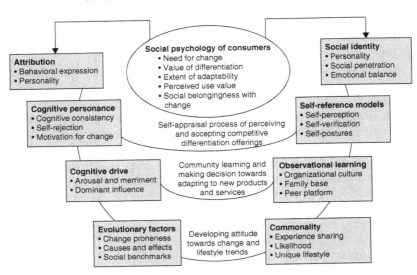

Figure 9.1   Linking consumer adaptability of competitive differentiation within social psychology theories

driven by arousal and merriment, and lean toward adapting differentiated products for gaining competitive advantages despite experiencing some negatives. Consumers also get involved in adapting new products out of "me too" feeling. The notion of commonality and sense of likelihood motivates consumers to go for differentiated products and share their experience. The change proneness attitude is also developed through a social evolutionary process and sets benchmarks for the adaptation and use of new products. Family, peers, and organizational cultures also motivate consumers in building positive intentions toward buying and using differentiated products. However, self-reference models and social identity factors also govern consumers' social psychodynamics toward new and competitively differentiated products. This process carries small changes into the wider social outreach, driving the butterfly effect efficiently.

Consumer culture

Consumer culture is an integrated pattern of behavior that is consistent and compatible in its components. It is not a collection of random behaviors of consumers, but rather behaviors that are related and integrated by firms in a marketplace. It is a learned behavior and not biologically transmitted. It depends on market environment and referrals. Consumer behavior is driven by the motivations of firms and consumer perceptions. Accordingly, a marketing manager of an international firm is supposed to be familiar with the reference groups, social class, consumption systems, family structure, and decision-making, adoption and diffusion, market segmentation, and consumer behavior in order to understand the consumer culture in a marketplace (Hoebel, 1969). Global firms make corporate culture visible to consumers and elevate it to priority status, often by highlighting desired values and behaviors that favor consumers. In 1994, the consumer products company Alberto-Culver North America developed an executive team and created the role of growth development leader, which helped sales grow by 83 percent and developed a positive consumer culture in the marketplace to ensure business growth in future (Lavin, 2001).

Many multinational firms that have been identified as high performers intend to perceive business insights as central to their culture, working approach, and strategy, and to believe that pro-brand consumer culture should be built to lead the market. However, there exists the challenge for consumer goods companies of building a pro-brand consumer culture and determining the impact of shopper-marketing efforts. Firms find that it is extremely challenging to forecast and track the impact of these efforts on performance indicators such as brand profitability and brand equity. Thus, companies with high-performing brand portfolios partner with retailers in key discount, grocery, and drug channels and to conduct experiments such as pilots or in-store simulations. Multinational firms develop their manufacturing and retailing strategies according to the pace of change in consumer tastes and technology, along with the nature of competition in the product categories where the company operates (Blair et al., 2007).

As consumption of cultural goods and services spreads all over the world, production itself tends to concentrate. This results in an oligopolistic market with a highly asymmetric structure. The effects of this market profile are as yet unknown; while we are aware that a large share of the cultural products circulating in most countries are produced elsewhere, we know very little about the impact of this global cultural market on citizens, audiences, businesses, and governments. The past few years have seen the emergence of a powerful interest in culture resulting from a combination of diverse phenomena such as globalization, regional integration processes, and cultures claiming their right to express themselves – all this in a context where cultural industries are progressively taking over traditional forms of creation and dissemination and bringing about changes in cultural practices. The issue of "culture and trade" has now acquired prime strategic significance. Cultural goods and services convey and construct cultural values, produce and reproduce cultural identity, and contribute to social cohesion; at the same time they constitute a key free factor of production in the new knowledge economy. Culture is an essential dimension of business development. Business solutions should be tailored to locally relevant traditions and institutions, and these activities should make use of local expertise and knowledge. An international company entering a host country should ensure that people, their cultures and society, and their organizations and institutions are taken into account in formulating business goals and operational strategies. Such development coordination with local culture improves the lives of people, especially the poor, and builds social capital for a company to sustain long in the host country (Rajagopal, 2007a).

Long before children enter school, most have already been socialized into play, social values, behaviors, attitudes, and linguistic repertoires shaped by videogames, television programs, and spin-off toys that constitute childhood experience. Childhood culture is an imaginary universe that connects TV programs to movies, videogames, toys, T-shirts, shoes, games, crayons, coloring books, bed linens and towels, pencil cases, lunch boxes, and even wallpaper. Beyond the merchandise transformations of movie or TV program characters, media icons extend to fast food chain or cereal box-top contests and special give-away deals, shopping mall entertainments featuring the recent cartoons Lion King, Ice Age or Spirit from Walt Disney productions, and contests such as a prize trip to Disney Land to meet the characters, create a business platform for the target group though cultural penetration. TV shapes the child's early age into narrative and consumption styles by being located in the center of family life, and by cross-referencing to other narrative forms such as movies, stories, comic books, videogames, music videos (often movie soundtracks), of which toys and teens' popular culture are an integral extension. In that regard TV serves as a kind of clearing house for both the verbal communication and artifacts of consumption. For children, the jump from narrative to commodities from Transformer cartoons to Transformer toys or from Disney cartoons to McDonald's giveaways of characters forms the background cultural tapestry that childhood is experiencing in Western countries inculcating consumption behavior. Besides, parents also show interest in taking their children to a fast-food corner and purchasing the latest collectibles, and buy the TV-advertised cereal or peanut butter that children insist on to avoid embarrassing conflicts in the supermarket. These everyday consumer and social practices constitute social and material relations between parents and children (Livingstone and Helsper, 2004).

Material culture includes the tools and artifacts – the material or physical things – in a society, excluding the physical things found in nature unless they undergo some technological procedure. For example, a tree per se is not part of a culture, but the Christmas tree is, and so is an orchard. Material culture affects the level of demand, the quality and types of products demanded, and their functional features, as well as the means of production of these goods and their distribution. Culture directly influences consumers in reference to what they understand, analyze, and adapt. Material culture exhibits the close relationship between consumers and goods as consumers redefine material objects to make them express themselves and their cultures. Such consumer behavior is revealed not only in personal tastes and attributes, but also moral principles and social ideals (Daniel, 1997).

Language is an important cultural tool for conducting international business in host countries effectively. Language has a deep-rooted sentiment in people. It is not just the spoken word, but also a symbolic communication of time, space, things, friendship, and agreements. The language people speak is part of the culture in which they were raised. Therefore, the language used in all marketing communications, including advertising, public relations, and general communications, should reflect the unique cultural expressions and values of the target locale. Nonverbal communication occurs through gestures, expressions, and other body movements. The language chosen for business should be regarded to offer the most appropriate sense of communication and should not be literally translated into the other language. Increasingly, managers of global firms and consumers all over the world speak a common language, and people everywhere can see what choices and preferences are in other countries. Companies need to learn to become insiders in the marketplace and develop an equidistant view of all customers (Kenichi, 1989).

Social interactions establish the roles that people play in a society and their authority/responsibility patterns. These roles and patterns are supported by society's institutional framework, which includes, for example, education and marriage. The recent concern of society on organic products has prompted a new thought process on green consumerism. Research into recent buyers of green products and empirical evidence suggests that the consumers most receptive to environmentally oriented marketing appeals are educated women aged 30–44 with household income of US$30,000 and above in the US. It has been observed that women consumers are in the forefront of green purchasing and contribute a considerable share of consumption of green products. Likewise, the adverse environmental impacts of plastic bags, including production energy costs, limited lifespan, increasing landfill content, and inability to biodegrade have driven throwaway consumer culture. Accordingly, the social and environmental awareness of the use of plastic bags is considered as one of the drivers in changing consumer behavior in line with sustainable development principles (Elaine et al., 2009).

Hispanic consumers spend heavily on the basics, including packaged goods and wireless phone services. Companies are funneling much of their Hispanic marketing budgets into Spanish-language TV. It is critical for retailers and marketers to understand the wide range of factors driving Hispanic consumers' shopping behavior. Retailing firms explore shopping behavior of Hispanic consumers in reference to their preferred buying place, buying practices, and the way retailers and marketers intend to adapt product offerings and promotions to satisfy this rapidly growing and diverse consumer segment. For Hispanic consumers, shopping is considered to be a family affair, an outing for all ages from grandparents to children. Retailers looking to attract the attention of Hispanic consumers create a family-friendly atmosphere, and providing rest areas for seniors in order to augment the shopping response. Retailing firms in the US train salespeople in managing customer relationships specifically with their Hispanic consumers. While respect is a fundamental of customer relations across the board, there is a certain reverence to be extended to elders within Hispanic culture and is observed by the sales staff in dealings with older shoppers.[1]

Human personality traits are determined by multi-dimensional factors like the individual's behavior, appearance, attitude and beliefs, and demographic characteristics. Based on trait theory, researchers have concluded that there are five stable personality dimensions, also called the "Big Five" human personality dimensions (Batra et al., 1993). The Big Five factors are extraversion, agreeableness, conscientiousness, neuroticism, and openness to experience. The relationship between point of sales promotions and retail buying decisions is largely governed by psychographic variables that can be measured broadly by the closeness and farness of the brand personality and the customer. The type

---

[1] Hispanic Business.com, Nielsen Reveals Hispanic Consumer Shopping Behavior Insights, September 24, 2007, http://www.hispanicbusiness.com/news/2007/9/24/nielsen_reveals_hispanic_consumer_shopping_behavior.htm

of relationship that customers possess with point of sales promotions offered by retail stores is largely based on loyalty levels (Rajagopal, 2007b). The new-generation marketing approaches include customer-focused, market-driven, outside-in, one-to-one, data-driven marketing, relationship and integrated styles, with integrated communications that emphasize two-way communication through better listening to customers and the idea that communication before, during, and after transactions can build or destroy important brand relationships. It has been observed that Hispanic consumers are sensitive to price while making buying decisions, and have a higher tendency to buy compulsively, are more prone to promotions, and are more likely to use online sales promotions (Vicdan et al., 2007).

Hispanic consumers are found to be attached firmly to their ethnic culture and tend to shop at the same store, especially those stores owned by members of the subculture and stores with Spanish-speaking salespeople (Saegert et al., 1985). Marketers reinforce the relationship between consumers and their stores by introducing periodic sales promotions. In general, Hispanic consumers show a tendency of buying products offered in sales promotions. In Latin America consumers' diversity is apparent and so is their attitude toward promotions. Consumers studied considered relative advantages in perceived price and product promotions, and preferred big bargains offered by retail stores. Retailers accrued higher benefits from such buying behavior of consumers while defining their promotional strategies, especially emphasizing an everyday low prices (EDLP) strategy, as in the case of Walmart (d'Andrea et al., 2006). Practically consumers react favorably to leisure sales campaigns of goods and services. However, customer value plays a decisive role in the shopping process. Sales promoters instill emotions among customers in terms of merchandise choice, visual merchandising, store environment, sales personnel attitude, pricing policies, and promotional activities during the pre-purchase stage. These factors are the very foundations of consumer satisfaction and decision drivers toward buying products (Otieno et al., 2005).

Behavioral and psychographic issues

Behavioral economists and social psychologists have been studying the individual's conceptual understanding of the causes and meanings of social communications. Both disciplines have focused primarily on process and outcomes in reference to the effects of the social communication of judgments. Often social media and the so-called communication grapevines of the topics of social interest cause a chaotic environment, and it is difficult for the recipients of the message to judge the contents and react. Such communications in social media may not only drive confusion among consumers but also leave companies unclear about the principal theme of a communication. Thus, the practice of mindful listening should be inculcated among peer groups and companies, in the sense of listening by being fully present to oneself and actualizing the contents to the current reference in mindful listening to social media. This embodies the practice of gaining insight and understanding and requires self-awareness, and awareness of the other players in the given situation (Ucok, 2006).

The traditional high esteem for the word in Europe is reflected, for instance, in the elaborate process of business correspondence. Europeans not only love to talk extensively in negotiations, they also draw up long minutes of meetings and letters of confirmation. They strive to put the progress of their business in exact words in order to keep going. Japanese enterprises, on the other hand, are not especially fond of correspondence. Compared to European business letters, Japanese letters tend to be brief and, in the European view, sometimes not sufficiently precise. Even differences in detail of communication may cause problems in business relationships. In Europe, contracts as a principle are put in writing, and written contracts are minutely drafted.

Consumer psychology is largely governed by perceptions on economic and relational variables as conceived by the buyers of products or services. The organizational values and consumer relationship approaches of the company also influence consumers to acquire higher values. The measure of consumer value as product efficiency may be viewed from the consumer's perspective toward a ratio of outputs (e.g., perceived use value, resale value, reliability, safety, comfort) that consumers obtain from a product relative to inputs (price, running costs) that consumers have to deliver in exchange. The efficiency value derived can be understood as the return on the consumer's investment. Products offering a maximum consumer value relative to all other alternatives in the market are characterized as efficient. Different efficient products may create value in different ways using different strategies (output–input combinations). Each efficient product can be viewed as a benchmark for a distinct sub-market. Jointly, these products form the efficient frontier, which serves as a reference function for inefficient products (Bauer et al., 2004).

There are some critical issues associated in price-sensitive consumer behavior, whether customers are equally price-sensitive while purchasing products for functional (e.g., purchasing frozen vegetables, toiletries or paper towels) versus hedonic (e.g., purchasing a high-technology computer or a video camera) consumption situations and whether perceived value derived during consuming the product influences price sensitivity. It may also be stated that higher price volatility makes consumers more sensitive to gains and less sensitive to losses, while intense price promotion by competing brands makes consumers more sensitive to losses but does not influence consumers' sensitivity to gains (Han et al., 2001). Companies may involve customers in the product-designing process and incorporate their preferences in order to optimize application-derived customer values.

A major intervening variable in behavioral manifestation today is the online social communities and postings that essentially define or redefine a product or service brand. Previous research studies have acknowledged that social intervention prompts asymmetrical performance of brands and determines the brand's market power (Sivakumar, 2004). It has been observed that there is a need for the forward integration of manufacturing companies into retailing, through the establishment of flagship stores, which provides such companies with an opportunity to provide a context consumer behavior and exercise a level of control over its manifestation. Behavioral manifestation reveals the brand health of the products. A set of consumer behavior elements serves as the leading indicators of sales risk and potential, include brand leadership, attractiveness, distinctiveness, satisfaction, and liabilities. The behavioral appearance influences brand image, whereas initial brand associations and perceived fit between new product and either remaining products (category fit) or brand image (image fit) are able to strengthen consumer attitudes.

Social institutions contribute substantially in nurturing cultural heritage, which is reflected in individual behavior. Such institutions as family, education, political structures, and the media, affect the ways in which people relate to one another, organize their activities to live in harmony with one another, teach acceptable behavior to succeeding generations, and govern themselves. The status of gender in society, the family, social classes, group behavior, age groups, and how societies define decency and civility are interpreted differently within every culture. Social institutions are a system of regulatory norms and rules of governing actions in pursuit of immediate ends in terms of their conformity with the ultimate common value system of a community. They constitute underlying norms and values making up the common value system of a society. Institutions are intimately related to and derived from the value attitudes common to members of a community. This establishes institutions as primarily moral phenomena, which leads to enforcing individual decisions on all human needs, including economic and business-related issues. The primary means for enforcement of norms is moral authority whereby an individual obeys the norm because that individual believes that the norm is good for its own sake. Urban and ethnic marketing strategies integrate consumer marketing solutions including the Internet and technology aspects within the cultural environment of the host country. An international marketer should evaluate the psychographic and demographic profiles that indicate the target market of urban and ethnic groups. The firm may choose to provide the marketing communication to target segments close to their lifestyle. Thus General Motors (GM) has made significant contributions to cultural life in its "America on the Move" exhibit at the Smithsonian Institution's National Museum of American History. GM has appeared to be the largest single donor ever contributing to a cultural group. This promotional strategy won the car company naming rights and a prominent place in promotions (Hostetter, 2003).

Companies could bring business and society closer together by creating shared value in association with consumers sharing marketing policies and business innovations. Such efforts would help firms to offer better economic value to consumers. Firms can create social value by analyzing social media conversations, reconceiving products and markets, developing customer-centric attributes in the value chain, and building supportive consumer clusters on virtual platforms. A number of leading firms have already embarked on such initiatives (Porter and Kramer, 2011). Ben & Jerry's, for example, has redesigned its consumer market on various social media platforms specific to consumer preferences for its ice creams for children, youth, gender-specific, and health-conscious consumers. However, not all companies are able to use social media to derive business benefit as well as create social value.

Some social media initiatives fail to bring benefits to companies because the initiatives are unable to create an emotional bonding between stakeholders and the company. However, social media has its limitation of trust, territory, and target just like any other media channel. Companies nonetheless can create a winning strategy using social media and focus on developing software to facilitate social networking and use the tools to build communities. Such practice may encourage stakeholders and employees of the company to be more productive and sincere. Though social media can catalyze in creating dynamic stakeholder relationships, deriving benefits with an online community requires firms to develop leadership in building emotional capital that values community-building as a means of creating economic value (Huy and Shipilov, 2012).

As social media is expanding manifold in the twenty-first century, social networks and word of mouth play a catalytic role in influencing consumer preferences and purchase decisions through online platforms. Companies such as Dell and eBay have adopted traditional unidirectional advertising messages, using them as a springboard to begin a two-way dialogue with consumers via social media platforms. Most marketers know that social media has emerged as a powerful way to generate sustainable, positive word-of-mouth marketing for the good of the business in a competitive marketplace. However, it is essential for firms to mark their success in business with social media, to select the right social media platform, develop and post the right messages, and engage the right users to interact on the issue and disseminate the message among peers. Firms may also take a fresh look into the possibilities of employing innovative metrics to exploit social media for achieving success in their marketing campaigns. Among such strategies firms may consider are developing an analysis of customers' influence effect, which could measure the influence a social media user has in simultaneous networks. Firms may also analyze the dynamics of social media users who actively discuss the company's products, services, and policies. In order to measure the effectiveness of social media, customer value could help the firm in finding out the monetary gain or loss realized by social marketing campaigns (Kumar and Mirchandani, 2012).

Although social networks have emerged as a significant tool for companies to expand their business, harnessing the power of social media platforms of such invisible groups creates a big challenge for firms to achieve organizational goals. It has been observed that there are no uniform directions available for firms to harness the social media. Thus, most efforts to promote collaboration with social media platforms are disorganized and are built on the logic that more connectivity on social media is a healthy sign for organizational growth. However, this might be a misnomer as, in general, networks create relational demands that could squeeze the time and energy of network participants and could affect the organization's interest adversely. Accordingly, it is often crucial for executives to learn how to promote connectivity only where it benefits both an organization and an individual, and to reduce the redundancy in communication as well as to limit the connectivity to selective networks.

Some of the best practices on social networking, as followed by Nestlé, Dell, and Kraft Foods, demonstrate that limiting their social media activities to a customized response network excels in framing the organizational interest and strategic innovation. Strategy consulting firms and new-product development groups also rely on this format. By contrast, surgical teams and law firms rely mostly on the modular response network, which works by encouraging customers to present their problems and get a reasonably good response. Such practice may help the organizations to build customer loyalty through the social networks and stay connected to reap competitive advantage against less social firms. Many firms believe that call centers could be useful in interacting on social media platforms. Social media collaboration does not occur spontaneously in the right places at the right times in an organization. Companies need to develop a strategic, nuanced view of collaboration by taking steps to ensure that companies support categorically the social networks that best fit their goals.

Perceptional mapping and the self-reference criterion

Despite the perpetual impact of market communication and advertising, word of mouth, and direct marketing, consumers largely make decisions based on their own conceptualization of issues. Such a self-analysis process can be called an "aura." In Roman mythology Aurora was the light of dawn, while in modern terms, an aura can be explained as an emotionally charged experience, for example, anxiety or supreme happiness. Thus, an aura is something that is created in the mind of the customer and has to do with customers' longing for adding attracting values to a company, product, or service (Bjorkman, 2002). Many consumers look for products that satisfy the needs that are important for their personality. Self-concepts or aura are developed among consumers as they live with products or they become the part of lifestyle. For example, some of the electro-domestic products such as the microwave and oven have become so essential for people that they have become a part of lifestyle. Use-aura is created when the customer gets more deeply involved with the product or service. This can be done in different ways. A person can have perhaps borrowed a car from a friend or been taking test-drive at a car dealer. Use-aura is in many ways a critical moment as it occurs during the moment the consumer undergoes the product test to derive his perceptions on its use value (Hill and Rifkin, 1999). A self-referencing criterion may be described as a process by which judgments on others are formed. It involves judging others' behavior against antecedents and experiences that are weighed on a preconceived platform of thinking. Before framing perceptions and conclusions, it would be wise to check with the people those are familiar with the culture of the host country, and perhaps debate the issues of concern on a knowledgeable base (Rajagopal, 2007b).

The concept of self-reference among consumers is a relevant framework for developing effective cognitive support toward buying decisions made on a particular product. Self-reference criteria are largely governed by social and economic factors such as the social status of owning the product, value for money, and perceived use value of the product. Some studies on consumer psychology have addressed these issues in the context of sense of control, beliefs about the length of association with the products, and the management of perceived value during the pre- and post-sales situations. Such experience tends to increase loyalty for products, brands, and firms, and also determine long-term lifestyle changes. Retailers attempt to create good feelings for the purchase of various consumer goods by engaging shoppers' attention on themes relating to social referents and family values. It is observed also that shopping items such as apparel and specialty items such as cosmetics offer prospects of titillating consumer motives of status and self-image enhancement, respectively, by engaging them with reputable merchandise in reputable settings (Miranda, 2009). However, in Western countries individualism dominates decision-making among consumers, unlike Oriental countries where family is considered to be the unit of consumption and plays an important role in deriving influences on consumer decisions. A lifestyle concept based on modern class structures is easily found in the context of social structures emerging out of urban geography. For example, home decoration and furnishing shows a less structured and more individualistic self-expressive approach to the lifestyle concept in terms of home and identity (Kirsten and Claus, 2004). It is observed that urban consumers largely build self-concepts on brands, products, and services on the basis of shopping orientation, importance of retail attributes, and beliefs about retail attributes. Retailing firms need to understand how consumers evaluate retail locations to develop their retail strategies in order to be competitive in the current market (Yan and Eckman, 2009).

Ethical consumerism and family consumer decision-making including the influence of children are emerging spheres of consumer behavior as the globalization effect advances across world markets. In family-led consumer decisions motivation to pursue an ethical lifestyle is an important attribute associated with an inheritance factor, where older members of family are awakened to ethical issues. However, the prominence of ethical trade-offs in consumer decision-making, ethical choices as normalizing behavior, and finally the presence of pester power in the ethical context also influence lifestyle and consumerism in the family (Carey et al., 2008). Self-reference criteria and lifestyle have driven many consumer decision-making styles, including recreational and hedonistic consciousness, perfectionism consciousness, habitual and brand loyalty, confusion by excess of choice, price and value consciousness, impulsiveness and carelessness, and brand and fashion consciousness behavior. In addition, eight lifestyle attributes have also emerged among urban consumers concerning the dimensions of activities, interests, and opinions; these are working activities, shopping activities, interests related to the home, interests related to the family, interests related to fashion, fashion as self-representation, opinions about themselves, and opinions about products (Kwan et al., 2008).

Urban shopping centers offer a variety of attributes to consumers to develop their perceptions toward buying products and services. Retail self-service stores that largely operate in chains are based on the rationale of *touch, feel, and pick*, which offers consumers a wide range of options to make buying decisions. Consumers find the environment significantly positive and exhibit higher levels of approach and impulse buying behaviors; they experience enhanced satisfaction when retail ambience is congruent with arousing qualities (Mattila and Wirtz, 2004). Visual effects associated with products often stimulate buying decisions among young consumers. Point of sales brochures, catalogues, and posters build assumptions on perceived use value and motivational relevance in product buying decisions. Emotional visuals exhibited on contextual factors such as proximity or stimulus size drive perception and subjective reactions on the utility and expected satisfaction of the products (Codispoti and de Cesarej, 2007). However, personal shopping motives, values, and perceived shopping alternatives are often considered as independent inputs into a choice model, being argued that shopping motives influence the perception of retail store attributes as well as the attitude toward retail stores.

Brand equity is the worth of an image and its strength as judged by its ability to remain unaffected by temporary changes in any of the comprising factors. Consumers have only one image of a brand, one created by the deployment of the brand assets at the firm's disposal: name, tradition, packaging, advertising, promotion posture, pricing, trade acceptance, sales force disciplines, customer satisfaction, repurchase patterns, etc. Clearly some brand assets are more important to product marketers than to service marketers, and vice versa. Some competitive environments put more of a premium on certain assets as well. Quality and price do not exist as isolated concepts in consumers' minds. They are interrelated. Research has shown that deep discounts do cause the consumer to believe that something is wrong. Frequent discounting serves to lower the value of the brand because of an almost subconscious reaction by the consumer who believes that quality also has been lowered (remember shirts with alligators on them?) or, in a "value rebound," consumers begin to perceive the everyday price as too high. The brand is then bought only as a deal.

Retailers may address the various interests of consumers through effective displays, designing appropriate retail ergonomics, easily identifiable packaging, making shopping exciting, and focusing in-store advertising to enhance arousal of young consumers (Quelch and Cannon, 1983). The three distinct dimensions of emotions, namely, pleasantness, arousal, and dominance, have been identified as major drivers for making buying decisions among adolescent consumers. The retail point of purchase is the time and place at which all the elements of a sale, the consumer, the money, and the product, converge. Marketers must make the most of the communications possibilities at this point to increase their sales (Rajagopal, 2006). There are some common strategies adopted by retailers to overcome the problems of fickle consumers, price-slashing competitors, and mood swings in the economy. Such wishful thinking holds that retailers will thrive only if they communicate better with young consumers through in-store amusement, recreation, and collaborative product demonstrations involving consumers, to help their purchase decisions. Retailers also offer buying incentives to develop conviction on buying such tried-out products (Berry, 2001). Satisfaction is the customer's perception of the value received in a transaction or relationship, and it helps in making re-patronage decisions on the basis of the customer's predictions concerning the value of a future product. Hence, many retailers develop innovative approaches to prospective new customers for new products by strengthening customer relationship and value management strategies.

10
Challenges of the Butterfly Effect

The butterfly effect emerging out of market chaos drives transformation in the business environment and consumer culture along the dimensions of geo-demographic reach, which can be evidenced in closeness to dense centers of population, and generate competition among firms to take advantage of scale and trade in specialized products. Firms prepare for going global by boosting their changes in marketing strategies of products and services and triggering impulses on shopping. This chapter addresses the challenges of companies competing in the market that face positive or negative butterfly effects. Multinational companies nurture a set of enterprise-wide mindsets that can maintain a uniformity of purpose while at the same time successfully adapt practices to diverse local economic and cultural conditions. The chapter also addresses emerging theories and practices, knowledge-sharing and building customer loyalty.

Transitional strategies

Globalization is characterized by increasing competition and continuous shifts in consumer preferences. Hence, most companies are always at the cutting edge of innovation and launching differentiated products and services for gaining competitive advantage and market leadership. The small changes that are introduced by the companies to offer differentiation advantages to consumers move from niches to a larger market space, carrying out the butterfly effect. New products in transition reflexively rely on the skills and strategies experienced in the market in the past, and companies tend to revise their mistakes and build an advantageous platform for consumers to accept the changes. Large companies moving into new roles attempt to gain a deep understanding of customer-centric as well as market-oriented situations on hand before experimenting with the competitive differentiation of products and services in the marketplace. To drive this task accurately companies tailor their strategies in tune with specific market requirements and competitive scenarios.

Companies should consider the STARS factors, namely, synchronizing innovation with needs, transition of innovation, accelerated growth, realignment with competitors, and sustainability of differentiation and new products. In this process companies face the challenges of launching a venture or differentiation project beginning from a niche and aiming at larger outreach to mass consumer markets. In managing such projects firms invest resources with an objective of rapid sales of differentiated products, re-energizing existing market segments, and driving efforts to be the leader of innovation in the market, leaving behind a strong legacy of success. Managers can accelerate the marketing of differentiated and competitively innovative products and build market leadership by efficiently managing the butterfly effect in creating supportive alliances across markets and consumer segments (Watkins, 2009).

The butterfly effect drives faster time to market, wider outreach of changes, and shorter product lifecycles for companies that are engaged in introducing new products more frequently. While new or competitively differentiated products can offer tremendous value, product introductions and transitions pose enormous challenges to managers. One of the common problems in managing butterfly effects across markets and consumer segments is consumer uncertainty toward making buying decisions on innovative products. Besides consumer indecisiveness, lack of a formal process to guide managerial decisions also makes companies struggle in marketing the differentiated products efficiently. There are always risks in managing a new products transition, and companies need to identify the critical factors across the departments tracking those risks. It is also necessary the companies to monitor the evolution of markets for new products over time and develop consumer cognitive mapping scenarios of risks and responses. Such strategies help a company to monitor new competitive products efficiently across the markets and lessen the chance and impact of unanticipated outcomes. This process can also assist managers in designing and implementing appropriate policies to boost sales for new products and maintain sales for existing products, balancing the supply and the demand for both so that combined sales can grow smoothly (Erhun et al., 2007).

Product differentiation by adopting new technologies is difficult for some firms owing to high cost involvement and low competencies in using the technologies for manufacturing at economies of scale. The Eastman Kodak Company filed a petition for solvency as it faced difficulties in growing in terms of streamlined manufacturing and marketing while its core business transitioned from an analog to a digital photographic equipment platform. Over more than a century, the company had developed complex manufacturing processes and high-speed coating technologies that offered it a near-monopoly market situation till the mid-1980s. At the same time the company had used high technology, which discouraged competitors challenging in its market. Kodak faced a particularly difficult analog-to-digital transition, like many companies that have faced the waves of creative destruction wrought by technological innovation since 2010 (Shih, 2012). The challenge for Kodak was the same challenge that companies in photo and video equipment manufacturing are facing, and telecom equipment companies are currently experiencing extreme changes in their underlying technology.

It is observed that whenever product differentiations with new technologies emerge in the global marketplace, it drives the butterfly effect and threatens many existing businesses. Many companies face a major dilemma whether to make a seamless transition to the change or to cordon their markets with existing products and plunge into a niche until they develop a new business model and new manufacturing process to cope with the technology change. However, at times neither strategies may sustain companies facing such change in the marketplace. It clearly indicates that managing transitions of technology, manufacturing processes, and carrying out competitive differentiations in products and services is a complex phenomenon. However, companies may adapt to a retrenchment to a niche of the traditional market, where the old technology has an advantage over the new in addressing customer needs, or relocate to a new market, where the old technology is inherently lauded by consumers (Adner and Snow, 2010). Any of these strategies require that a company demonstrates high competency in managing the transitional crisis and building capabilities to absorb market shocks.

Most firms believe that competing through business models is critical for success, but developing appropriate business strategies to push technology and innovations through such business models is a difficult task. Technology firms focus on creating innovative models and evaluating their efficacy. However, the success or failure of a company's business model depends largely on how it interacts with players within the industry and the competitive marketplace. Any business model will perform efficiently in a pure monopolistic or temporary-monopolistic market conditions. As firms build technology- and innovation-based products in isolation of market competition, they routinely deploy conventional business models. Moreover, many companies ignore the dynamic elements of business models and fail to realize that they can design business models to generate winner-takes-all effects similar to the network externalities that high-tech companies such as Microsoft, eBay, and Facebook often create. A good business model creates sustainable cycles that, over time, result in competitive advantage (Casadesus-Masanell and Ricart, 2011).

Contemporary global business models explain that firms tend to structure themselves as one of four organizational types, namely, international, multi-domestic, global, and transnational. Depending on the type, a company's assets and capabilities are either centralized or decentralized, knowledge is developed and diffused in either one direction or in many, and the importance of the overseas office to the home office varies. International marketing refers to exchanges across national boundaries for the satisfaction of human needs and wants. The various marketing functions coordinated and integrated across the multiple country markets may be referred as global marketing. The process of such integration may involve product standardization, uniform packaging, and homogeneity in brand architecture, identical brand names, synchronized product positioning, and commonality in communication strategies or well-coordinated sales campaigns across the markets of different countries. The term "global" does not convey the literal meaning of penetration into all countries of the world, and needs to be understood in a relative sense – even regionalization or operating in a cluster of countries may also be taken as a global operation in an applied perspective. Regional marketing efforts like Trans-Asian or Pan-European marketing operations may also be viewed as examples of global marketing. The suppliers of products ranging from Budweiser beer to BMW cars have been able to keep growing without succumbing to the pricing pressures of an intensely promotional environment. A strong brand can also open the door when growth depends on breaking into new markets. Starbucks Corporation (Khermouch, 2002), among the fastest-growing global brands, recently set up shop in Vienna, one of Europe's café capitals, with among 400 new stores planned at overseas locations. Companies can succeed in regional integration across multiple countries as they follow similar strategies and management principles.

The global corporation operates at relatively low costs with international standardization. The Coca-Cola and Pepsi-Cola companies have standardized their products globally according to the regional and ethnic preferences of consumers. The most effective world competitors integrate quality and trust attributes into their cost structure. Such companies compete on the basis of appropriate value of price, quality, trust, and delivery systems. These values are considered by the companies in reference to product design, function, and changing consumer preferences like fashion. Multinational corporations have deep knowledge of the business environment in a country, put their efforts into adapting to the given environment, and set out on a gradual penetration process in the country. On the other hand, global corporations also recognize the absolute need to be competitive and drive through lower prices by standardizing their marketing operations (Rajagopal, 2008).

Despite the globalization skills of many companies while introducing a new technology, managers implementing the change strategies must bridge the gap between the differentiation designs, technologies, and the users of the innovated or competitively differentiated products to make the transition smooth without affecting existing market and consumer segments. This task becomes complex when met with implementation incongruity, lack of competence of employees, and consumer resistance (Leonard-Barton and Kraus, 1985). Most companies attempt to change in response to market calls for competitive differentiation through shifts in technology or customer demands. In fairly stable markets, companies can manage transitions in an effective way to deal with change but successful companies in rapidly changing, intensely competitive industries change proactively. Companies that carry out changes in tune with market needs build momentum, and companies that effectively manage transitions sustain in conditions of market competition (Eissenhardt and Brown, 1998).

Shifts in consumer culture

Culture is getting more complex every day as it is increasingly influenced by market trends and the interactivity of social media. Global competition has driven continuous innovations in products that are supplemented with the mass promotions strategy of companies, and have induced an obsessive and compulsive consumption culture among consumers. Such a phenomenon is apparent in the food products, apparel, and fashion accessories segments. In the twenty-first century, management thinkers are running into contemporary debates about excessive consumption and critically examining a set of sensitive social practices derived from the sociocultural behavior of consumers. The challenges for marketing laid by contemporary debates on material-ism and excessive consumption make a greater dent in driving the consumption decisions of consumers (Kjellberg, 2008). In the current scenario of global competition and struggle of companies to acquire and retain consumers, marketers need to recognize the changing pri-orities of consumption. Companies should develop strategies along-side consumer beliefs to motivate them to have an ever-greater array and quantity of goods and services with total satisfaction. Consumers are increasingly looking to companies and markets that can provide resources and technologies to enable them to achieve rewarding and sustainable states of consumption and accordingly cultivate a consump-tion culture (Shankar and Fitchett, 2002).

Manufacturers and marketers of consumer products develop their strategies through four processes in order to induce change in consumer culture. These comprise chartering, learning, mobilizing, and realigning to pave the way for successful institutionalization of a strategic change initiative. These elements rely much more on an understanding of the mix of task-related, emotional, and behavioral factors than is fashion-able in today's metrics-driven environment. This also drives the shift in conventional wisdom about programmatic change, arguing that managers need to set in motion a series of processes right at the start if widespread changes are to stick (Roberto and Levesque, 2005). The cultural change in buying consumer goods from low-price brands to high-technology brands in emerging markets has been institutionalized through a family environment. It has been observed that parental and sibling influences decreased with age, whereas peer and media influ-ences expanded with increasing age. Television and celebrities also play a significant role in influencing adolescents' clothing choices irrespec-tive of gender categories. Among the most common two forms of media that children use are magazines and television, while teens are primarily influenced by visual merchandising, hands-on experience, and copying fashion apparel users (Seock and Bailey, 2009).

The local culture is embedded in urban settings that are evolved his-torically. Interaction and local culture are essential parts of the business community and play a guiding role in measuring consumer behavior to develop marketing strategies by firms. Street markets have emerged not only as a social meeting place for people but are also considered as political grassroots to institutions to propagate ideologies and debates on current issues. These markets reflect the characteristics of users, varying degrees of accessibility to diverse populations, and state poli-cies toward markets. The differences in shopping behavior correspond to clear differences in prices between grocery and food stores serving the two shopping cultural groups. However, some supermarkets also have lower prices across a range of food products but may not be able to simulate the ethnic surroundings of street markets (Ackerman and Tellis, 2001).

The extent of personal involvement in products, brands, and services also determines the buying attitudes of consumers. Companies engaged in gaining market share amidst competition drive consumer involvement through experience-sharing, such as consumers sharing a test drive experience of automobiles, social media dialogs, interactive product websites such as Nintendo, and so on. Consumer involvement commonly builds a positive attitude toward the products and services. Consumers may have low or high involvement with objects for sale to perceive value, competitive advantage, and an attitude toward buying them. Bottled water is a low-involvement product for which a purchase decision is made without much thought or emotional involvement, while a body lotion is a high-involvement product prompting consumers to review established opinions and suitability for various skin types. Such involvement of consumers in products largely requires persuasion to build as well as change the consumer attitudes. Analysis of consumer attitudinal metrics indicates that liking, market attraction, and price make a substantial impact on forming buying attitude among consumers. As consumers are largely driven by product attractiveness and marketing tactics of competitors, liking and price appear to have the highest elasticity (Stillerman, 2006).

Social consciousness among consumers toward consumption of socially supported products and services has a sustainable effect in building involvement, attitude, and behavior toward the consumption of such products. There is a strong agreement across the European Union about the ethics of environmentally friendly products as consumers endorse that using these is "the right thing to do," and their family and friends would think it was good if they could buy these products. Consumer attitudes can be built toward various physical and social objects including products, brands, models, stores, and people. Some consumers have the attitude of buying products with the same salesperson in a store or getting a haircut from the same barber. Multinational companies invest substantial resources in building consumer attitudes toward their products and services in the marketplace. Hence, many consumers are influenced by marketing strategy, like an announcement of discount in price in food products or an advertisement anchored by a public celebrity.

The complexities of choice facing consumers have led to product standardization strategies by multinational companies. Over the years standardization has become a powerful strategy in consumer markets, although high standardization levels have also been rejected by consumers as negating the possibility of a customization to their choice. Thus, in the twenty-first century the standardization approach has reached the point of diminishing returns. In order to drive consumer preferences, visual merchandising and developing retail outlets in attractive locations has emerged as a strategy of the new era. However, social activists often regard plans for constructing new shopping malls critically from the environment and social security perspectives. From California to Florida to New Jersey, neighborhoods are passing ordinances that dictate the sizes and even architectural styles of new shops. Most consumer goods companies have now begun to use clustering techniques for making decision-making easy and to focus their efforts on the relatively small number of buying purchasing variables. The customization-by-clusters approach, which began as a strategy for grocery stores in the mid-1990s, has since proven effective in drugstores, department stores, mass merchants, big-box retailers, restaurants, apparel companies, and a variety of consumer goods manufacturers (Vishwanath and Rigby, 2006).

Product and market complexities

Globalization can be seen as being encompassed by three rings of risks, comprising product, technology, and innovation shifts. Product complexity and market dynamics dramatically changed over the twentieth century and most companies are facing an uphill task to adjust to technology, consumer preferences, and trends of product differentiation in competitive markets. Hence, companies need to redefine the extent of complexity in managing product differentiation and its related butterfly effect to maximize their outreach. It is also necessary for firms to measure the intensity of market shifts and increasing product development agility to measure long-term business growth and sustainability (Thonke and Reinertsen, 1998). The product and market complexities have increased in the era of globalization alongside the parallel growth of disruptive technologies, product piracy, and gray markets. Gray markets, where branded products of global companies are sold or resold through unauthorized distributors, have increased manifold. They exist for both products and services, including massive products such as automobiles and construction equipment. Companies engaged in manufacturing mass consumer products such as watches and cosmetics also face intensive threats of innovative disruptions and gray channels. Gray markets have become the part of the business arena and they need to be accepted as local channels. They pose continuous threats to upcoming innovations and persist in the marketplace as value-added resellers. Among the major market complexities faced by companies engaged in launching competitive products with sustainable differentiation are price differentials and value-added services for the products. Most gray markets cater to the convenience of consumers and offer value-added services to disruptive or counterfeit products. In many situations, their sales outstrip the sales of the original products. Most companies encounter enormous stress in the market as they face their inability to compete with gray markets. The sale of legitimate products in the wrong place or through the wrong channel poses unique problems for companies (Anita et al., 2004). Companies can resolve the gray market complexity by selecting the right approach to develop price-setting decisions based on local resources and the nature of the product's market. It is also necessary for companies to adapt the following strategies to overcome the threats by local market players:

- Understand the market, but work with the predetermined corporate goals.
- Adapt to local conditions, but implement global standards.
- Pay for performance, but build a customer-centric marketplace.
- Drive costs down, but maintain quality, services, and customer value.
- Recognize complexity in managing butterfly effects in low-end markets, but define clear priorities.

In order to succeed with the butterfly effects in low-end markets, companies are required to develop cultural understanding and adaptability, market intelligence and knowledge, and the ability to sense and respond to rapid change (Paine, 2010).

Product differentiation or reconstruction involves a continuum of activities from recycling to refurbishing to innovation or cosmetic differentiation that allow companies to sell high-performance goods at competitive prices and realize high profits. Product differentiation may open new markets for companies but simultaneously call for taking all precautions to protect the products from counterfeiting and disruptive marketing. Companies should work out their product differentiations primarily to cater to the needs of the following taxonomy of consumers:

- Those who need to retain the differentiated product because it has a high perceived use value.
- End-users who are critical to change and tend to gather more approval from peers.
- Customers who make low utilization of differentiated products but love to have the products as a lifestyle.
- Those who wish to continue using a product that has become obsolete in the market but for whom differentiated products may work as a substitute.
- People who simply want to be experimental toward new products.
- Customers who are interested in change and value-added products.

In order to overcome competition complexity in the market, companies must meticulously analyze consumer attitudes on product differentiation and develop an efficient sales force that has abilities to acquire customers (Pearce, 2009). Market complexities in rapidly shifting global competitive conditions are also caused by customer location, market competition, product utility, price, and services availability. The key factors that affect decisions of companies on market intervention through competitive product differentiation include customer value, price, complementarity, and lifecycle of intervening or new products. Because of the complexity involved in setting marketing goals of differentiated products, strategic or tactical, the key risk factors inherent in the competitive markets, such as consumer defection, tactical promotions, offering value-added benefits to the channel, and aggressive sales by competing companies, need to be addressed by companies engaging in differentiation.

Evolution of markets, chaos, and Darwinism

The evolution of markets over the centuries has been a perennial phenomenon congruent with shifts in social, economic, and technological knowledge in society. The evolution of business and growth has promoted economic behavior to explore markets. Sociologically the evolution of markets was based on the understanding that individuals are embedded in various cognitive structures involving business activities. Shifts in market processes of society are induced by fundamental beliefs and shared assumptions, and resemble elements of social culture defining norms of markets, expected behavior, and thought. Such business evolution paradigms are resistant to minor discrepancies between their fundamental models and contradictory (potentially empirical) evidence. Thus, discrepancies in market behavior are considered as socioeconomic abnormalities, paradoxes or puzzles in a given place and time (Hedaa and Ritter, 2005).

Historical documentation reveals that market evolution is a long process with some causal attribution (Goldthrope, 2000). Historical analysis can sometimes enable identification of the reasons for important transitions by highlighting key events that triggered change and their patterns. Marketing patterns in society are commonly believed to have evolved through five distinct phases of growth over the ages. These phases can be categorized as the simple trade era, the production era, the sales era, the marketing department era, and the marketing company era. Markets and society have faced significant changes in the global marketplace, which resulted in the economic dynamism of both developed and developing economies across the continents. Accordingly many countries jumped into the market fray and started to produce a larger variety of products, making them more substitutable, raising the price elasticity of demand, and strengthening competition. Such market development had driven higher competition in modern growth, and competitive firms have aimed at larger territorial expansion with lower markups and prolonged breakeven prices. As firms become larger, they find it easier to cover the fixed costs of innovation and technology diffusion and adaptation. When the size of the market is large, with a significant competitive driving force, market innovation grows endogenously. This, in turn, pushes the market to grow exponentially, providing additional incentives to mount competition. The market economy thus graduates in the global marketplace to the era of competition and contests determining the Darwinian theories of struggle for existence and survival of the fittest.

In growing market competition small firms always face major threats from large firms as the latter possess more resources (physical, finance, human, and technology) as against the smaller firms. Hence, most smaller firms develop a cocooning attitude and confine themselves to a niche as they know they could not continue their struggle for existence in the marketplace. Most companies at the bottom of markets fall into the cocooning pattern, which leads to continuous struggling to establish their posture in a given marketplace. It may be observed that large firms often enter into new market niches created by small firms through technological innovation and ingest the market share of these small firms. In view of the Darwinian theory it may be argued that market conditions and company-specific characteristics explain entry timing and underlying goals of the large firms, and such entry might be a continuous process for large firms in different marketplaces. The dominating behavior of large firms is more likely to be backed by innovations in the industry in response to competing firms. Small firms are affected by the entry of firms that are similar in size and resources. When a highly similar company enters a new market, it raises the probability that it is entering beyond levels based solely on the attractiveness of the market (Debruyne and Reibstein, 2005). Hence, small firms adopt both aggressive and defensive strategies to stay in the marketplace despite competitive attacks by new entrants. A consortium of small firms manufacturing identical products also pose a major threat to large firm in sustaining the competitive marketplace.

Darwinian model of fitness in market evolution argues that when consumers increase, more varieties of products and services penetrate the market, driving more demand. Such market thrust in positioning products and services increases the price elasticity of demand. Some management studies exploit this feature, and show in a one-period model how the higher elasticity of demand, arising from a larger population or more liberalized trade, facilitates innovation (Desmet and Parente, 2010). As trade liberalization continues in the globular marketplace, transforming the regional markets, multidimensional growth appears to be a strong catalytic thrust in the economy of developing countries. Multidimensional growth, in which a corporate firm manages relatively freestanding business units, was the most successful design of the marketing organizations of the twentieth century. However, some firms have evolved organizational designs that signal a new way of resolving the market competition. These firms are organized around multiple dimensions, such as region, product, services, and account, that are able to hold different strategies accountable for performance on these dimensions. The multidimensional growth of marketing organizations is best understood as the next step in the evolution from a resource-centric business model to a customer-centric knowledge-sharing model. It is a way of managing competitive markets that is particularly well adapted to stimulating market leadership that is necessary to create economic value in complex markets (Strikwerda and Stoelhorst, 2009).

The continuum of market evolution across regions, products, and services had driven the rapid diffusion of new products in the marketplace. Quicker time to market and shorter product lifecycles are pushing companies to introduce new products more frequently in the global marketplace. While new products intend to offer high value, product introductions and transitions pose enormous challenges to managers. Drawing from research at Intel and examples from General Motors and

Cisco Systems, it may be argued that the risks impacting a transition identify a set of factors across departments tracking those risks, monitors the evolution of these factors over time, and develops playbook mapping scenarios of risks and responses in the market. This process of market evolution by nurturing the demand for new product helps firm's expectations in the marketplace, lowers the chance and impact of unanticipated outcomes, and helps synchronize responses among different consumer segments (Erhun et al., 2007).

Increasing competition in the global marketplace has induced large companies with high market share and brand equity to expand their market operations spatially. In this process large companies tend to acquire smaller firms or get them merged with larger organizations in win–win negotiations. Although such a process has been established in the global marketplace as an effective strategy for the growth of business for larger companies, it has been seen as a matter of survival for smaller and weak companies in the market. In the context of global competition this approach may be considered as a process of cannibalization. At the lower end of the market, value-added resellers (VAR) also catalyze cannibalization of the global market. Remanufactured products do not always cannibalize new product sales. To minimize cannibalization and create additional profits, firms need to understand how consumers value remanufactured products. This is not a static consumer decision and should be re-evaluated over the entire product lifecycle. While firms exhibit responsibility to maximize profits for the firm, this is not necessarily equivalent to maximizing new product sales. A portfolio that includes remanufactured products can enable firms to reach additional market segments and help block competition from new low-end products or third-party remanufacturers (Atsu et al., 2010).

The role of brand prices contributes toward product cannibalization in the market. Price elasticity of competing firms poses a major threat in the market and induces cannibalization. It has been observed that new entrants cannibalize market share of a large company's brand by growing sales of low-cost brands (Meredith and Maki, 2001). Hence, there is a growing need for studying the effects of cannibalization and its importance, as established in the literature, especially since an assessment of the expected cannibalization effect of a new product can help in deciding on suitable times for new product introduction and promotions. Successful companies encounter unique competitive challenges to grow in the competitive market. However, there are several product strategy initiatives that are relevant to all organizations seeking to develop market-driven strategies. Key initiatives include leveraging the business design, recognizing the growth mandate, developing market vision, achieving a capabilities and value match, exploring strategic relationships, building strong brands, brand leveraging, and recognizing the advantages of proactive cannibalization (Cravens et al., 2000).

Cannibalization in the global marketplace is common in the liberal entry policies adopted by many countries in response to globalization. The expansion of product lines and continuous innovations drive cannibalization not only for competing products but also within the product line of a company. Companies often design product lines by segmenting their markets on quality attributes that exhibit a "more is better" or "value for money" property for all consumers. Since products within a product line with marginal differentiation are close substitutes, and consumers can self-select the products they want to purchase, there is often a threat of competition among products within the product line. Multiproduct firms need to meticulously address the cannibalization problem in designing their product lines and avoid product overlaps. It has been observed that if lower-quality products are attractive, consumers with the concern for "value for money" may find it beneficial to buy lower-quality products rather than the higher-quality products targeted to them. Accordingly, lower-quality products can potentially cannibalize higher-quality products. The cannibalization problem forces a firm to provide only the highest-valuation segment with its preferred quality while other segments get lower qualities than anticipated. The firm may not serve some of the lowest-valuation segments when the cannibalization problem is very severe. However, not much is known about how and when the cannibalization problem affects product line design in an oligopoly. Also, consumers may differ not only in their quality valuations but also in their taste preferences (Desai, 2001).

Cannibalization has also become a critical phenomenon in selling products and services of identical nature in the competitive consumer segment. Consider a seller who faces two customer segments with differing valuations of quality of a durable product where demand is stationary and known, the technology exists to release two products simultaneously, and the seller can commit in advance to subsequent prices and qualities. Should he introduce two differentiated products simultaneously? Under the simultaneous strategy, the lower quality would cannibalize demand for the higher quality. To reduce cannibalization, the seller could lower the quality of the low-end model and reduce the price of the high-end model. Alternatively, he could increase the quality of the low-end model, but delay its release (Moorthy and Png, 1992).

Firms cannibalize in the marketplace to seize each other's market share using different approaches. Large firms adopt long-terms plans as their competitive strategies while small firms follow tactical and myopic approaches to gain higher market share in the short term thus surpassing existing firms. The common attributes of cannibalization include use of disruptive technology, engaging in price wars, introduction of new products, developing extensive customer loyalty programs, improving customer services, enhancing quality, and augmenting value for money. The firms that have innovative strategies also exhibit cannibalization attributes. The success of such attackers in gaining market share has created a dilemma for established companies. Established companies can potentially take advantage of a great growth opportunity by embracing the new business models that the innovators have introduced in their markets. These new business models often conflict with established ones. It has been observed that the challenge for companies is to balance the benefits of keeping the new and existing business models separate while at the same time integrating them enough so as to allow them to exploit synergies with one another (Markides and Charitou, 2004).

Large firms operate on economies of scale in the market with low costs and high differentiation of products and services. Such a strategy leads firms in the mass market and drives them to gain high market share. Many firms operate at the same time in a given marketplace, and competition among the firms turns fierce. Some firms operate at high cost but also go for high differentiation of products and services. Firms with such attributes locate themselves in the premium market and struggle to achieve high brand equity. On the other hand, firms that have low differentiation of products and services and low cost of marketing operate in niches by following defensive marketing strategies. Where firms have low differentiation of products and services at a high cost of marketing, business growth becomes sluggish, affecting the brand equity of the firm. If this situation prevails for a long time with such firms, it may cause disaster. Many small firms that have high cost and low differentiation stay out of market competition and become extinct over a period either by shutting down operations or merging with stronger firms.

Many firms stay in global competition believing that they need to develop innovative products or leading brands before venturing abroad. Some firms become global players in their industries by excelling in old-fashioned capabilities. They skip the risky, expensive strategy of opening their own facilities and extend their reach through acquisitions and alliances. Speed of innovation also appears to be an important factor in the success of newly emerging firms. Faster and appropriate customer-centric business strategies allow new entrants to pull ahead of competing firms and drive vertical integration. Newly emerging firms with such attributes are able to move products quickly and cost-effectively to far-flung customers (Guillen and Garcia-Canal, 2010).

To survive in a competitive marketplace it is important for firms to have an obvious sense of advantage and to drive the business to achieve its predefined objective. Defining objective, scope, and advantage requires managing trade-offs amidst market competition. If a firm pursues growth or size, profitability will be jeopardized, and when the firm chooses to serve institutional clients, this may ignore retail customers. Hence, trade-offs in the marketplace will bounce if appropriate decisions are not taken by firms to sustain the market competition. On the other hand, a firm may derive its competitive advantage from economies of scale and may not be able to accommodate idiosyncratic customer needs. Accordingly, growth of local firms may emerge with high brand equity in niches amidst the threats of large firms while large firms can follow a combination of long-run and short-run strategies to outwit regional firms.

In this way local firms struggle for existence while large firms may be consistent with the Darwinian theory of survival of the fittest in a given competitive marketplace. Local firms that demonstrate long-run effective strategy but appear weak on the tactical front to gain short-run competitive advantage should look at diversifying their business activities. In the contemporary global marketplace, the smartest organizations recognize that workforce diversity can be a source of competitive strength. It has been observed that the increasing diversity of the firm in a competitive marketplace leverages it to explore new market opportunities and work with most of them. Emerging firms should learn how industry giants IBM and Merck harnessed their employees' diverse backgrounds and perspectives to gain competitive edge. Diversity of firms helped them to sustain the competition and increase their life span in the market (Park, 2008). Whereas firms that could not manage diversity succumb to ineffective strategies and inefficient tactics over the period.

In the global marketplace market competition accelerates as knowledge on innovation, strategy, and tactics is disseminated. The speed of competition increases in accordance with the dynamics of innovation and technology. Firms in market competition manage their processes strategically and maximize their knowledge development capabilities to the full in creating and exploiting business opportunities.

Emerging firms with strong market orientation identify their speed of organizational transition as the single biggest issue underpinning their successful development, accompanied by the determination and exploitation of strategic processes as key creative ingredients for success (Chaharbaghi and Nugent, 1996). Successful challenger firms in market competition pursue dynamic market share and high brand equity by following aggressive marketing strategies in order to manage the high speed of competition and predetermined targets of high sales and market share. Though firms with such competitive power are susceptible to the intermittent threats of small firms penetrating locally using disruptive technology (like imitations, reviving obsolete technology products, and offering low-cost ad hoc solutions), products, and services. It may be observed that speed in new product introduction is a critical dimension of competition many firms face in high-tech industries. This is especially becoming evident with shorter technological lifecycles and increasing global competition. In the present scenario of global competition, it appears that there is a significant influence on firms' ability to develop as global market leaders in reference to technological familiarity, product differentiation, competitive intensity, internal research, development, and innovative skills (Yeoh, 1994).

Many firms enter at an appropriate time when there is relatively slow speed of competition and leverage higher sales and their market share target. Such a strategy may be considered as opportunistic penetration in the market. Such firms become market leader within a short period, cordon their market share from new entrants in the market, and exhibit monopolistic attributes implicitly or explicitly. Firms with such market orientation appear consistent with the Darwinian theory of survival of the fittest. Contrary to this business situation, firms in market competition need to explore the possibility of diversities to sustain the competition. For instance, with the costs of servicing the grocery industry rising at an alarming rate, many smaller manufacturers are likely to go out of business. Too many supplier companies are willing to do business with the top multiples and achieve high volume sales but remain totally unprofitable (Madigan, 1980). Such market pressures dump weak firms in growing market competition as they lack in innovation and diversity, and are incapable of managing long-run minor attacks of competing firms, which may be considered as guerilla marketing. Firms that face difficulties in coping with market competition, instability in the market, and diminishing returns, may face the consequences of slow death in the marketplace. Under such circumstances, many firms become extinct in the market by shutting down their production and business operations or opt for a merger with a stronger firm contending in the market. Large firms will keep an eye on such firms on the brink of extinction and propose their acquisition to get the advantage of their mobile and immobile assets, including skilled human resources.

Co-creation of ideas

In the digital age, firms are recognizing the power of the Internet as a platform for co-creating value with customers. The Internet has impacted the process of collaborative innovation as a key process in value co-creation. Distinctive capabilities of the Internet as a platform for customer engagement include interactivity, enhanced reach, persistence, speed, and flexibility, suggesting that firms can use these capabilities to engage customers in collaborative product innovation through a variety of Internet-based mechanisms. Network mechanisms can facilitate collaborative innovation at different stages of the new product development process and for differing levels of customer involvement. Ducati, a manufacturer of motorbikes, and Eli Lilly, a multinational pharmaceutical company, have been actively engaged in encouraging customer involvement in developing their new products (Sawhney et al., 2005). In pursuing growth through product innovation, companies should look at their customers as partners in creating and building value. Consumers today have near-instant access to all the information they need on virtually any product. Moreover, they are using this information to influence product development as individuals and, more importantly, through user communities and review groups (Johnson, 2006). Most companies ask their customers about their needs. Customers offer solutions in the form of products or services. Companies then deliver these tangibles, and customers just don't buy. The product research and development team of the company should work with customers to find appropriate solution. Customers should be asked only about the final product they want to use.

Co-creation has become an effective value-embedded marketing strategy in many companies across countries in the global marketplace arena. The new generation of performance management systems is largely based on the co-creation process, either in an organization engaged in innovative products development or a marketing company aiming to be market leader by achieving higher market share. The co-creative performance management system uses the traditional structure of the balanced scorecard, engaging the various stakeholders in unique ways for creating vivid results for consumer-oriented companies.

Social networks are one of the most effective digital media, via Facebook, YouTube, and common interest blogs, to float ideas, reviews, and comments on product differentiation, new products, or product reconstructs in the new paradigm known of co-creation markets. Such platforms, which earlier used to survive in the consumer niche through word of mouth, now exist in the global system as digital networks. Co-creation is the process by which products, services, and experiences are developed jointly by companies and their stakeholders, creating competitive advantage and enhanced customer value. The co-creating strategy is being increasingly employed by progressive organizations by coordinating between employees of the company and stakeholders, and defining the need for differentiation in competitive marketplace. Companies must seek to engage consumers as active co-creators of value and manage co-creating unique strategies to stand out with products and services differentiations to outperform competitors in the market. Customer-centric companies can cultivate a co-creative engagement platform based on the cognitive-management integration model comprising dialog, access, risk–reward assessment, and transparency determinants. Companies can grow an unbeatable competitive strength by taking consumers into confidence through co-creating competitive differentiations and sustainable business policies (Ramaswamy, 2009).

Firms are required to employ economic value-added analysis and strategic value assessments, such as customer preferences, the rate of change of underlying technology, and competitive position in the marketplace. Most multinational firms are targeting bottom-of-the-pyramid market segments to acquire higher market share in the mass market, and these firms are fostering a sustainable value chain by building local capacity through the "4As" comprising awareness, acceptance, adaptability, and affordability. Firms also invest in educating local market players and alliance partners, developing infrastructure, and providing basic community services. Large firms also create shared-value opportunities by improving products and reorganizing market segments, redefining productivity in the value chain, and enabling local cluster development. Large and emerging firms also aim at co-creation of products and business models to upgrade shareholder value and enhance the value-creation process. Emerging companies like AXA Group, dealing with financial and insurance business, are engaged in dramatically redesigning both upper- and lower-end value chain architecture by reinventing the concept of customer value. Companies should focus not only on operational efficiencies, but also modify their activities in the value chain to reach low-income consumers or small suppliers (Anderson and

Billou, 2007). The creation and governing value chains in firms will be critical to successful implementation of strategy for effective backward and forward linkages. Firms should stay in the marketplace, constantly innovating new products and processes, and understand the changing behavior of markets to develop long-term customer-centric strategies and efficient value chain models (Esko et al., 2013).

Innovation in business either in strategy, operations, technology, new products or services, is a complex phenomenon that involves the entire organization. It is necessary to involve senior management early in the innovation process when most of the major strategy and resource decisions are still easy to change, and to generate awareness about the innovation project among all role players within the organization. Such integration of knowledge with the employees of the company would help in developing a product innovation process. Success of innovation does not come with a single best effort but firms need to create multiple prototypes and conduct market tests. For instance, I-Robot Company developed several prototypes of automatic vacuum cleaning machines to conduct market tests and launched the best product as a breakthrough innovation with technology. The recent trend of product innovation advocates co-creation with consumers. Large multinational companies involve consumers early and often, despite threats from potential competitors, and make efforts to protect the confidentiality of information on innovation. Innovations to drive new products and services need subject matter experts, and firms should bring them within the organizational gamut to facilitate working teams on innovation projects. It may be complex for a person to be both the facilitator of the process and the leader of discussions and decisions about the business (Rajagopal, 2014).

Successful innovation leads to customer involvement and profits, which can be achieved through co-creation by aligning consumers and market players in the innovation process. Some multinational companies have invested resources by taking advantage of social media to diffuse new ideas and stimulate co-creation of innovative products and services. For many companies, developing new products does not occur as a matter of chance or coincidence but rather innovative products emerge through careful attention to many important criteria. Firms should analyze their innovation practices and capabilities to become more effective in driving innovation as a breakthrough and gain competitive advantage. For most firms, services innovation generally means making incremental improvements to existing services. Though focus of firms on improving the quality of existing services certainly makes a difference in the competitive marketplace, firms should also make efforts to overcome gaps in innovation capabilities by delimiting new ideas. Multinational firms focus on improving service capabilities to address the fundamental needs of their customers and develop services innovations through shared solutions with customers. Firms with co-creation strategies are able to create effective breakthrough products and processes. Such a process of service innovation results in value co-creation, which makes a significant difference to customers and to competing services products in the marketplace (Bettencourt et al., 2013).

Several explanations of consumer behavior have been advanced over time, but the expectations–disconfirmation paradigm has contributed significantly to research over time. The economic perspectives of consumer behavior have been explored in research studies through various models during post-globalization shifts in the market through interrelated variables including lifecycle consumption patterns, life-styles, brand loyalty, choice of features, and search behavior. Consumer research addressing the sociocultural, experiential, symbolic, and ideo-logical aspects of consumption has also been addressed in conceptual research studies, which have reviewed the literature since the mid-1980s and argued over enduring misconceptions about the nature and ana-lytic orientation of Consumer Culture Theory (Arnould and Thompson, 2005). Companies are trying to understand consumer needs by involv-ing them in developing desired products, by competitive differentiation in existing products, and by customer-focused new products to acquire customer support in marketing products in competitive marketplaces. These days more companies are frequently engaging consumers in design products. By focusing on improving the experiences of everyone involved, such firms are achieving breakthrough insights, lower costs, new revenues, and new business models.

References

Foreword

Appelo, J. (2011), *Management 3.0: Leading Agile Developers, Developing Agile Leaders*, Boston, MA: Addison-Wesley.

Ariely, D. (2010), *Predictably Irrational: The Hidden Forces that Shape Our Decisions*, New York: Harper Perennial.

Lorenz, E. (1972), *Predictability: Does the flap of a butterfly's wings in Brazil set off a tornado in Texas?* Speech before the American Academy for the Advancement of Science (http://eaps4.mit.edu/research/Lorenz/Butterfly_1972.pdf [Retrieved on November 06, 2014].

Sterman, J. (2000), *Business Dynamics: Systems Thinking and Modeling for a Complex World*, Burr Ridge, IL: McGraw Hill.

Weinberg, G. M. (1992), *Quality Software Management*, Vol. 1, New York: Dorset House.

1 Chaos in Markets

Abell, P. (2000), Sociological Theory and Rational Choice Theory, in Bryan S. Turner, *The Blackwell Companion to Social Theory*, 2nd ed., Malden, MA: Blackwell Publishers.

Abrahamson, E. (2004), Avoiding repetitive change syndrome, *MIT Sloan Management Review*, 45 (2), 93–95.

Alden, D.L., Steenkamp, J.B., and Batra, R. (1999), Brand positioning through advertising in Asia, North America, and Europe: The role of global consumer culture, *Journal of Marketing*, 63 (1), 75–87.

Alden, D.L., Steenkamp, J.B., and Batra, R. (2006), Consumer attitudes toward marketplace globalization: Structure, antecedents and consequences, *International Journal of Research in Marketing*, 23 (1), 227–239.

Ali, A. and Hang, L. (2006), Economic reforms and bank efficiency in developing countries: The case of the Indian banking industry, *Applied Consumer Economics*, 16 (9), 653–663.

Barton, D., Grant, A., and Horn, M. (2012), Leading in the twenty first century, *McKinsey Quarterly*, June (retrieved on June 23, 2014, http://www.mckinsey.com/insights/leading_in_the_21st_century/leading_in_the_21st_century).

Blumenthal, D. (2002), Beyond 'form versus content': Simmelian theory as a framework for adaptive brand strategy, *Journal of Brand Management*, 10 (1), 9–18.

Bremmer, I. (2014), New rules of globalization, *Harvard Business Review*, 92 (1), 103–107.

Coca-Stefaniak, J. A., Blackwell, M., Codato, G., and Estevan, F. (2010), European approaches to creative urban revitalisation – A critical study of the applicability of key performance indicators to the socio-economic, branding and environmental evaluation of culture-led community engagement programmes and festivals, *Proceedings of the 5th World Congress for Downtowns and Town Centres*, London, June 16–19.

Davies, A. (2004), Moving base into high-value integrated solutions: A value stream approach, *Industrial and Corporate Change*, 13 (5), 727–756.

Dawar, N. (2013), When marketing is strategy, *Harvard Business Review*, 91 (12), 100–108.

Donner, J. and Tellez, C. (2008), Mobile banking and economic development: Linking adoption, impact, and use, *Asian Journal of Communication*, 18 (4), 318–332.

Dubey, J. and Patel, R. P. (2004), Small wonders of the Indian market, *Journal of Consumer Behaviour*, 4 (2), 145–151.

Durkin, M. (2007), Understanding registration influences for electronic banking, *The International Review of Retail, Distribution and Consumer Research*, 17 (3), 219–231.

Economic Intelligence Unit (2005), *Business 2010: Embracing the Challenge of Change*, White Paper, Economist Intelligence Unit, New York, February.

Ger, G. (1999), Localizing in the global village: Local firms competing in global markets, *California Management Review*, 41 (4), 64–83.

Ger, G. and Belk, R. W. (1996), Cross-cultural differences in materialism, *Journal of Economic Psychology*, 17 (1), 55–77.

Goldstein, D. G., Johnson, E. J., Herrmann, A., and Heitmann, M. (2008), Nudge your customers toward better choices, *Harvard Business Review*, 86 (12), 99–105.

Hansen, G. E. (2002), *The Culture of Strangers – Globalization, Localization and the Phenomenon of Exchange*, New York: University Press of America.

Homans, G. (1961), *Social Behaviour: Its Elementary Forms*, London: Routledge & Kegan Paul.

Jullens, J. (2013), How emerging giants can take on the world, *Harvard Business Review*, 91 (12), 121–125.

Khanna, T. and Palepu, K. G. (2006), Emerging giants: Building world-class companies in developing countries, *Harvard Business Review*, 84 (10), 60–70.

Khanna, T., Palepu, K. G., and Sinha, J. (2005), Strategies that fit emerging markets, *Harvard Business Review*, 83 (6), 63–74.

Kim, W. C. and Mauborgne, R. (2004), Blue ocean strategy, *Harvard Business Review*, 82 (10), 76–84.

Kogut, B. (1999), What makes a company global, *Harvard Business Review*, 77 (1), 165–170.

Kotabe, M. and Helsen, K. (2010), *Global Marketing Management*, 5th ed., Hoboken, NJ: John Wiley & Sons, Inc.

Levitt, T. (1983), Globalization of markets, *Harvard Business Review*, 61 (3), 92–102.

Liu, W., Guillet, B. D., Xiao, Q., and Law, R. (2014), Globalization or localization of consumer preferences: The case of hotel room booking, *Tourism Management*, 41 (2), 148–157.

Markides, C.C. (1999), A dynamic view of strategy, *MIT Sloan Management Review*, 40 (3), 55–63.

Meyer, A. D., Loch, C. H., and Pich, M. T. (2002), Managing project uncertainty, *MIT Sloan Management Review*, 43 (2), 60–67.

Piccoli, G., Brohman, M. K., Watson, R. T., and Parasuraman, A. (2009), Process completeness: Strategies for aligning service systems with customers' service needs, *Business Horizons*, 52 (4), 367–376.

Potter, D. (2004), Confronting low-end competition, *MIT Sloan Management Review*, 45 (4), 73–79.

Prahalad, C. K. and Lieberthal, K. (2003), End of corporate imperialism, *Harvard Business Review*, 76 (4), 68–79.

Prashantham, S. and Birkinshaw, J. (2008), Dancing with gorillas: How small companies can partner effectively with MNCs, *California Management Review*, 51 (1), 6–23.

Rajagopal (2012), *Darwinian Fitness in the Global Marketplace: Analysis of Competition*, Basingstoke: Palgrave Macmillan.

Rajagopal (2014), *Architecting Enterprise: Managing Innovation, Technology, and Global Competitiveness*, Basingstoke: Palgrave Macmillan.

Raphael, A. and Christoph, Z. (2012), Creating value through business model innovation, *MIT Sloan Management Review*, 53 (3), 41–49.

Ritzer, G. (2007), *The Globalization of Nothing 2*, Thousand Oaks, CA: Pine Forge Press.

Robertson, R. (1987), Globalization and societal modernization: A note on Japan and Japanese religion, *Sociological Analysis*, 47, 35–43.

Robertson, R. (1995), Glocalization: Time–space and homogeneity–heterogeneity, 25–44, in Featherstone, M., Lash, S., and Robertson, R. (Eds), *Global Modernities*, London: Sage.

Sawhney, M. and Prandelli, E. (2000), Communities of creation: Managing distributed innovation in turbulent markets, *California Management Review*, 42 (4), 24–54.

Scott, J. (2000), *Understanding Contemporary Society: Theories of The Present*, edited by Browning, G., Halcli, A., and Webster, F., London: Sage Publications.

Stalk, G. and Lachenauer, R. (2004), Hardball – Five killer strategies for trouncing the competition, *Harvard Business Review*, 82 (4), 62–71

Steenkamp, J. B. and De Jong, M. G. (2010), A global investigation into the constellation of consumer attitudes toward global and local products, *Journal of Marketing*, 74 (6), 18–40.

Sullivan, T. (2011), Embracing complexity, *Harvard Business Review*, 89 (9), 89–92.

Sutthijakra, S. (2011), Managing service subsidiaries through an innovation perspective: A case of standard interpretation in multinational hotels, *The Service Industries Journal*, 31 (3/4), 545–558.

Tate, W. L., Ellram, L. M., Schoenherr, T., and Petersen, K. J. (2014), Global competitive conditions driving the manufacturing location decision, *Business Horizons*, 57 (3), 381–390.

Wang, Z. (2005), *Technology Innovation and Market Turbulence: A Dot com Example*, Federal Reserve Bank of Kansas City, Payments System Research Working Paper # PSR-WP-05-02, 1–49.

Wheeler, M. A. (2004), Turn chaos to your advantage, *Harvard Business Publishing Newsletters*, April 01.

Wood, I. J. and Grosvenor, S. (2003), Chocolate in China: The Cadbury experience, *Australian Geographer*, 28 (2), 173–184.

Yousafzai, S., Pallister, J. and Foxall, G. (2009), Multi-dimensional role of trust in Internet banking adoption, *Service Industries Journal*, 29 (5), 591–605.

Yu, Y. C., Byun, W. H., and Lee, T. J. (2014), Critical issues of globalization in the international hotel industry, *Current Issues in Tourism*, 17 (2), 114–118.

Zachary, G. P. (1999), Many industries are congealing into a lineup of few dominant giants, *The Wall Street Journal*, March 08.

Zou, S. and Cavusgil, S. T. (2002), The GMS: A brand conceptualization of global marketing strategy and its effect on firm performance, *Journal of Marketing*, 66 (4), 40–56.

2 Reasoned Action and Planned Behavior

Acito, F., McDougall, P. M., and Smith, D. C. (2008), One hundred years of excellence in business education: What have we learned?, *Business Horizons*, 51 (1), 5–12.

Aizen, I. (1991), The theory of planned behavior, *Organizational Behavior and Human Decision Processes*, 50 (2), 179–211.

Amit, R. and Zott, C. (2012), Creating value through business model innovation, *MIT Sloan Management Review*, 53 (3), 41–49.

Boden, R. and Nevada, M. (2010), Employing discourse: Universities and graduate employability, *Journal of Education Policy*, 25, 37–54.

Bone, P. F. (1995), Word-of-mouth effects on short-term and long-term product judgments, *Journal of Business Research*, 32 (3), 213–223.

Brown, J. S. and Duguid, P. (1998), Organizing knowledge, *California Management Review*, 40 (3), 90–111.

Brown, T. (2008), Design thinking, *Harvard Business Review*, 86 (6), 84–92.

Buckingham, M. (2005), What great managers do, *Harvard Business Review*, 83 (3), 70–80.

Doherty, A. M. (2009), Market and partner selection processes in international retail franchising, *Journal of Business Research*, 62 (5), 528–534.

Drayton, B. and Budinich, V. (2010), A new alliance for the global change, *Harvard Business Review*, 88 (9), 56–64.

Eisenhardt, K. M. and Sull, D. N. (2001), Strategy as simple rules, *Harvard Business Review*, 79 (1), 106–116.

Ennew, C. T., Banerjee, A. K., and Li, D. (2000), Managing word-of mouth communication: Empirical evidence from India, *International Journal of Bank Marketing*, 18 (2), 75–89.

Ferguson, R. J., Paulin, M. and Bergeron, J. (2010), Customer sociability and the total experience: Antecedents of the positive word-of-mouth intentions, *Journal of Services Management*, 21 (1), 25–44.

Fishbein, M. and Ajzen, I. (1975), *Belief, Attitude, Intention, and Behavior: An Introduction to Theory and Research*, Reading, MA: Addison-Wesley.

Garvin, D. A. (1993), Building a learning organization, *Harvard Business Review*, 73 (4), 78–91.

Ghemawat, P. (1985), Building strategy on experience curve, *Harvard Business Review*, 63 (2), 143–149.

Ghemawat, P. (2007), Managing differences: The central challenge of global strategy, *Harvard Business Review*, 85 (3), 59–68.

Ghoshal, S. and Gratton, L. (2002), Integrating the enterprise, *MIT Sloan Management Review*, 44 (1), 31–38.

Goldman, E. F. (2007), Strategic thinking at the top, *MIT Sloan Management Review*, 48 (4), 75–81.

Hanna, R. C., Rohm, A., and Crittenden, V. L. (2011), We're all connected: The power of the social media ecosystem, *Business Horizons*, 54 (3), 265–273.

Isenberg, D. J. (2008), The global entrepreneur, *Harvard Business Review*, 86 (12), 107–111.

Izosimov, A. V. (2008), Managing hyper-growth, *Harvard Business Review*, 86 (4), 121–127.

Kalyanam, K. and Zweben, M. (2005), Perfect message at the perfect moment, *Harvard Business Review*, 83 (11), 112–120.

Keidel, R. W. (2013), Strategy made simple: Think in threes, *Business Horizons*, 56 (1), 105–111.

Kiron, D. (2012), How IBM builds vibrant social communities, *MIT Sloan Management Review*, 54 (1), 1–6.

Klarl, T. (2009), *Knowledge Diffusion and Knowledge Transfer: Two Sides of the Medal*, Working paper 09-080, Center for European Economic Research, 1–24.

Kuemmerle, W. (2005), Entrepreneur's path to global expansion, *MIT Sloan Management Review*, 46 (2), 42–49.

Lapre, M. A. and Van Wassenhove, L. N. (2003), Managing learning curves in factories by creating and transferring knowledge, *California Management Review*, 46 (1), 53–71.

Lester, R. K., Piore, M. J., and Malek, K. M. (1998), Interpretive management: What general managers can learn from design, *Harvard Business Review*, 76 (2), 86–96.

Malhotra, A., Malhotra, C. K., and See, A. (2012), How to get your messages retweeted, *MIT Sloan Management Review*, 53 (2), 61–66.

May, M. E. (2012), *Observe First, Design Second: Taming the Traps of Traditional Thinking*, Working Paper, Rotman School of Management, April, 01.

Mintzberg, H. and Westley, F. (2001), Decision making: It's not what you think, *MIT Sloan Management Review*, 42 (3), 89–93.

Nayar, V. (2010), *Employees First, Customers Second: Turning Conventional Management Upside Down*, Boston, MA: Harvard Business School Press.

Procter, J. and Richards, M. (2002), Word-of-mouth marketing: Beyond pester power, *Young Consumers: Insights and Ideas for Responsible Marketers*, 3 (3), 3–11.

Rajagopal (2009), *Globalization Thrust: Driving Nations Competitive*, Hauppauge, NY: Nova Publishers.

Rajagopal (2011), Impact of radio advertisements on buying behavior of urban commuters, *International Journal of Retail and Distribution Management*, 39 (7), 480–503.

Report (2000), Companies on a learning curve, *Journal of European Industrial Training*, 24 (8), 5–6.

Sharma, P., Hoy, F., Astrachan, J. H., and Koiranen, M. (2007), The practice-driven evolution of family business education, *Journal of Business Research*, 60 (10), 1012–1021.

Steffes, E. M. and Burgee, L. E. (2009), Social ties and online word-of-mouth, *Internet Research: Electronic Networking and Applications and Policy*, 19 (1), 42–59.

Storey, J. and Barnett, E. (2000), Knowledge management initiatives: Learning from failure, *Journal of Knowledge Management*, 4 (2), 145–156.

Sull, D. N. (2003), Managing by commitments, *Harvard Business Review*, 81 (6), 82–91.

Sweeney, J. C., Soutar, G. N., and Mazzarol, T. (2012), Word-of-mouth: Measuring the power of individual messages, *European Journal of Marketing*, 46 (1), 237–257.

Wilton, N. (2008), Business graduates and management jobs: An employability match made in heaven?, *Journal of Education and Work*, 21 (2), 143–158.

Wollan, R., Smith, N., and Zhou, C. (2011), *The Social Media Management Handbook: Everything You Need to Know to Get Social Media Working in Your Business*, Hoboken, NJ: John Wiley & Sons, Inc.

Yu, L. (2007), The quality effect on word-of-mouth, *MIT Sloan Management Review*, 49 (1), 6–8.

3 Managing Market Shifts

Armstrong, J. S. (1988), Review of Alfie Kohn's book, *No Contest, Journal of Marketing*, 52 (4), 131–132.

Baldwin, C. Y. and Clark, K. B. (1997), Managing in an age of modularity, *Harvard Business Review*, 75 (5), 84–93.

Borison, A. and Hamm, G. (2010), Prediction markets: A new tool for strategic decision making, *California Management Review*, 52 (4), 51–57.

Carter, T. (2006), Sales management coaching: A model for improved insurance company performance, *Journal of Hospital Marketing & Public Relations*, 16 (1), 113–125.

Carswell, Peter (2005), The financial impact of organizational downsizing practices: The New Zealand experience, *Asia Pacific Journal of Management*, 22 (1), 41–63.

Chaudhry, A. S. (2005), Knowledge sharing practices in Asian institutions: A multi-cultural perspective from Singapore, In *Proceedings of 71th IFLA General Conference and Council*, Oslo, Norway, August 14–18.

Christensen, C. M., Marx, M., and Stevenson, H. H. (2006), Tools of cooperation and change, *Harvard Business Review*, 84 (10), 72–80.

Darr, A. (2003), Control and autonomy among knowledge workers in sales: An employee perspective, *Employee Relations*, 25 (1), 31–41.

Davies, A. (2004), Moving base into high-value integrated solutions: A value stream approach, *Industrial and Corporate Change*, 13 (5), 727–756.

Edmondson, A. C., Bohmer, R. M., and Pisano, G. P. (2001a), Disrupted routines: Team learning and new technology implementation in hospitals, *Administrative Science Quarterly*, 46 (4).

Edmondson, A. C., Bohmer, R. M., and Pisano, G. P. (2001b), Speeding-up team learning, *Harvard Business Review*, 64 (5), 66–73.

Fahey, L. (1999), *Competitors: Outwitting, Outmaneuvering and Outperforming*, New York: John Wiley and Sons.

Farrell, M. (2005), The effect of a market-oriented organizational culture on sales-force behavior and attitudes, *Journal of Strategic Marketing*, 13 (4), 261–273.

Fine, C. H., Vardan, R., Pethick, R., and El-Hout, J. (2002), Rapid-response capability in value-chain design, *MIT Sloan Management Review*, 43 (2), 69–75.

Garvin, D. A., Edmonson, A. C. and Gino, F. (2008), Is yours a learning organization?, *Harvard Business Review*, 86 (3), 109–116.

Hong, D., Suh, E., and Koo, C. (2011), Developing strategies for overcoming barriers to knowledge sharing based on conversational knowledge management: A case study of a financial company, *Expert Systems with Applications*, 38 (12), 14417–14427.

Hurley, R. F. and Hult, G. T. (1998), Innovation, market orientation, and organizational learning: An integration and empirical examination, *Journal of Marketing*, 62 (3), 42–54.

Jacobides, M. G. and MacDuffie, J. P. (2013), How to drive value your way, *Harvard Business Review*, 91 (7), 92–100.

Johnson, G., Yip, G. S., and Hensmans, M. (2012), Achieving successful strategic transformation, *MIT Sloan Management Review*, 53 (3), 25–32.

Jones, G. R. (2007), *Organizational Theory, Design and Change*, 5th ed., Upper Saddle River, NJ: Prentice Hall.

Kim, W. C. and Maubourge, R. A. (1999), Creating new market space, *Harvard Business Review*, 77 (1), 83–93.

Kohn, A. (1988), *No Contest: The Case Against Competition*, Boston, MA: Houghton Mifflin.

Lacity, M. C. and Willcocks, L. P. (2013), Outsourcing business processes for innovation, *MIT Sloan Management Review*, 54 (3), 63–69.

MacMillan, I. C. and McGrath, R. G. (1997), Discovering new points of differentiation, *Harvard Business Review*, 75 (4), 133–142.

Neely, A. and Al Najjar, M. (2006), Management learning not management control: The true role of performance management?, *California Management Review*, 48 (3), 101–14.

Pascale, R. T. and Sternin, J. (2005), Your company's secret change agents, *Harvard Business Review*, 83 (5), 72–81.

Potter, D. (2004), Confronting low-end competition, *MIT Sloan Management Review*, 41 (3), 41–49.

Rajagopal and Rajagopal, A. (2008), Team performance and control process in sales organizations, *Team Performance Management*, 14 (1), 70–85.

Rust, R. T., Zeithaml, V. A., and Lemon, K. N. (2004), Customer centered brand management, *Harvard Business Review*, 82 (9), 110–118.

Sargut, G. and McGrath, R. G. (2011), Learning to live with complexity, *Harvard Business Review*, 89 (9), 69–76.

Schein, E. H. (1996), Three cultures of management: The key to organizational learning, *MIT Sloan Management Review*, 38 (1), 9–20.

Schoemaker, P. J. H. and Day, G. S. (2011), Innovating in uncertain markets: 10 lessons for green technologies, *MIT Sloan Management Review*, 52 (4), 37–45.

Therin, F. (2002), Organizational learning and innovation in high-tech small firms, in *Proceedings of the 36th International Conference on System Sciences*, Hawaii, IEEE Computer Society, 1–8.

Vila, J. (2012), Normalize innovation to transform your firm, *IESE-Insight Magazine*, 14, 36–43.

Wenger, E. and Snyder, W. M. (2000), Communities of practice: The organizational frontier, *Harvard Business Review*, 78 (1), 139–145.

Williams, M. J. (1997), Agility in learning: An essential for evolving organizations and people, *Harvard Business School Newsletter*, May, 01.

4   Market Trend Analysis

Ahmed, A., Ahmed, N., and Ahmed, S. (2005), Critical issues in packaged food business, *British Food Journal*, 107 (10), 760–780.
Axarloglou, K. (2003), The cyclicality of new product introductions, *Journal of Business*, 76 (1), 29–48.
Bertot, J. C., Jaeger, P. T., and Hansen, D. (2012), The impact of polices on government social media usage: Issues, challenges, and recommendations, *Government Information Quarterly*, 29 (1), 30–40.
Black, J. S. and Morrison, A. J. (2010), A cautionary tale for emerging market giants, *Harvard Business Review*, 88 (9), 99–105.
Bower, J. L. and Christensen, C. M. (1995), Disruptive technology: Catching the wave, *Harvard Business Review*, 73 (1), 43–53.
Christensen, C. M. and Overdorf, M. (2000), Meeting the challenge of disruptive change, *Harvard Business Review*, 78 (2), 66–76.
Cowen, T. (2002), *Creative Destruction: How Globalization Is Changing the World's Cultures*, Princeton, NJ: Princeton University Press.
Davenport, T. H., Prusak, L., and Wilson, J. H. (2003), Who's bringing you hot ideas, *Harvard Business Review*, 81 (2), 58–64.
de Jonge, J., van Trijp, H., Jan, R. R., and Frewer, L. (2007), Understanding consumer confidence in the safety of food: Its two-dimensional structure and determinants, *Risk Analysis*, 27 (3), 729–740.
Denstadli, J. M., Lines, R., and Grønhaug, K. (2005), First mover advantages in the discount grocery industry, *European Journal of Marketing*, 39 (7–8), 872–884.
Dilek, C., Bülent, C., and Serdar, B. O. (2005), Competition through collaboration: Insights from an initiative in the Turkish textile supply chain, *Supply Chain Management – An International Journal*, 10 (4), 238–240.
Dubey, J. and Patel, R. P. (2004), Small wonders of the Indian market, *Journal of Consumer Behaviour*, 4 (2), 145–151.
Griener, L. E. (1998), Evolution and revolution as organizations grow, *Harvard Business Review*, 76 (3), 55–63.
Hofman, J. D. and Orlikowski, W. J. (1997), Improvisational model for change management: The case of groupware technologies, *MIT Sloan Management Review*, 38 (2), 11–22.
Ibeh, K. I. N., Essam, I., and Panayides, P. M. (2006), International market success among smaller agri-food companies: Some case study evidence, *International Journal of Entrepreneurial Behaviour and Research*, 12 (2), 85–104.
Kim, W. C. and Mauborgne, R. (2005), *Blue Ocean Strategy: How to Create Uncontested Market Space and Make the Competition Irrelevant*, Boston, MA: Harvard Business School Press.
Kumar, S. and Krob, W. (2007), Phase reviews versus fast product development: A business case, *Journal of Engineering Design*, 18 (3), 279–291.
Lilien, G. L. and Yoon, E. (1990), The timing of competitive market entry: An exploratory study of new industrial products, *Management Science*, 36, 568–585.

Paladino, A. (2007), Investigating the drivers of innovation and new product success: A comparison of strategic orientations, *Journal of Product Innovation Management*, 24 (6), 534–553.

Petiot, J. F. and Grognet, S. (2006), Product design: A vectors field-based approach for preference modeling, *Journal of Engineering Design*, 17 (3), 217–233.

Radas, S. and Shugan, S. M. (1998), Seasonal marketing and timing new product introductions, *Journal of Marketing Research*, 35, 345–360.

Rajagopal (2006), Measuring consumer value gaps: An empirical study in Mexican retail markets, *Economic Issues*, 11 (1), 19–40.

Rajagopal (2007), Stimulating retail sales and upholding consumer value, *Journal of Retail and Leisure Property*, 6 (2), 117–135.

Rajagopal and Rajagopal, A. (2007), Competition vs. cooperation: Analyzing strategy dilemma in business growth under changing social paradigms, *International Journal of Business Environment*, 1 (4), 476–487.

Salmi, L. and Holmström, J. (2004), Monitoring new product introductions with sell-through data from channel partners, *Supply Chain Management: An International Journal*, 9 (3), 209–212.

Salonen, M., Holtta, O. K., and Otto, K. (2007), Effecting product reliability and life cycle costs with early design phase product architecture decisions, *International Journal of Product Development*, 5 (1–2), 109–124.

Samiee, S. (2008), Global marketing effectiveness via alliances and electronic commerce in business-to-business markets, *Industrial Marketing Management*, 37 (1), 3–8.

Sharan, J., Jedidi, K., and Jamil, M. (2007), A multi-brand concept-testing methodology for new product strategy, *Journal of Product Innovation Management*, 24 (1), 34–51.

Sirkin, H. L., Keenan, P., and Jackson, A. (2005), Hard side of change management, *Harvard Business Review*, 83 (10), 108–118.

Sobreman, D. A. (2003), Role of differentiation in markets driven by advertising, *California Management Review*, 45 (3), 1–17.

Teratanavat, R. and Hooker, N. H. (2006), Consumer valuations and preference heterogeneity for a novel functional food, *Journal of Food Science*, 71 (7), 533–541.

Wilson, L. O. and Norton, J. A. (1989), Optimal entry timing for a product line extension, *Marketing Science*, 8 (1), 1–17.

Yu, D. and Hang, C. C. (2010), A reflective review of disruptive innovation theory, *International Journal of Management Review*, 12 (4), 435–452.

5 Consumer Value Management

Abraham, Z. (2004), Managers and leaders: Are they different?, *Harvard Business Review*, 82 (1), 74–81.

Ahmed, J. U. (1996), Modern approaches to product reliability improvement, *International Journal of Quality & Reliability Management*, 13 (3), 27–41.

Anderson, J. and Billou, N. (2007), Serving the world's poor: Innovation at the base of the economic pyramid, *Journal of Business Strategy*, 28 (2), 14–21.

Baker, T. L. Jr., Cronin, J. J., and Hopkins, C. D. (2009), The impact of involvement on key service relationships, *Journal of Services Marketing*, 23 (2), 114–123.

Bauer, H. H., Hammerschmidt, M., and Staat, M. (2004), *Analyzing Product Efficiency: A Customer Oriented Approach*, University of Mannheim, February.

Bhatt, G. (2000), Organizing knowledge in the knowledge development cycle, *Journal of Knowledge Management*, 4 (1), 15–26.

Brucks, M., Zeithaml, V. A., and Naylor, G. (2000), Price and brand name as indicators of quality dimensions of customer durables, *Journal of Academy of Marketing Science*, 28 (3), 359–374.

Bruhn, M. (2003), *Relationship Marketing: Management of Customer Relationships*, Harlow: Pearson.

Cardy, R. L. and Selvaraj, T. T. (2006), Competencies: Alternative frameworks for competitive advantage, *Business Horizon*, 49 (3), 235–245.

Carswell, Peter (2005), The financial impact of organizational downsizing practices: The New Zealand experience, *Asia Pacific Journal of Management*, 22 (1), 41–63.

Chan, K. W. and Mauborgne, R. A. (1999), Creating new market space, *Harvard Business Review*, 77 (1), 83–93.

Chang, T. Z., Mehta, R., Chen, S. J., Polsa, P., and Mazur, J. (1999), The effects of market orientation on effectiveness and efficiency: The case of automotive distribution channels in Finland and Poland, *Journal of Services Marketing*, 13 (4–5), 407–418.

Chung, J., Jin, B., and Sternquist, B. (2007), The role of market orientation in channel relationships when channel power is imbalanced, *International Review of Retail, Distribution and Consumer Research*, 17 (2), 159–176.

Cristiano, J. J., Liker, J. K., and White III, C. C. (2000), Customer-driven product development through quality function deployment in the US and Japan, *Journal of Product Innovation Management*, 17 (4), 286–308.

Dash, S., Bruning, E., and Guin, K. K. (2009), A cross-cultural comparison of individualism's moderating effect on bonding and commitment in banking relationships, *Marketing Intelligence & Planning*, 27 (1), 146–169.

Davies, P. 2004, Is evidence-based policy possible?, *The Jerry Lee Lecture*, Campbell Collaboration Colloquium, Washington, February 18–20.

Deshpande, R., Hoyer, W., and Donthu, N. (1986), The intensity of ethnic affiliation: A study of the sociology of Hispanic consumption, *Journal of Consumer Research*, 13 (2), 214–221.

Dong, A. (2005), The latent semantic approach to studying development team communication, *Design Studies*, 26 (5), 445–461.

Draganska, M. and Jain, D. C. (2005), Product line length as a competitive tool, *Journal of Economics and Management Strategy*, 14 (1), 1–28.

Drucker, P. F. (1998), Discipline of innovation, *Harvard Business Review*, 76 (6), 149–157.

Edmondson, A. C. (2008), The competitive imperative of learning, *Harvard Business Review*, 86 (7), 60–67.

Erhun, F., Concalves, P., and Hopman, J. (2007), Art of managing new product transitions, *MIT Sloan Management Review*, 48 (3), 73–80.

Esko, S., Zeromskis, M., and Hsuan, J. (2013), Value chain and innovation at the base of the pyramid, *South Asian Journal of Global Business Research*, 2 (2), 230–250.

Fine, C. H., Vardan, R., Pethick, R., and El-Hout, J. (2002), Rapid-response capability in value-chain design, *MIT Sloan Management Review*, 43 (2), 69–75.

Garcia, R. and Calantone, R. (2002), A critical look at technological innovation typology and innovativeness terminology: A literature review, *Journal of Product Innovation Management*, 19 (2), 110–132.

Gary, L. (2003), Ambidextrous innovation, *Harvard Business Publishing Newsletter*, April 01.

Goldstein, D. G., Johnson, E. J., Herrmann, A., and Heitmann, M. (2008), Nudge your customers towards better choices, *Harvard Business Review*, 86 (12), 99–105.

Hanninen, S. and Sandberg, B. (2006), Consumer learning roadmap: A necessary tool for new products, *International Journal of Knowledge and Learning*, 2 (3), 298–307.

Heiko, G., Regine, K., and Elgar, F. (2008), Exploring the effect of cognitive biases on customer support services, *Creativity and Innovation Management*, 17 (1), 58–70.

Hirunyawipada, T. and Paswan, A. K. (2006), Consumer innovativeness and perceived risk: Implications for high technology product adoption, *Journal of Consumer Marketing*, 23 (4), 182–198.

Hulten, Bertil (2007), Customer segmentation: The concepts of trust, commitment and relationship, *Journal of Targeting, Measurement and Analysis for Marketing*, 15 (4), 256–269.

Hultink, E. J. and Atuahene-Gima, K. (2000), The effect of sales team adoption on new product selling performance, *Journal of Product Innovation Management*, 17 (6), 435–450.

Hunt, S. D. and Morgan, R. M. (1995), The comparative advantage theory of competition, *Journal of Marketing*, 59 (2), 1–15.

Lamming, R. C., Johnsen, T. E., Harland, C. M., and Zheng, J. (2000), Managing in supply networks: Cascade and intervention, *9th International Annual IPSERA Conference*, University of Western Ontario, Canada, May 24–27.

Locke, C. (2000), Smart customers, dumb companies, *Harvard Business Review*, 78 (6), 187–191.

Maaike, K., Buijs, J., and Valkenburg, R. (2010), Understanding the complexity of knowledge integration in collaborative new product development teams: A case study, *Journal of Engineering and Technology Management*, 27 (1–2), 20–32.

Maylor, H. (2001), Assessing the relationship between practice changes and process improvement in new product development, *Omega*, 29 (1), 85–96.

McGrath, R. G. and MacMillan, I. C. (1997), Discovering new points of differentiation, *Harvard Business Review*, 75 (3), 133–145.

Mascarenhas, B., Baveja, A., and Jamil, M. (1998), Dynamics of core competencies in leading multinational companies, *California Management Review*, 40 (4), 117–132.

Nagle, T. T. and Holden, R. K. (2002), *The Strategy and Tactics of Pricing*, Englewood Cliffs, NJ: Prentice Hall.

Normann, R. and Ramirez, R. (1993), From value chain to value constellation – designing interactive strategy, *Harvard Business Review*, 71 (4), 65–77.

Oakley, P. (1996), High tech NPD success through faster overseas launch, *European Journal of Marketing*, 30 (8), 75–91.

Payne, A. and Frow, P. (2005), Strategic framework for customer relationship management, *Journal of Marketing*, 69 (4), 167–176.

Prahalad, C. K. and Hamel, G. (1990), Core competency of the corporation, *Harvard Business Review*, 68 (3), 79–93.

Rajagopal (2007), Sales management in developing countries: A comparison of managerial control perspectives, *Journal of Asia Pacific Business*, 8 (3), 37–61.

Rajagopal and Rajagopal, A. (2008), Team performance and control process in sales organizations, *Team Performance Management – An International Journal*, 14 (1), 70–85.

Rajagopal and Sanchez, R. (2004), Conceptual analysis of brand architecture and relations within product categories, *The Journal of Brand Management*, 11 (3), 233–247.

Reichheld, F. F. and Sasser, W. E. (1990), Zero defections: Quality comes to services, *Harvard Business Review*, 68 (5), 105–111.

Slater, S. and Narver, J. (1995), Market orientation and the learning organization, *Journal of Marketing*, 59 (3), 63–74.

Suarez, F. F. and Lanzolla, G. (2005), The half truth of first mover advantage, *Harvard Business Review*, 83 (4), 121–127.

Tsai, W. M. H., MacMillan, I. C., and Low, M. B. (1991), Effects of strategy and environment on corporate venture success in industrial markets, *Journal of Business Venturing*, 6 (1), 9–28.

Weick, K. E. and Roberts, K. H. (1993), Collective mind in organizations: Heedful interrelating on flight decks, *Administrative Science Quarterly*, 38 (4), 357–381.

Werther, W. B. and Kerr, J. L. (1995), The shifting sands of competitive advantage, *Business Horizons*, 38 (3), 11–17.

6 Darwinism in the Marketplace

Adner, R. and Snow, D. C. (2010), Bold retreat: A new strategy for old technologies, *Harvard Business Review*, 88 (3), 76–81.

Anderson, J. E. (1979), A theoretical foundation for the gravity equation, *American Economic Review*, 69 (1), 106–116.

Atsu, A., Guide, V. D. R., and Wassenhove, L. N. V. (2010), So what if remanufacturing cannibalizes my new product sales?, *California Management Review*, 52 (2), 56–76.

Blumenthal, D. (2002), Beyond "form versus content": Simmelian theory as a framework for adaptive brand strategy, *Journal of Brand Management*, 10 (1), 9–18.

Clayton, C. M. (2003), *Beyond the Innovator's Dilemma*, Harvard Business Publishing Newsletter, March 01, Boston, MA.

Cravens, D. W., Piercy, N. F., and Prentice, A. (2000), Developing market-driven product strategies, *Journal of Product and Brand Management*, 9 (6), 369–388.

Cruickshank, J. A. (2009), A play for rurality: Modernization versus local autonomy, *Journal of Rural Studies*, 25 (1), 98–107.

Debruyne, M. and Reibstein, D. J. (2005), Competitor see, competitor do: Incumbent entry in new market niches, *Marketing Science*, 24 (1), 55–66.

Desai, P. S. (2001), Quality segmentation in spatial markets: When does cannibalization affect product line design?, *Marketing Science*, 20 (3), 265–283.

Desmet, K. and Parente, S. L. (2010), Bigger is better: Market size, demand elasticity, and innovation, *International Economic Review*, 51 (2), 319–333.

Doz, Y. L. and Hamel, G. (1998), *Alliance Advantage: The Art of Creating Value through Partnerships*, Boston, MA: Harvard Business School Press.

Dubey, J. and Patel, R. P. (2004), Small wonders of the Indian market, *Journal of Consumer Behaviour*, 4 (2), 145–151.

Erhun, F., Concalves, P., and Hopman, J. (2007), Art of managing new products transition, *MIT Sloan Management Review*, 48 (3), 73–80.

Flores, F., Letelier, M. F., and Spinosa, C. (2003), Developing productive customers in emerging markets, *California Management Review*, 45 (4), 77–103.

Ganesh, J. (2004), Managing customer preferences in a multi-channel environment using Web services, *International Journal of Retail & Distribution Management*, 32 (3), 140–146.

Goldthorpe, J. H. (2000), Globalization and social class, *West European Politics*, 25 (3), 1–28.

Hayes, J. B., Alford, B. L., Silver, L., and York, R. P. (2006), Looks matter in developing consumer–brand relationships, *Journal of Product and Brand Management*, 15 (5), 306–315.

Hedaa, L. and Ritter, T. (2005), Business relationships on different waves: Paradigm shift and marketing orientation revisited, *Industrial Marketing Management*, 34 (7), 714–721.

Hwang, A. (2010), More than 20 companies join Taiwan Blu-ray Disc Consortium, *DIGITIMES*, Taipei, April 29.

Kapferer, J. N. (2000), *Strategic Brand Management*, 2nd ed., London: Kogan Press, 125–140.

Levitt, T. (1960), Marketing myopia, *Harvard Business Review*, 38 (4), 45–56.

Li, W. (1999), A tale of two reforms, *Rand Journal of Economics*, 30 (1), 120–136.

MacMillan, I. C. and McGrath, R. G. (1997), Discovering new points of differentiation, *Harvard Business Review*, 75 (4), 133–145.

Medlin, B. Dawn and Romaniello, Adriana (2008), The cost of electronic retailing: Prevalent security threats and their results, *International Journal of Electronic Marketing and Retailing*, 2 (1), 80–96.

Meredith, L. and Maki, D. (2001), Product cannibalization and the role of prices, *Applied Economics*, 33 (14), 1785–1793.

Moorthy, K. S. and Png, I. P. L. (1992), Market segmentation, cannibalization, and the timing of product introductions, *Management Science*, 38 (3), 345–359.

Prahalad, C. K. (2002), Strategies for the bottom of the economic pyramid: India as a source of innovation, *Reflections: The SOL Journal*, 3 (4), 6–18.

Prahalad, C. K. and Hammond, A. (2002), Serving the world's poor, profitably, *Harvard Business Review*, 80 (9), 48–58.

Prahalad, C. K. and Lieberthal, K. (2003), The end of corporate imperialism, *Harvard Business Review*, 81 (8), 109–117.

Quinn, R. S. (1985), Managing innovation: Controlled chaos, *Harvard Business Review*, 63 (3), 73–84.

Rajagopal (2006), Brand excellence: Measuring impact of advertising and brand personality on buying decisions, *Measuring Business Excellence*, 10 (3), 55–65.

Rajagopal (2009), Branding paradigm for bottom of the pyramid markets, *Measuring Business Excellence*, 13 (4), 58–68.

Rajagopal and Rajagopal, A. (2007), Architecting brands: Managerial process and control, *Journal of Transnational Management*, 12 (3), 25–37.

Reed, G., Story, V., and Saker, J. (2004), Information technology: Changing the face of automotive retailing?, *International Journal of Retail & Distribution Management*, 32 (1), 19–32.

Sabharwal, A. P., Gorman, M. E., and Werhane, P. H. (2004), Case study: Hindustan Lever Limited and marketing to the poorest of the poor, *International Journal of Entrepreneurship and Innovation Management*, 4 (5), 495–511.

Sehrawet, M. and Kundu, S. C. (2007), Buying behaviour of rural and urban consumers in India: The impact of packaging, *International Journal of Consumer Studies*, 31 (6), 630–638.

Soberman, D. A. (2003), Role of differentiation in markets driven by advertising, *California Management Review*, 45 (3), 130–146.

Strikwerda, J. and Stoelhorst, J. W. (2009), The emergence and evolution of the multidimensional organization, *California Management Review*, 51 (4), 11–31.

The Economist (1998), Asia's brand barons go shopping, March 28, 60.

Thomas, R., Tillmann, W., and Fawcett, S. (2008), Project management in retailing: Integrating the behavioral dimension, *International Review of Retail, Distribution and Consumer Research*, 18 (3), 325–341.

7 Business Growth and Local Effects

Aaker, D. A. and Joachimsthaler, E. (1999), The lure of global branding, *Harvard Business Review*, 77 (6), 137–146.

Adler, R. (2010), Enhancing business success: The role of performance management, *Business Horizons*, 53 (4), 331–333.

Ashkenas, R. (2007), Simplicity minded management, *Harvard Business Review*, 85 (12), 101–109.

Asian Development Bank (2003), Drivers of change, globalization, technology and competition, Section III, *Competitiveness in Developing Asia*, Asian Development Outlook, 2003.

Bonabeau, E. (2007), Understanding and managing complexity risk, *MIT Sloan Management Review*, 48 (4), 62–68.

Braglia, M., Grassi, A., and Montanari, R. (2004), Multi-attribute classification method for spare parts inventory management, *Journal of Quality in Maintenance Engineering*, 10 (1), 55–65.

Crittenden, V. L. and Crittenden, W. F. (2012), Corporate governance in emerging economies: Understanding the game, *Business Horizons*, 55 (6), 576–574.

Davenport, T. H., Prusak, L., and Wilson, J. H. (2003), Who's bringing you hot ideas?, *Harvard Business Review*, 81 (2), 58–64.

Davies, A. (2004), Moving base into high-value integrated solutions: A value stream approach, *Industrial and Corporate Change*, 13 (5), 727–756.

Dobson, J. (2007), Aesthetics as a foundation for business activity, *Journal of Business Ethics*, 72 (1), 41–46.

Erhun, F., Concalves, P., and Hopman, J. (2007), Art of manufacturing new product transitions, *MIT Sloan Management Review*, 48 (3), 73–80.

Fixson, S. K. (2005), Product architecture assessment: A tool to link product, process, and supply chain design decisions, *Journal of Operations Management*, 23 (3–4), 345–369.

Ger, G. (1999), Localizing in the global village: Local firms competing in global markets, *California Management Review*, 41 (4), 64–83.

Gottfredson, M. and Aspinall, K. (2005), Innovation versus complexity: What is too much of a good thing?, *Harvard Business Review*, 83 (11), 62–71.

Gottfredson, M. and Schwedel, A. (2008), Cut complexity and costs, *Harvard Business Publishing Newsletters*, August 01.

Hausman, A., Johnston, W. J., and Oyedele, A. (2005), Cooperative adoption of complex systems: A comprehensive model within and across networks, *Journal of Business & Industrial Marketing*, 20 (4), 200–210.

Hayes, R. H. and Wheelwright, S. C. (1979), Link manufacturing process and product life cycles, *Harvard Business Review*, 57 (1), 133–140.

Hoe, S. L. (2001), Weaving complexity and business: Engaging the soul at work, *Leadership & Organization Development Journal*, 22 (6), 301–303.

Ibeh, K. I. N., Essam, I., and Panayides, P. M. (2006), International market success among smaller agri-food companies: Some case study evidence, *International Journal of Entrepreneurial Behavior and Research*, 12 (2), 85–104.

Johnson-Cramer, M. E., Parise, S., and Cross, R. L. (2007), Managing change through networks and values, *California Management Review*, 49 (3), 85–109.

Keil, M. and Montealegre, R. (2000), Cutting your losses: Extricating your organization when a big project goes awry, *MIT Sloan Management Review*, 41 (3), 55–68.

Kishnan, V. and Ulrich, K. T. (2001), Product development decisions: A review of literature, *Management Science*, 47 (1), 1–21.

Lager, T. and Hörte, S. Å. (2002), Success factors for improvement and innovation of process technology in process industry, *Integrated Manufacturing Systems*, 13 (3), 158–164.

McGrath, R. G. (2011), Failing by design, *Harvard Business Review*, 89 (4), 76–83.

Moon, Y. (2005), Break free from the product life cycle, *Harvard Business Review*, 83 (5), 86–94.

Prewitt, E. (1998), Fast cycle decision making, *Harvard Business Publishing Newsletters*, August, 01.

Rajagopal (2008), Measuring brand performance through metrics application, *Measuring Business Excellence*, 12 (1), 29–38.

Ramus, C. A. (2001), Organizational support for employees: Encouraging creative ideas for environmental sustainability, *California Management Review*, 43 (3), 85–105.

Reilly, R. R., Lynn, G. S., and Aronson, Z. H. (2002), The role of personality in new product development team performance, *Journal of Engineering and Technology Management*, 19 (1), 39–58.

Sargut, G. and McGrath, R. G. (2011), Learning to live with complexity, *Harvard Business Review*, 89 (9), 68–76.

Stone, D. N. (1994), Overconfidence in initial self-efficacy judgment – effects on decision-processes and performance, *Organizational Behavior and Human Decision Processes*, 59 (3), 452–474.

Teratanavat, R. and Hooker, N. H. (2006), Consumer valuations and preference heterogeneity for a novel functional food, *Journal of Food Science*, 71 (7), 533–541.

van Stel, A. and Stunnenberg, V. (2006), Linking business ownership and perceived administrative complexity, *Journal of Small Business and Enterprise Development*, 13 (1), 7–22.

Werker, C. (2003), Innovation, market performance, and competition: Lessons from a product life cycle model, *Technovation*, 23 (4) 281–290.

8   Sustainable Marketing

Armstrong, J. S. (1988), Review of Alfie Kohn's book, *No Contest*, *Journal of Marketing*, 52 (4), 131–132.
Badarcco, Jr, J. L. (1988), *General Motor's Asian Alliance*, Cambridge, MA: Harvard Business School Press.
Bauer, H. H., Hammerschmidt, M., and Staat, M. (2004), *Analyzing Product Efficiency: A Customer Oriented Approach*, University of Mannheim, February.
Berman, B. and Thelen, S. (2004), A guide to developing and managing a well-integrated multi-channel retail strategy, *International Journal of Retail & Distribution Management*, 32 (3), 147–156.
Bickle, M., Buccine, R., Makela, C., and Mallette Dawn (2006), Consumers' uniqueness in home décor: Retail channel choice behaviour, *The International Review of Retail, Distribution and Consumer Research*, 16 (3), 317–331.
Billington, J. (1996), Five keys to keeping your best customers, *Harvard Business Publishing Newsletters*, July, 01.
Charlesworth, W. R. (1996), Co-operation and competition: Contributions to an evolutionary and developmental model, *International Journal of Behavioral Development*, 19 (1), 25–38.
Crittenden, V. L. and Wilson, E. J. (2002), Success factors in non-store retailing: Exploring the great merchants framework, *Journal of Strategic Marketing*, 10 (4), 255–272.
Daghfous, A. (2004), Organizational learning, knowledge and technology transfer: A case study, *Learning Organization: An International Journal*, 11 (1), 67–83.
Davies, A. (2004), Moving base into high-value integrated solutions: A value stream approach, *Industrial and Corporate Change*, 13 (5), 727–756.
Dempster, N., Freakley, M., and Parry, L. (2001), The ethical climate of public schooling under new public management, *International Journal of Leadership in Education*, 4 (1), 1–12.
Denstadli, J. M., Lines, R., and Grønhaug, K. (2005), First mover advantages in the discount grocery industry, *European Journal of Marketing*, 39 (7–8), 872–884.
Deshpande, R. (2014), *Marketing Reading: Customer Centricity*, Cambridge, MA: Harvard Business School Press.
Encaoua, D. and Hollander, A. (2002), Competition policy and innovation, *Oxford Review of Economic Policy*, 18 (1), 63–79.
Ganesh, J. (2004), Managing customer preferences in a multi-channel environment using web services, *International Journal of Retail & Distribution Management*, 32 (3), 140–146.
Haanaes, K., Michael, D., Jurgens, J., and Rangan, S. (2013), Making sustainability profitable, *Harvard Business Review*, 91 (3), 110–115.
Hall, J. K., Daneke, G. A., and Lenox, M. J. (2010), Sustainable development and entrepreneurship: Past contributions and future directions, *Journal of Business Venturing*, 25 (5), 439–448.
Holliday, C. (2001). Sustainable growth, the DuPont way, *Harvard Business Review*, 79 (8), 129–132.

Hopkins, M. S. (2009), 8 Reasons sustainability will change management, *MIT Sloan Management Review*, 51 (1), 27–30.

Ibeh, K. I. N., Essam, I., and Panayides, P. M. (2006), International market success among smaller agri-food companies: Some case study evidence, *International Journal of Entrepreneurial Behavior and Research*, 12 (2), 85–104.

Ingenbleek, P., Debruyne, M., Frambach, R. T., and Verhallen, T. (2003), Successful new product pricing practices: A contingency approach, *Marketing letters*, 14 (4), 289–305.

Jindal, R. P., Reinartz, W., Krafft, M., and Hoyer, W. D. (2007), Determinants of the variety of routes to market, *International Journal of Research in Marketing*, 24 (1), 17–29.

Kohn, A. (1986), *No Contest: The Case Against Competition*, Boston, MA: Houghton Mifflin.

Krubasik, E. G. (1988), Customize your product development, *Harvard Business Review*, 66 (6), 46–52.

Landers-Potts, M. and Grant, L. (1997), Competitive climates, athletic skill, and children's status in after-school recreational sports programs, *Social Psychology of Education*, 2 (3), 297–313.

Lee, H. H. and Kim, J. (2008), The effects of shopping orientations on consumers' satisfaction with product search and purchases in a multi-channel environment, *Journal of Fashion Marketing and Management*, 12 (2), 193–216.

Levitt, T. (2004), Marketing myopia, *Harvard Business Review*, 82 (7), 138–149.

Liu, G. S. and Garino, G. (2001), Privatization or competition?: A lesson learnt from the Chinese, *Economics of Planning*, 34 (1), 37–51.

McGoldrick, P. J. and Collins, N. (2007), Multichannel retailing: Profiling the multichannel shopper, *The International Review of Retail, Distribution and Consumer Research*, 17 (2), 139–158.

Nicholson, M., Clarke, I., and Blakemore, M. (2002), "One brand, three ways to shop": Situational variables and multichannel consumer behavior, *The International Review of Retail, Distribution and Consumer Research*, 12 (2), 131–148.

Narver, J. C., Jacobson, R. L., and MacLachlan, D. L. (2004), Responsive and proactive market orientation and new-product success, *Journal of Product Innovation Management*, 21 (5), 334–347.

Nunes, P. and Breene, T. (2011), Reinvent your business before it's too late, *Harvard Business Review*, 89 (1), 80–87.

Pine II, B. J., Peppers, D., and Rogers, M. (1995), Do you want to keep your customers forever?, *Harvard Business Review*, 73 (2), 103–114.

Potter, D. (2004), Confronting low-end competition, *MIT Sloan Management Review*, 45 (4), 73–78.

Rajagopal (2008), Consumer response and cyclicality in new products management, *Journal of Customer Behavior*, 7 (2), 165–180.

Rajagopal and Rajagopal, A. (2007), Competition vs. cooperation: Analyzing strategy dilemma in business growth under changing social paradigms, *International Journal of Business Environment*, 1 (4), 476–487.

Rajagopal and Sanchez, R. (2005), Analysis of customer portfolio and relationship management models: Bridging managerial gaps, *Journal of Business and Industrial Marketing*, 20 (6), 307–316.

Samiee, S. (2008), Global marketing effectiveness via alliances and electronic commerce in business-to-business markets, *Industrial Marketing Management*, 37 (1), 3–8.

Seelos, C. and Mair, J. (2005), Social entrepreneurship: Creating new business models to serve the poor, *Business Horizons*, 48 (3), 241–246.

Tu, H. S., Kim, S. Y., and Sullivan, S. E. (2002), Global strategy lessons from Japanese and Korean business groups, *Business Horizons*, 45 (2), 39–46.

Verma, R. and Rajagopal (2013), Conceptualizing service innovation architecture: A service-strategic framework, *Journal of Transnational Management*, 18 (1), 3–22.

Vrontis, D. and Thrassou, A. (2007), A new conceptual framework for business–consumer relationships, *Marketing Intelligence & Planning*, 25 (7), 789–806.

Wallace, D. W., Giese, J. L., and Johnson, J. L. (2004), Customer retailer loyalty in the context of multiple channel strategies, *Journal of Retailing*, 80 (4), 249–263.

Webb, J. W., Ketchen Jr, D. J., and Ireland, R. D. (2010), Strategic entrepreneurship within family-controlled firms: Opportunities and challenges, *Journal of Family Business Strategy*, 1 (2), 67–77.

Yan, R. (1998), Short-term results: The litmus test for success in China, *Harvard Business Review*, 76 (5), 61–69.

Zheng, W., Yang, B., and McLean, G. N. (2010), Linking organizational culture, structure, strategy, and organizational effectiveness: Mediating role of knowledge management, *Journal of Business Research*, 63 (7), 763–771.

9   Social Psychology of Consumers

Batra, R., Lehmann, D., and Singh, D. (1993), The Brand Personality Component of Brand Goodwill: Some Antecedents and Consequences, in Aaker, D. A. and Biel, A. L. (eds): *Brand Equity and Advertising: Advertising's Role in Building Strong Brands*, Hillsdale, NJ: Lawrence Erlbaum Associates, 83–95.

Bauer, H. H., Hammerschmidt, M., and Staat, M. (2004), *Analyzing Product Efficiency: A Customer Oriented Approach*, University of Mannheim, February.

Berry, L. L. (2001), The old pillars of new retailing, *Harvard Business Review*, 79 (4), 131–137.

Bjorkman, I. (2002), Aura: Aesthetic business creativity, *Consumption, Markets and Culture*, 5 (1), 69–78.

Blair, C., Gordon, J. W., and Mulder, S. R. (2007), How consumer goods companies are coping with complexity, *McKinsey Quarterly*, May.

Carey, L., Shaw, D., and Shiu, E. (2008), The impact of ethical concerns on family consumer decision-making, *International Journal of Consumer Studies*, 32 (5), 553–556.

Cayla, J., Beers, R., and Arnould, E. (2014), Stories that deliver business insights, *MIT Sloan Management Review*, 55 (2), 55–62.

Codispoti, M. and de Cesarei, A. (2007), Arousal and attention: Picture size and emotional reactions, *Psychophysiology*, 44 (5), 680–686.

D'Andrea, G., Schleicher, M., and Lunardini, F. (2006), The role of promotions and other factors affecting overall store price image in Latin America, *International Journal of Retail & Distribution Management*, 34 (9), 688–700.

Daniel, M. (1997), *Material Culture and Mass Consumerism*, New York: Wiley-Blackwell.

Elaine, R., Carol, B., and Calum, M. (2009), Plastic bag politics: Modifying consumer behavior for sustainable development, *International Journal of Consumer Studies*, 33 (2), 168–174.

Han, S., Gupta, S., and Lehmann, D. R. (2001), Consumer price sensitivity and price thresholds, *Journal of Retailing*, 77 (4), 435–456.

Heidrich, B. (2002), Business as unusual: The role of national cultural background in corporate life, *European Integration Studies*, 1 (2), 25–36.

Hill, S. and Rifkin, G. (1999), *Radical Marketing*, New York: Harper Business.

Hoebel, A. (1969), *Man, Culture and Society*, New York: Oxford University Press.

Hofstede, G. (1993), Cultural constraint in management theories, *Academy of Management Executive*, 7 (1), 81–94.

Hostetter, M. (2003) The marketing of culture, *Gotham Gazette*, Internet Edition, October, http://www.gothamgazette.com/article/20031023/1/580.

Huy, Q. and Shipilov, A. (2012), The key to social media success within organizations, *MIT Sloan Management Review*, 54 (1), 73–81.

Kenichi, O. (1989), Managing a borderless world, *Harvard Business Review*, 67 (3), 152–159.

Kirsten, G. H. and Claus, B. D. (2004), House, home and identity from a consumption perspective, *Housing, Theory and Society*, 21 (1), 17–26.

Kumar, V. and Mirchandani, R. (2012), Increasing the ROI of social media marketing, *MIT Sloan Management Review*, 54 (1), 55–61.

Kwan, C. Y., Yeung, K. W., and Au, K. F. (2008), Relationships between consumer decision-making styles and lifestyle characteristics: Young fashion consumers in China, *Journal of the Textile Institute*, 99 (3), 193–209.

Lavin, B. C. (2001), When your culture needs a makeover, *Harvard Business Review*, 79 (6), 53–61.

Livingstone, S. and Helsper, E. (2004), *Advertising Foods to Children: Understanding Promotion in the Context of Children's Daily Lives*, Department of Media and Communications, London School of Economics and Political Science, London, May.

Mattila, A. S. and Wirtz, J. (2004), Congruency of scent and music as a driver of in-store evaluations and behavior, *Journal of Retailing*, 77 (2), 273–289.

Miranda, M. J. (2009), Engaging the purchase motivations to charm shoppers, *Marketing Intelligence & Planning*, 27 (1), 127–145.

Otieno, R., Harrow, C. and Lea-Greenwood, G. (2005), The unhappy shopper, a retail experience: Exploring fashion, fit and affordability, *International Journal of Retail & Distribution Management*, 33 (4), 298–309.

Porter, M. E. and Kramer, M. R. (2011), Creating shared value, *Harvard Business Review*, 89 (1), 62–77.

Quelch, J. A. and Cannon-Bonventre, K. (1983), Better marketing at the point of purchase, *Harvard Business Review*, 61 (6), 162–169.

Rajagopal (2006), Leisure shopping behavior and recreational retailing: A symbiotic analysis of marketplace strategy and consumer response, *Journal of Hospitality Management*, 15 (2), 5–31.

Rajagopal (2007a), *International Marketing: Global Environment, Corporate Strategy and Case Studies*, New Delhi: Vikas Publishing House.

Rajagopal (2007b), Influence of brand name in variety seeking behavior of consumers: An empirical study, *International Journal of Management Practice*, 2 (4), 306–323.

Roberts, J. A. (1996), Green consumers in the 1990s: Profile and implications for advertising, *Journal of Business Research*, 36 (3), 217–231.

Saegert, J., Hoover, R. J., and Hilger, M. T. (1985), Characteristics of Mexican American consumers, *Journal of Consumer Research*, 12, 104–109.

Sivakumar, K. (2004), Manifestations and measurement of asymmetric brand competition, *Journal of Business Research*, 57 (8), 813–820.

Ucok, O. (2006), Transparency, communication and mindfulness, *Journal of Management Development*, 25 (10), 1024–1028.

Vicdan, H., Chapa, S., and de Los Santos, G. (2007), Understanding compulsive buyers' online shopping incidence: A closer look at the effects of sales promotions and bargains on Hispanic Americans, *Journal of Customer Behaviour*, 6 (1), 57–74.

Weston, H. (1999), *Mary Kay Cosmetics – Sales Force Incentives*, Cambridge, MA: Harvard Business School Press.

Yagi, T. (2003), *Effect of Cultural Influence on Market Expansion*, Working Paper, Doshisha University, Kyoto, Japan.

Yan, R. N. and Eckman, M. (2009), Are lifestyle centres unique? Consumers' perceptions across locations, *International Journal of Retail & Distribution Management*, 37 (1), 24–42.

10   Challenges of the Butterfly Effect

Ackerman, D. and Tellis, G. (2001), Can culture affect prices? A cross-cultural study of shopping and retail prices, *Journal of Retailing*, 77 (1), 57–82.

Adner, R. and Snow, D. C. (2010), Bold retreat: A new strategy for old technologies, *Harvard Business Review*, 88 (3), 76–81.

Anderson, J. and Billou, N. (2007), Serving the world's poor: Innovation at the base of the economic pyramid, *Journal of Business Strategy*, 28 (2), 14–21.

Antia, K. D., Bergen, M., and Dutta, S. (2004), Competing with grey markets, *MIT Sloan Management Review*, 46 (1), 63–69.

Arnould, E. J. and Thompson, C. J. (2005), Consumer Culture Theory (CCT): Twenty years of research, *Journal of Consumer Research*, 31 (4), 868–882.

Atasu, A., Guide, V. D. R., and Wassenhove, L. N. V. (2010), So what if remanufacturing cannibalizes my new product sales?, *California Management Review*, 52 (2), 56–76.

Bettencourt, L. A., Brown, S. W., and Sirianni, N. J. (2013), The secret to true service innovation, *Business Horizons*, 56 (1), 13–22.

Casadesus-Masanell, R. and Ricart, J. E. (2011), How to design a winning business model, *Harvard Business Review*, 89 (1–2), 100–107.

Chaharbaghi, K. and Nugent, E. (1996), A new generation of competitors, *Management Decision*, 34 (10), 5–10.

Cravens, D. W., Piercy, N. F., and Prentice, A. (2000), Developing market-driven product strategies, *Journal of Product and Brand Management*, 9 (6), 369–388.

Debruyne, M. and Reibstein, D. J. (2005), Competitor see, competitor do: Incumbent entry in new market niches, *Marketing Science*, 24 (1), 55–66.

Desai, P. S. (2001), Quality segmentation in spatial markets: When does cannibalization affect product line design?, *Marketing Science*, 20 (3), 265–283.

Desmet, K. and Parente, S. L. (2010), Bigger is better: Market size, demand elasticity, and innovation, *International Economic Review*, 51 (2), 319–333.

Eisenhardt, K. M. and Brown, S. L. (1998), Time pacing: Competing in markets that won't stand still, *Harvard Business Review*, 76 (2), 59–70.

Erhun, F., Concalves, P., and Hopman, J. (2007), Art of managing new product transitions, *MIT Sloan Management Review*, 48 (3), 73–80.

Esko, S., Zeromskis, M., and Hsuan, J. (2013), Value chain and innovation at the base of the pyramid, *South Asian Journal of Global Business Research*, 2 (2), 230–250.

Goldthorpe, J. H. (2000), Globalisation and social class, *West European Politics*, 25 (3), 1–28.

Guillen, M. F. and Garcia-Canal, E. (2010), How to conquer new markets with old skills, *Harvard Business Review*, 88 (11), 118–122.

Hedaa, L. and Ritter, T. (2005), Business relationships on different waves: Paradigm shift and marketing orientation revisited, *Industrial Marketing Management*, 34 (7), 714–721.

Johnson, L. K. (2006), Harnessing the power of the customer, *Harvard Business Publishing Newsletter*, November, 1–2.

Khermouch, G. (2002), The best global brands, *Business Week Online*, August, 05.

Leonard-Barton, D. and Kraus, W. A. (1985), Implementing new technology, *Harvard Business Review*, 63 (6), 102–110.

Kjellberg, H. (2008), Market practices and over-consumption, *Consumption Markets & Culture*, 11 (2), 151–167.

Madigan, M. (1980), Small food firms fight for survival, *International Journal of Retail & Distribution Management*, 8 (5), 59–65.

Markides, C. and Charitou, C. D. (2004), Competing with dual business models: A contingency approach, *The Academy of Management Executive*, 18 (3), 22–36.

Meredith, L. and Maki, D. (2001), Product cannibalization and the role of prices, *Applied Economics*, 33 (14), 1785–1793.

Moorthy, K. S. and Png, I. P. L. (1992), Market segmentation, cannibalization, and the timing of product introductions, *Management Science*, 38 (3), 345–359.

Paine, L. (2010), The China rules, *Harvard Business Review*, 88 (6), 103–108.

Park, A. (2008), Making diversity a business advantage, *Harvard Business Publishing Newsletter*, April 01, 5–7.

Pearce, J. A. (2009), The profit-making allure of product reconstruction, *MIT Sloan Management Review*, 50 (3), 59–65.

Rajagopal (2008), *Globalization Thrust: Driving Nations Competitive*, Hauppauge, NY: Nova Science Publishers.

Rajagopal (2014), *Architecting Enterprise: Managing Innovation, Technology, and Global Competitiveness*, Basingstoke: Palgrave Macmillan.

Ramaswamy, V. (2009), Are you ready for the co-creation movement?, *IESE-Insight Magazine*, 2, 29–35.

Roberto, M. A. and Lynne, C. L. (2005), Art of making change initiative sticks, *MIT Sloan Management Review*, 46 (4), 53–60.

Sawhney, M., Verona, G., and Prandelli, E. (2005), Collaborating to create: The Internet as a platform for customer engagement in product innovation, *Journal of Interactive Marketing*, 19 (4), 4–17.

Seock, Y. K. and Bailey, L. R., (2009), Fashion promotions in the Hispanic market: Hispanic consumers' use of information sources in apparel shopping, *International Journal of Retail & Distribution Management*, 37 (2), 161–181.

Shankar, A. and Fitchett, J. A. (2002), Having, being and consumption, *Journal of Marketing Management*, 18 (5–6), 501–516.

Shih, W. (2012), *Competency-Destroying Technology Transitions: Why the Transition to Digital Is Particularly Challenging*, Background Note, Cambridge, MA: Harvard Business School Press.

Stillerman, J. (2006), Private, parochial, and public realms in Santiago, Chile's retail sector, *City & Community*, 5 (3), 293–317.

Strikwerda, J. and Stoelhorst, J. W. (2009), The emergence and evolution of multidimensional organizations, *California Management Review*, 51 (4), 11–31.

Thonke, S. and Reinertsen, D. (1998), Agile product development: Managing development flexibility in uncertain environments, *California Management Review*, 41 (1), 8–30.

Vishwanath, V. and Rigby, D. K. (2006), Localization: Revolution in consumer markets, *Harvard Business Review*, 84 (4), 82–92.

Watkins, M. D. (2009), Picking the right transition strategy, *Harvard Business Review*, 87 (1), 46–53.

Yeoh, P. L. (1994), Speed to global markets: An empirical prediction of new product success in the ethical pharmaceutical industry, *European Journal of Marketing*, 28 (11), 29–49.

Index

CPSIA information can be obtained
at www.ICGtesting.com
Printed in the USA
BVOW06*1814060917
494141BV00006B/29/P

9 781137 434951